AN AFGHANISTAN PICTURE SHOW

OR, HOW I SAVED THE WORLD

WILLIAM T. VOLLMANN

FARRAR, STRAUS AND GIROUX

NEW YORK

Library of Congress Cataloging-in-Publication Data
Vollmann, William T.
An Afghanistan picture show ; or, how I saved the world / William
T. Vollmann.
P. cm.
1. Afghanistan—History—Soviet occupation, 1979–1989—Personal
narratives, American.   2. Afghanistan—Description and travel—1981–
3. Vollman, William T.—Journeys—Afghanistan.   I. Title.
DS371.2.V65 1992   958.104′5—dc20   92-7415   CIP

*This book is dedicated
to all who try to help others,
whether they succeed or fail*

CONTENTS

II: THE REFUGEES

Appendix

And I have admitted that the foreigner will probably pronounce a sentence differently if he conceives it differently; but what we call his wrong conception *need* not lie in anything that accompanies the utterance . . .

Wittgenstein, Philosophical Investigations, I.20

ADVERTISEMENT FOR THE REVISION

Ten years ago, when Soviet troops were airlifted to Kabul, the radio spoke in shocked tones. This afternoon it seemed to me somewhat reconciled, for the invaders were now called "government spokesmen," and the Afghans had become "Muslim extremists." As for me, during this decade I have thought much on Afghanistan and accomplished nothing; and so the Young Man has become the Thirty Years' Bore. This work for its part has been similarly revised, ossified and prissified. I hope that it is still honest nonetheless. And I pray that this record of my failures may somehow in its negative way help somebody.

W.T.V. (1989)

PREFACE

We are all disposed to live in comfort; and when some people shun the chilly slopes of Lofty Principle, preferring to watch those beneath them from the comfortable plateau of High Dudgeon, we had best forgive; we may not be able to shove them off, as they will have fortified their camp. Their opinion of us is very important, of course: — in metaphors like this one we are all, for some never explained reason, trying hard to work our way up the mountain; and as *they* have mined all the lower passes, we must be civil and request their escort. I myself, like many a milksop before, chose the path of altruism, on whose more fatiguing switchbacks one may encounter starving children, and lean one's weight on their little heads in the guise of patting them. The question for me was whom to aid; for I could see the sun shining on the rifle sights of the folks whose opinion of me was of so much consequence. It was not that any of them was *particular* to excess; in fact, they were a very tolerant lot, believing in democracy, so that they generously allowed among their number many with whom they fought to the death; and thanks to this admirable diversity of view one could never be sure who was currently at the rifle sight. I recollected that the contingent which controlled this one pass was devoutly anti-Soviet (according to latest report), which meant that every Afghan I assisted would make me look so much better than I was; and who knew? — I might even be able to *help* somebody. I would write a book, I would; that was always safe.

I purchased two cameras, three lenses and forty rolls of film, and proceeded into the foothills, via Pakistan.

W.T.V.   (1982)

AN AFGHANISTAN PICTURE SHOW

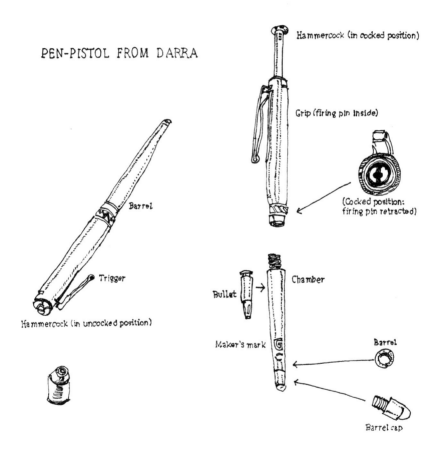

PEN-PISTOL FROM DARRA

Hammercock (in cocked position)

Grip (firing pin inside)

(Cocked position:
firing pin retracted)

Barrel

Trigger

Hammercock (in uncocked position)

Bullet

Chamber

Maker's mark

Barrel

Barrel cap

From an interview with Leonid Brezhnev (1980)

. . . "Today the opponents of peace and détente are trying to speculate on the events in Afghanistan. Mountains of lies are being built up around these events, and a shameless anti-Soviet campaign is being mounted. — What has really happened in Afghanistan?

"A revolution took place there in April 1978.* The Afghan people took their destiny into their hands and embarked on the road of independence and freedom. As it has always been in history, the forces of the past ganged up against the revolution. But from the very first days of the revolution it encountered an external aggression and rude interference from outside into their internal affairs.†

"Thousands and thousands of insurgents, armed and trained abroad, and whole armed units were sent into the territory of Afghanistan. In effect, imperialism, together with its accomplices, launched an undeclared war against revolutionary Afghanistan.

"Afghanistan persistently demanded an end to the aggression and that it be allowed to build its new life in peace. Resisting the internal aggression, the Afghan leadership, during the lifetime of President Taraki and then later, repeatedly asked the Soviet Union for assistance. On our part, we warned those concerned that if the aggression did not stop, we would not abandon the Afghan people at their time of trial. As is known, we stand by what we say."

---

* For those interested in teleological history, I have furnished a chronology of events from the Russian conquests in Kazakhstan in 1734 to the pullout of Soviet troops in 1989. It may be useful when reading the section entitled "A Matter of Politics."

† It is no fault of Brezhnev's that the translated syntax here reminds one of the ultimatum of the Japanese to MacArthur: "The outcome of the present combat has already been decided, and you are cornered to the doom . . . Dear Filipino soldiers! We repeat for the last!"

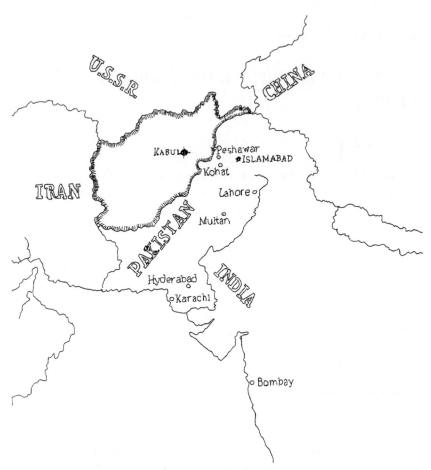

The Young Man's sketch map of Afghanistan

Looking due north from Peshawar (1982)

Now, on our left we have **AFGHANISTAN**, which is to say **RUSSIA**, which is to say a hostile country, and up ahead of us, long before we could ever get clear and free to, for example, Polaris, we have **CHINA**, which is to say a neutral with its own

problems, which is to say (in this instance) a hostile country; and
on our right we have **INDIA**, which has got to be practical, as
we all do, so here we have another hostile country, and behind
us, as a reminder that not only people are hostile, is the Arabian
Sea. (But everybody knows that all environments are hostile in
the long run.) So the refugees from our side of Afghanistan tend
to stay in Pakistan. A few have gone to Delhi, it is true, where
they experience difficulties at the hands of those who want to be
counted on the winning side. Some enter **IRAN** through Baluchistan, but it is said that their ultimate situation is not happy. A
very few (the rich, claim the ones who remain) are given asylum
in the United States or the Federal Republic of Germany. There
is much talk about going back to Afghanistan to fight, and an
impressive number actually do it. And **PAKISTAN**, a country
as gracious in spirit as it is poor, takes in all the others—who
number more than three million.

Looking around us, then, we have quite a vista—a bit disheart-
ening, maybe, but if there were no problems what would we do
with the people who wanted to solve them? And—speak of the
altruist!—I do believe that I can see our Young Man from America
down there at this very moment, just dying to be of use, and
wishing he *could* just die, for he has dysentery.*

Sketch maps have been furnished for your reference. A glossary
of Pushto (or, if you prefer, Pashto, Pushtu, Pukhto or Pakhto)
words and expressions has been omitted. Going in the summer is
not advised on account of the heat.

---

* Diagnosed in due time as *Giardia lamblia* and *Rare entamoeba something-or-other* (cysts
indicated).

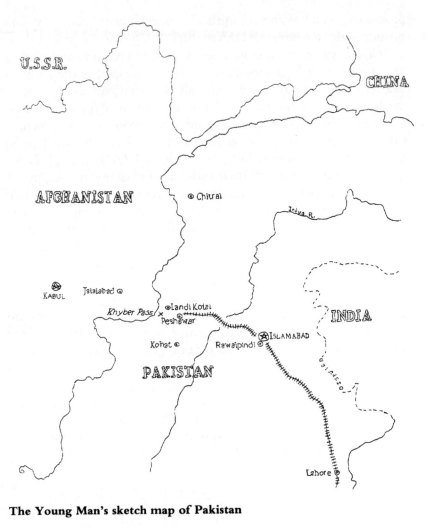

The Young Man's sketch map of Pakistan

I
THE BORDER

1

SURELY THY LORD

(1982)

Then she conceived him; and withdrew with him
to a remote place. And the throes of childbirth
drove her to the trunk of a palm-tree. She said:
Oh, would that I had died before this, and had
been a thing quite forgotten!

So a voice came to her from beneath her: Grieve
not, surely thy Lord has provided a stream
beneath thee. And shake towards thee the
trunk of the palm-tree, it will drop on thee fresh
ripe dates.

QUR'ĀN, XVI: 19: 16–23

Surely thy Lord [1]

It was his first hour in the country. He picked up his luggage and went to the door marked EXIT. The customs officials stared after him sternly.

Immediately as he stepped outside he had the sense of being crowded by something. He stood there in the night until he could see, hearing patient, deferential breathings and rustlings of garments on either side of him. He saw that the sidewalk in front of the terminal had a low fence on his right and his left, like a slaughter chute. Pressed up against the fence were hundreds of men, calling out softly: "A nickel, please?" — "Taxi, sir?" — They awaited his pleasure. Step by step he traversed the protected space, trying to look straight ahead of him and hoping that he would see a sign directing him to official transportation of some kind. Fifty feet ahead, the railings ended at the street curb. The Pakistanis stood waiting for him. He was by himself; the other passengers, who were all native to the place, had been cleared quickly and had gone. He had never been to Asia before. What should he do? Would they rob him there in the dark when he came in among them? — He continued walking. Having worked for a year in a reinsurance firm to finance his visit to the battlefields (which were still a thousand miles away), he had drawn up and balanced out to zero a list of his assets and liabilities:

ASSETS	LIABILITIES
1. My what-the-hell attitude.	1. The same.
2. My meager need for comfort. (Call this "stamina.")	2. The steady decay of my immune system.
3. Lack of much hunger.	3. Lack of much money.
4. Prudence.	4. The same. (Call it "cowardice.")
TOTALS: 0	0

He concentrated on that first item, his what-the-hell attitude, and took his last few steps.

The red hill [1]

Once upon a time there was a Young Man who wanted to be more than he really was. This made him unhappy. He decided to go to Afghanistan and take pictures of the bullets whizzing past his ears. Unfortunately he had a stomach ache.

The red hill [2]

Once there was a Young Man who wanted to go to war. Unfortunately, no one would take him at first. — "Well," he reflected in his hotel room, "it could have been worse. They could have taken me and gotten me killed."

Still and all, he thought, choking down a kebab at the Lone Star Café, he felt like a failure; for he had tried and tried to go. — What a panting puppy! — Had he been called upon to fetch newspapers for any master, oh! he would have run across the lawn of politics, tail a-wagging, like that breathless zigzagger Lukács, that silly noser-around in satellite countries, trying desperately to implement his convictions with any ready-to-hand artillery clip, even obligingly changing the convictions themselves as required by Stalin & Co. (At least, thought the Young Man, if any creepy organization is breathing down my neck at the moment, *I'm* on the other side!)—and always missing the democratic revolutionary boat, poor György, always getting short-circuited in the Great Electrification; for whenever he got his revolver out and aimed at the head of the oppressor class he would be informed of dismaying changes in the curriculum, so that all his efforts to raise the toiling masses and other Igor beavers up to social consciousness succeeded no more than any other type of levitation— and every time he got expelled from the people's this and the people's that, until he was left with nothing to do, finally, but talk about praxis in nineteenth-century novels. Stupid bastard. — Well, he wasn't going to end up like that, the Young Man vowed,

no sirree; why, he'd grab one of these here *topaks* all cocked and loaded with *golai* swiped from some Soviet ammunition dump, knock out the lights and maybe shoot somebody's cap off just for effect (if only he could shoot!), assume command, lead the Mujahideen to the battlefront like Lawrence of Arabia, capture a helicopter in Kabul and proceed to Moscow, rotoring comfortably along below the radar line; and then he'd strafe the Kremlin roof and interrupt any number of important meetings. Oho, he'd change the objective conditions of history, he would; he'd make the materialists acknowledge the mud that they were made of—

And if he had been a Soviet Young Man, he would have gone to Nicaragua.

His little fiancée bought him sausage, and shortbread, and marzipan, and chocolate, and fancy crackers, convinced as she was that she would never see him again. He put it all in his camera duffel, which he then in military fashion STOWED beneath his feet on the plane. As one kind of cloud gave way to another beside his window seat, he drank ginger ale. He imagined calling his fiancée from each stop—New York, Frankfurt, Karachi—getting successively worse connections, having less and less to say. Mainly, however, he let himself be pampered by a benign blankness of thought, as if the ever-changing clouds had wandered in behind his eyes, and the blue lucidities between them were vacant. — He passed out of Swiss airspace. The clouds were thicker over Yugoslavia, and it was raining in Istanbul during the refueling. He stayed in the plane and watched a blue tank stenciled **POLIS** amble around the runway, with two white helmets sticking out from the hatch.

Coasting from time zone to time zone, he presently found himself sitting next to an ex-ambassador who was going home to India to do some trout fishing. The plane was almost empty. At midnight the blackness in the windows was challenged by rare small patterns of brightness from the United Arab Emirates. Two hours later came the descent, the lights of Karachi extending indefinitely beneath the window in all directions like electric pushpins marking the spread of cholera. The plane stopped, the door opened, and from the Arabian Sea came a fishy, sulphurous steam, like a malfunctioning boiler, that made the stewardesses' uniforms stick to their bodies. The Young Man picked up his duffel, hands sweating, and got off the plane.

2

THE LAND OF
COUNTERPANE
(1959–81)

Ephraim herds the wind, and pursues the east
wind all day long . . .

BIBLE, HOSEA: 12.1

The Land of Counterpane

It is part of the fragmentation of life that certain states of existence can barely be recalled in others, as to a storybook sailor long away the feel of walking in the street drains first from his mind, which can conceive of only present time; and then gradually from his hands, which once flashed in free arcs at his sides and now must always be grasping stanchions or rigging; and finally from his legs and feet, which, having through greatest proximity become most accustomed to the confidently repetitive action of striding over the unmoving pavement, are the slowest to forget; and at last the sensation of walking on land becomes an abstraction, like the mountains of some country beyond the horizon. This was especially true for me when as a child I was ill. — I would wake up feeling hot and nauseous; the breakfast which my mother had made me I was unable to eat, and there was no talk of my going to school. My father, who sometimes suspected me of malingering, would study me sharply, but in the end my pallor and forehead heat would convince even him, and I would be sent back to bed for the day. I would lie there, and watch the sun slowly ascend in the sky, the other children going off past my window with their schoolbooks slung under their arms if they were boys, or held tightly against their chests if they were girls; and then I lay still and watched the clock beside me change the position of its hands with all the monotonous slowness of the great geological epochs. At five of eight the hands began to move faster; eight o'clock was the fatal hour when school began, and I knew that if I jumped out of bed even now, and dressed and ran off to school breakfastless, then I might perhaps arrive before the teacher called off my name, which, beginning as it did with "V," was at the bottom of the attendance list. And I knew that my father, too, if he had not already left for the office, was also looking at the clock, thinking that it might not be too late to force me out of bed and take me to school in the car; but he did his best to judge my case fairly, and reconsidered the evidence which he had seen me exhibit: Was my temperature genuinely high, and did I look all that pale? Eventually he decided that yes, I was sick; or that at any rate it would be difficult to establish that I was not well; and it would certainly be too late to take me to school; for achieving that would involve first confronting and then besting my mother, who stood with her back toward him, also looking at the clock, but only unobtrusively, between the breakfast dishes, so as not to give my father an excuse for reopening the subject; and then eight o' clock had come and the issue was decided. It was only then that the hands of the clock stopped once again, and I became completely absorbed in my state of sickness.

The world outside blurred in the sunlight, in the same way that a streetlamp, seen through tears, becomes a bright, vague star; and this lack of definition seemed to me a *force* with a self, swelling until it pushed against my windowpane, halted at first by the smooth, cold surface, but waiting there, growing stronger and more determined, until it was able to seep in through some edge-crack. My desk, my schoolbooks and the few toys which I had not yet given up slowly became enveloped in its luminous sparkle; the closet's black mouth filled with it; and then it flowed around me from three sides, and into me. Charged with it, I began to forget the cues and sensations of health, as in health I could not imagine myself as feeling sick, nor could I have much empathy for my sister Julie when she had the measles, nor keep from getting angry at my teacher when she did not come in that day and we had to have a substitute. The idea of a world beyond the window, which was now a translucent slab of light, or for that matter of any other possibility than that of lying in my bed immobile, became as dry and strange as some ontological argument of the Middle Ages, and by degrees ever less likely, until when at mid-morning, my mother came in to bring me a cup of tea or some soup, I refused politely, in the same way that I would have done if she'd come to ask whether I would be willing to study law at the university. This inability to grasp my own state of existence of the day before would have possessed me so much that by midafternoon, when my mother came in to read to me, I no longer shifted my position beneath the blankets at all, but lay absolutely still in the hot faintness of my malady as though I were one of those people one reads about in old books, who are always getting becalmed in the tropics.

As soon as I was old enough to read by myself I stopped having my mother read to me at night, because I always disagreed with my sister as to what should be read to us that evening; and it was so much better for me to read what I wished, while Julie sat on my mother's lap and listened to her reading from *Just So Stories* or a poem from *A Child's Garden of Verses* (both of which I now found childish) in her slow, soft voice; and when I was sick my mother would simply buy me a book, such as *Captains Courageous*, which I was too proud to ask her to read to me. But when I did still like having my mother read everything to me, and I was absorbed by poems like the one about the fight between the gingham dog and the calico cat, or the one that described a voyage to Africa, in which the traveler sees the knotty crocodile of the Nile (but I used to think that it was the NAUGHTY CROCODILE that had eaten people up and so must be spanked), and he finds the toys of the old Egyptian boys and all the other things which rhyme—there was still one poem which I dreaded. It was called "The Land of Counterpane," and it recounted the fantasy of a child who is sick and abed with his toy soldiers. This "Land of Counterpane" is simply the topography of the wrinkled and up-thrust blankets; and the child marches his soldiers up and down the quilt-patterned hills, skirmishes them on whatever rare plains there may be, and sets up ambushes and rescues at the mouths of little vales formed by pinching the sheets into contours of sufficient exactitude. My mother could never understand why it was that I so disliked this poem,★ but, accepting my detestation as she would have accepted one of my father's pronouncements on some mechanical matter, she did not read the poem to me, and I felt grateful, dreading the sight of the very poem that preceded it as my mother slowly turned the pages, which were as colorful as butterflies' wings; and feeling the smug contentment of one who has arrived alive, most bones intact, after a session or two on the rack, when we were safely a couple of poems beyond. The truth of the matter, which I was always ashamed to explain, was that the image of the wrinkles terrified me, I having just become aware of the correlation between the wrinkles on the faces of my grandparents and the fact that they were going to die within the next several decades; and

---

★ The dislikes we have are such a mystery! My friend Seth was always terrified of whales, although he never met any, and I once met a little Afghan girl who screamed whenever she heard an airplane. Later I found out that an airplane had killed her parents and transformed her into a paraplegic.

once I had been prevailed upon to accept the fact of my own death, I started feeling my face every day for wrinkles, knowing that one day they would come; and I watched my parents closely, noticing with horror the ever-lessening resemblance between my mother and her bridal picture in the family album, and the fact that my father's hair was slowly graying; and when I lay in bed all day, the eerie luminescence of my sickness in me and all about me, my inability to recall my healthy state in any real sense made the wrinkles of my own "Land of Counterpane" seem a menacing *memento mori*.

Antarctica

But I wanted to go to Antarctica. In New England there was the snow and the woods, but it was gloomy among the trees and when I went sledding with Julie we would always crash into old stone walls. Antarctica sounded much better; my father told me that hardly anyone lived there. I imagined a sunny space of snow, a smoothness of ice that sparkled blue and green. There were penguins, of course. Icebergs moved through the ocean like ships, and far away could be seen jumping porpoises, and I could build snow castles and have my own ice-cream mine. One needed a parka to live there, but it was not too cold, especially when the sun was out in the afternoons and the ice was like a mirror. I would come out of school sometimes in February or March, almost understanding fractions. Those were warm days for winter; the snow was a little sticky, and it packed perfectly. They were building tall snow sculptures on the green. On my way home I walked past fields with the grass coming up golden through the snow, and that was territory belonging to Antarctica.

Indiana

When I looked out the window of our new house the yard was just like a photograph. The trees and shrubs were various shades of green against the yellow-brown lawn (which I had just mowed). The sky was cloudless, naturally. Other houses in the neighborhood maintained the still solidarity of the nouveaux riches. I had a plenitude of time, and time being, like all things which have been thought on and settled, value-free, I could, I suppose, have made those free afternoons and evenings into delightful baskings in supra-conscious temporality as well as I did make them into hours of boredom and horror.

My first demonstration

After some discussion, my friend and I agreed to put two hours' worth of coins in the parking meter. It was a hot day, and neither of us thought that we would want to stay any longer than that.

"Should I lock my door?" I said.

"Yes, please," my friend said.

We walked over to the ornamental fountain where the demonstration was scheduled to begin, and children came up to give us pamphlets. The man with the bullhorn said that if we were united we would never be defeated. The shouting procession began. Nobody saw us. Sweat was in our eyes. My friend and I walked listlessly. We were both feeling very tired. After two blocks we went back to the car.

The red hill [3]

I̶t is part of the fragmentation of life that after the Soviets invaded Afghanistan I wanted to go there. It sounded like a treasure-trove of nightmares. Allow me to quote briefly from the *Encyclopaedia Britannica* to set my expectations' scene:

A kingdom in . . . For information about border disputes . . . great central range of mountains . . . a series of deep ravines and broken ridges . . . more than 115° F in the summer, while in the highlands of Kabul . . . to − 15° F in February . . . the influence of the southwest monsoon hardly extends beyond Jalalabad in eastern Afghanistan . . . a dry, invigorating atmosphere . . . periodic blizzards . . . large forest trees . . . The lowest terminal ridges, especially toward the west, are naked in aspect . . . Wild animals include the wolf, fox, hyena, wild dog, wildcat, common leopard, mongoose, wild sheep, mole, shrew, hedgehog, bat, several species of jumping mouse, jerboa and pika hare. Bears are found in the forests and the Mongolian tiger is said to inhabit the thick reed country of the Amu-darya . . . The Pathans, i.e. the Afghans proper . . . dark hair and . . . The Tajiks . . . The Hazaras, also, are part of the far-flung Mongolian race. They are glabrous, short-haired . . . Different forms of the vendetta exist . . . the protagonist hops on one leg . . . involves the attempt to retrieve a decapitated calf's body from a ditch, on horseback, and carry it to the goal, hundreds of riders participating in the contest . . . singing in a chorus accompanied by native instruments . . . an Iron Age settlement at Balkh with plain buffware . . . few remains of the early Muslim invaders . . . the Hephthalite domination . . . when already Arab armies . . . descended upon the city . . . Mongol hordes . . . no living thing was to be spared. The beautiful city of Balkh was utterly . . . The horrors of the Mongol invasion were then repeated, though on a lesser scale . . . peace and prosperity . . . was parceled between the Mughals of India and . . . were slaughtered . . . The Russians . . . Internal strife . . . Meanwhile . . . blinded and imprisoned . . . indolent ruler . . . Napoleon . . . but instead the Sikh ruler robbed him of the famous Koh-i-Nor diamond . . . the unfortunate minister to be cut to pieces . . . holy war in 1836 . . . A British army . . . honorably treated . . . who killed him with his own hands . . . a speedy but peaceful settlement of the Afghan question . . . annihilated . . . evacuated . . . machinery and other modern appliances . . . assassinated . . . the national awakening . . . independence . . . a group of reactionaries who . . . a reign of terror . . . Unfortunately, this steady progress was interrupted by . . .

Internal peace was maintained, and steady progress . . . neutrality . . . friction between Afghanistan and Pakistan . . . agreements with certain foreign governments . . . a motorway and . . . the new constitution . . . rioting by students . . . the assembly . . . social welfare centers . . . a military academy at Kabul . . . facilities for jet bombers.

It all sounded quite interesting, especially since I had just realized that open space was not in fact the life-pervaded medium which I had imagined. The softness of blown grass or willows or evergreens is not a genuine softness, because gravity and death make all living things hard. We do not all have skeletons, of course, for in marine environments particularly, where both of these rather stern considerations are harder to keep sight of in that hazy green light, any competent researcher can find the octopi, say, or the many phyla of benthic worms which do seem to manage without, but we are given a clue, by virtue of the documented failures of arthropoda and cartilaginous fishes, that all is *not* well nonetheless. And indeed, on consideration we see that even an octopus (most marvelously developed eyes of any of the invertebrates, said my biology teacher, Dr. Mawby) often lives and hides in a nice hard little GROTTO or CORAL FORMATION somewhere. It follows from my presentation that we are (all of us, vegetables, protists and animals alike) members of a great fraternity of scavengers—that we are either patches of mold or ants crawling through the fissures of some immense decaying skull: a familiar central range of mountains, their contours almost memorized now after long nights of study in the desert, eyes aching over the textbook . . . a series of deep ravines and broken ridges, the lowest of which, especially toward the west, are naked in aspect because we have picked them clean . . . a dry, invigorating atmosphere, at least where we are, in our bone-ivory tower built some distance above that rather creepy-looking eye socket (please, God, don't let *that* be on Dr. Mawby's exam): in short, the Land of Counterpane.

Sitting at my bleached college desk one summer evening, waiting to graduate on Sunday, I looked out the window, which was hung with white drapes, and could see only the night leaves (backlit by streetlights) and the articulated branches from which they fanned like the skeleton of a hand. Everything was quiet, and I finally closed my eyes, sustained by the humidity that impinged on marine benthic organisms as currents bearing to eager gill slits the dissolved nutrients of rotting things in their richness—and that brushed, too, about the lonely corpse of that Russian cosmonaut, faintly crackling between the stars, as that scientifically undetectable but nonetheless palpable Ether that everybody had once believed in, and its swirlings made the frost sparkle now and then beneath his cracked and darkened helmet—what was his name? —as he circled round and round the deserts and poles of the world in a people's soviet socialist tin can. — Had this really happened, or did it come from a science-fiction book I'd read? I didn't even know that much.

Explanations [1]

"I still don't understand why you want to go to Afghanistan," my father said. "I guess I'll never understand it."

Actually it was very simple. I just wanted to comprehend what had happened there. Then I would put myself at someone's service. I meant to be good, and was prepared to do good.

In my notebook, on the page of questions to be answered, I wrote: *Is it possible that the invasion will be beneficial in the long run (increasing literacy through compulsory schooling, etc.)?* For it was and is my habit to take everything at face value first.

> Take religion, Lenin had said, or the denial of rights to women, or the oppression and inequality of the non-Russian nationalities . . . In our country they have been settled completely by the legislation of the October Revolution. We have fought and are fighting religion in earnest. We have granted *all* the non-Russian nationalities *their own* republics or autonomous regions. We in Russia no longer have the base, mean and infamous denial of rights to women or inequality of the sexes, that disgusting survival of feudalism and medievalism, which is being renovated by the avaricious bourgeoisie . . .

I had never been to the Soviet Union, although I had always wanted to see Tashkent with its fountains and roses, Gorki, Leningrad, Western Siberia ("the land is fabulously rich in reindeer and luxurious furs") . . . So it was possible that face value was honest value, that this multinational republic had succeeded in ending starvation, in making books available to all, in giving women a fairer chance (*we* could not even pass the Equal Rights Amendment!), and that the Afghans, too, could hope someday to serve on the Supreme Soviet in their national costumes—and why shouldn't Afghan women be granted formal equality? — But maybe that consideration did not apply in Afghanistan; maybe wearing the veil was what was right there. If so, the Soviet re-educators should leave them alone. — And what about this business of "fighting religion in earnest"? I did not much like that. It seemed wrong to strike at someone else's faith (if, indeed, that was what the Soviets were doing, for again our newspapers might be distorting things). Most disturbing, of course, was the fact that the upward evolution had to be forcibly sponsored.

At the university I had met an old Maoist who was visiting through some exchange program or other; in the kitchen late one night I asked him about the liquidation of the landlords in China, for I was sure that that had not been right.

We were alone, and the kitchen light was very bright. The night was hot. Crickets chirped. The professor said, "Maybe it could have been done eventually without the liquidations. But I doubt it. Once their land was expropriated, would they have been content with that? Why did they have more land than the small peasants in the first place? If we left them there to make trouble in the villages, you can be assured that they would have gotten their neighbors in debt to them again; they would have *schemed* to do it. The land would become theirs again. So there was no other way to do it."

"Do you think that the executioners should have been sorry?"

"No," he said, "I don't think so. But I had nothing to do with it."

Later I remembered Vlad IV of Romania, who had abolished poverty by burning up the poor. I wondered how well and for how long this had worked.

3

DIFFICULTIES OF THE MIRACLE WORKER

(1982)

And when they meet those who believe, they say,
We believe; and when they are alone with their
devils, they say: Surely we are with you; we
were only mocking.

Allah will pay them back their mockery, and He
leaves them alone in their inordinacy, blindly
wandering on.

QUR'ĀN, II: 2: 14–15

Difficulties of the miracle worker

King's "Restaurant" for lunch. He ordered chicken fry with *nan*.* The chicken was literally a skeleton in chicken-flavored oil. Evidently the bird had been boiled and boiled into soup, and somebody else had ordered the soup. — As he was a foreigner, he was brought a knife and fork. The waiter and the owner stared with almost religious interest at his attempts to eat with these utensils, which he had seen before in this life, but which had never been applied by him to such difficult usages. The skeleton swam about halfheartedly (if that is the right word) when his proxies pursued it through its frictionless bath. The liquid ran through the tines of his fork. A perfect drop of oil remained on each point after immersion, so every now and then he raised the fork to his mouth coolly, as if he were getting somewhere, and sucked at it. It tasted as if they had cooked the entrails and feathers along with the bones. Fishing politely for a velvety snippet of blood clot or rooster's comb at the bottom of the dish, he accidentally over-turned the skeleton and discovered some meat on the wing. The fork and knife could not pull it loose, however, as he hadn't been raised in France or Italy, where in the afternoons you could watch old men peal a peach with their silverware, wasting scarcely a molecule of fruit-flesh as the skin came perfectly off; no, the Young Man was an American, and so finally he plunged his hand into the lukewarm oil to get at the skeleton, and he disarticulated the wing joint so as to free that sliver of meat. — The unsprung bone snapped fiercely against the dish, and his table jerked. — The waiter tch-tch'ed, though whether out of pity or offense it was impossible to say.

"Very sorry, sir," the owner said from behind the counter. "Very fresh." — He was a bald old man in the uniform of the

---

* *Nan* and *dordai* are the equivalents of pita bread. *Nan* is Pakistani; *dordai* is Afghan—very similar to *nan*, but thicker.

Indian Army. Watching his almost empty establishment from the
back of the room, he played a cassette over and over. Whenever
it reached the end of a side, he flipped it again. The sound was a
muffled drumming of static within static, with remnants of calliope
in as much evidence as a whore's hymen.

Well, the Young Man thought, giving up on the meat and
dipping little bits of *nan* into the oil, at least they were subservient
instead of inquisitive here; they said they were sorry, so, okay,
okay; and believe you me, there's no finer sight than a thousand
waiters tacking into the wind, running for water at the snap of a
finger or a waved rupee note, lighting cigarettes for the customer,
his napkins blowing like racing pennants in the wind of the *pukkas*★
as he steams on, crunching another bone, skipper of his appetite,
proud, great and Yankee come to help the Third World.

THE BUFFALO-MILK CANDY

. . . Stomach aching heartily after partaking of a nauseating sweet
composed of fermented buffalo milk—what *wouldn't* he do for
courtesy? . . . It had been a wedding reception, at the home of
relatives of General N., and everybody was very nice; they took
him in to see the bride in her ceremonial costume of golden fringe,
with her yellow glass bangles; they found an American program
on television for him, they showed off the family's young sons,
the host let him handle the guns of the household, and Wife Number Two waited on him constantly with this delicacy and that. He
liked the family very much. He had had a lot of diarrhea that day,
with blood, and the thought of eating anything at all made him
want to throw up, but he would not insult them. Manfully he ate
the meat and picked at his *nan*. They had honored him; his portion
was the biggest and the most limpid with grease. The vegetables
were good, and the water potable, but meanwhile they had
brought him sweets, each more sickening than the one before.
There were hard, stale orange pretzels so sweet that his teeth ached.
Then came red things that were glazed rock-solid on the outside,
but burst in his mouth like cockroaches, running with sour-sweet
syrup supersaturated with sugar, so that crystals of it stuck to his

---

★ Fans.

gums and under his tongue, and his breath began to stink in his throat. Finally they hauled out the buffalo-milk candy—a platter of it, stacked with whitish, crumbly squares, each as big as his hand. He had been taking very small portions all evening, and could see their growing disappointment with him. So this time, instead of breaking off a corner of a piece and hiding it in his pocket later, he grabbed the biggest piece he could see and opened his mouth wide. Everyone beamed. It took him half an hour to finish it.

"My dear brother," said the Afghan Brigadier the following afternoon, selecting his words with great care from his small English repertoire, "please come outside." — But the Young Man was in agonies just then from what he was sure was the buffalo sweet, and could only sit up in bed and pat his stomach feebly. — "Uh, good afternoon," he told the Brigadier, pretending not to understand (people often did that to *him*). The Brigadier shook his head slowly and went out.

It was quiet. The Brigadier spent his days sitting in a lawn chair, his feet in another, his cheek and mouth resting against his hand as he looked at nothing, crowded by busy birds. A big vein ran down his temple like a bolt of lightning. The morning breeze stirred the air between them when they took their breakfast together, but his white prayer cap and his gray hair remained still. He had a deep, sad crease on either side of his mouth.

The Brigadier put his hand to his forehead that afternoon, waited, and finally got to his feet, crossing his arms behind his back. He walked away around the corner of the hedge. The Young Man lay watching through the window. A little later, when it had become horribly hot, the Brigadier came back to take his siesta. He slept with the same benign expression as he sat all day, the expression of someone whom months of unproductive waiting are slowly bringing to seed. Finally the Young Man's own eyes closed.

FRIENDS

General N.'s guest room had only one large bed, in which the Young Man and the Brigadier both slept. At first the Young Man felt uncomfortable with this arrangement. Like most males from his country, he believed that close and prolonged proximity to an older man might well presage homosexuality. He did not like it when old men held his hand to guide him through the bazaars. He felt as a Pakistani woman might have felt if her husband had taken her hand in public. None of this was right or wrong. He who adapts insufficiently to an alien society is a sort of evolutionary failure, condemned to isolation, sterility and extinction; he who adapts too much defaces the self he was born with. The Young Man, being young, should have adapted substantially; he had less previous self to deny. He did his best. In Karachi he'd met two men who befriended him. They paid for his lunch (*nan*, oil and curried egg), bought him a leaf-wrapped packet of betel nut to chew, showed him the tomb of Mr. Jinnah, the founder of Pakistan, and took him on a bus ride to Clifton Beach, where in September the giant sea tortoises came to lay their eggs. "It's a fascinating spectacle on a moonlit night," the guidebook said. Unfortunately, this was the middle of a 125-degree afternoon (so it seemed) in the middle of June.

The buses were painted in a hundred gorgeous ways: blue and silver, like the turquoise jewelry of the American Southwest, red diamonds with yellow centers (buttercups in poppy fields, the Young Man thought), emerald-glazed ivy patterns . . . They never stopped. You ran behind one for a block or so, dodging the cars and motor-rickshaws and the carts of the spitting camel-drivers, until there was a wagon blocking the intersection ahead, or the conductor felt sorry for you, and then the bus slowed. The conductor held out his hand. You grabbed it as the bus picked up speed, got a foot in and jumped. Inside it was dark. The floor was wet with spittle. His two new friends, Akbar and Muhammed Ibrahim, stood protectively on either side. Muhammed Ibrahim insisted on carrying his pack for him. The Young Man, who'd spent hours in the heat trying to get his railway ticket to Peshawar, being bullied by people who wanted to do him expensive services, terrified by wailing beggar-women who pantomimed that they were dying of hunger (were they? how could he tell? why was it his fault?), cheek-stroked by smiling prostitutes, reviled by the men in official red uniforms (COOLIE NO. 17302) because he would not let his pack be carried by them; baffled by everything, thirsty, but afraid to drink for fear of disease (by the end of that first day in the country he was drinking a Sprite every hour and a half, plus water when he had to; he usually had to), sweating in crowded lines, always in the wrong line, until finally a man in the line got his ticket for him, saying, "You are a guest of our country; I *must* help you!"—all this with a gentle smile that confounded the Young Man with gratitude and guilt, for then his benefactor must go once again to the end of the line to get his own ticket; as for the Young Man, his train didn't leave until ten that night and somehow he had to last till then, so he moved through the long confusion of that afternoon like a restless fly afraid of being swatted, knowing that whenever he stopped, the beggars, prostitutes, arrangers and desperate children would come; gasping, he hailed a rickshaw and roared off to the bazaars, those unknown fixed points devoid for him of any content; while the ride lasted it was marvelous because no one could bother him and he enjoyed the hot wind against his ears in that flimsy taxi, which was simply a Suzuki motor and two seats nested beneath an aluminum canopy painted with some movie star's likeness; but then they got to the bazaars, and as soon as he got out the problem of not being left alone reasserted itself, so he couldn't stop anywhere; didn't know what to do, poor helpless yoyo; walked the sunny, steamy streets, making a show of looking at straw mats and lovely plastic water coolers, becoming more and more exhausted and afraid of having his blood sucked by all these people who grasped at him and whom he refused—the Young Man, then, was happy to be in someone's keeping. — There were so many passengers on the bus that it was impossible to sit down. Strong-looking, swarthy men stood all around, rubbing their beards and conversing in low, serious voices. They looked at the Young Man, but left him to himself. Akbar and Muhammed Ibrahim smiled at him kindly. That made him feel guilty again, because he had presented himself to them falsely. Since he could be arrested for trying to cross the Afghan border, he'd told everyone who asked that his purpose was to visit Pakistan. When Akbar and Muhammed Ibrahim discovered that he did not intend to go on to India, they were astonished and touched by his interest in their country. The Young Man, who had never given much thought to Pakistan before he came there, decided then and there to make his interest sincere, and at the close of his journey he reckoned that that was one of the few good things that he had actually done. — The bus lurched on. — "Cal-*lif*-lif-lif-lif-lif, Cal-*lif*-lif-lif-lif-lif, Cal-*lif*-lif-lif-lif-lif, Ca-*lif*ton!"

the conductor sang out the door. Passengers leaped on and off. They passed a billboard for Sprite; the picture showed a veiled woman pouring the bubbling stuff into a glass. The afternoon had changed its character; feeling safe, he had begun to enjoy himself. — Here he was, in an Oriental city as fabulous as the Land of Counterpane, and he was riding toward the shores of the Arabian Sea; with him, two new friends; around him, exotic-looking personages in bright pajamas, talking in Urdu! (What else ought they to have been speaking, after all? But it must be admitted that the Young Man's attitude was endearing.)

BEGGARS AND CHOOSERS [1]

Akbar directed his attention to all the most interesting things: over there, the pillars proclaiming the Islamic virtues of FAITH, UNITY, and DISCIPLINE; over there, the new hospital for tuberculosis patients; then the almost completed Holiday Inn. — "Cal-*lif*-lif-lif-lif-lif, Ca-*lif*ton!" called the conductor. — Just ahead, a checkered cab smashed into a donkey. For a moment the great traffic-pulse seemed to miss a beat; and he could hear, as he had early that morning, the songs of tropical birds. — No, perhaps he had imagined the accident, for in less than an instant everything began again, the cab and the donkey going their separate ways; and now came half a dozen embellished rickshaws, nephews or cousins of the one he had ridden, all empty; and an old man dashed across the street, pulling behind him a wheelbarrow full of lemons. — The bus was passing along a wide street, evidently of Empire construction, lined with the canvas lean-tos of clothes vendors. The whining calls of these salesmen stung through the traffic like bees. — The Young Man's sense of well-being began to dissolve. Everything seemed strange to him; he was so far from home! He dug through the compost layers of his education, looking for familiar correspondences, and though he found them it did not matter in the least. — A leper jumped aboard, moving his silvery cattish head from side to side. He took in the Young Man almost at once. The other men stopped talking, watching to see what would happen. — "He want you give him money," Akbar said. — "Do I need to?" said the Young Man, wondering if he was being taken advantage of. — "No, no," said Akbar politely, holding out a few paisa, and the leper took the money without saying anything and jumped off the moving bus . . .

POST MORTEM

Should I have given the leper money, or did I in fact present an appearance of courageous steadfastness by being selfish? (I should make the record accurate by confessing that I did not in fact come to a decision; in this case, "not to decide was to decide.") If I was in fact obligated to give him money, should I have also accepted those many services offered to me by the coolies, tour-guides and prostitutes until my money was gone? And if I was obligated to give *them* money, should I not have been more obligated to give all my money to my poorest neighbors in America? If I'd stayed home, I could have given away the cost of my plane ticket. — But no! How could I have Saved The Afghans then? And, being no longer at home, I had to hoard my money; I did not know how much it would cost to Save Them.

BEGGARS AND CHOOSERS [2]

Clifton was the end of the line. Everybody got off. The Young Man and his companions passed through a British pavilion in memory of Lady So-and-so, and down a long, gentle flight of steps to the beach. It stank there. Akbar and Muhammed Ibrahim stopped so that he could admire everything. A quarter mile out, a twin-masted ship had run aground or been abandoned. The wreck was canted and decaying. To the right, and possibly a bit farther out (it was hard to tell), was a pair of islets, or rather—if one were mean-spirited—rocks. For the sake of saying something, he asked if anyone ever went there. Akbar gave him a look which he thought might be contemptuous. — "Smugglers go there." — "Oh," the Young Man said. — Families squatted along the beach, roasting what looked like Indian corn over open fires. On the little bluff between him and the ocean stood the booths of the banana and mango sellers, faithfully attended by swollen flies. Sweat ran down the Young Man's back.

Akbar insisted that the Young Man have a camel ride. The camel crouched in the warm sand by its master. Its fur was matted with little dried balls of mud or dung where it had rolled on the ground. The Young Man took his pack off and clambered onto the place that Akbar directed, just below the hump. — "You want by yourself, or you lonely?" Akbar said to him. — "Lonely," the Young Man said, feeling that not to have replied so would have been impolite. — Akbar got on behind him and held on to him tightly. The owner of the camel, a bitter-looking fellow with a mustache, kicked the camel in the throat until it stood up. Then he led it down a path to the waves. Muhammed Ibrahim came smiling behind with the Young Man's pack. After the camel ride he carried it for the rest of the day, despite the Young Man's embarrassed protests.

Later they walked along the beach, ignoring the beggars. People approached the Young Man with various commercial offers, but his two guardians motioned them away, until presently no one importuned him anymore. (Nonetheless he knew that the whole mass remained aware of him, that if he were for a moment left to himself then the consequences would be the same as that morning. He tried to imagine a comparable situation for a foreigner in America—being stuck in the middle of a ten-lane superhighway, maybe. But maybe there was none.)

Akbar and Muhammed Ibrahim invited him to go out wading with them, but he declined, knowing that salt water was bad for his cameras, which he would need to take pictures of famous battles; so his friends went out into the breakers alone and had him take a picture of them.

"You will send to us?" Akbar said.

"Yes, I'll send it."

"If you no to send, we will be sad. Very sad."

"I'll send it," he said.

"We will write to you letter. You will please to answer our letter? You will send to us?"

"I'll send it. Don't worry."

They never wrote him later. So he didn't have their address. So he didn't send it.

They took him on the merry-go-round, from which he had a whirling view of that tawny, canvas-colored beach whose camels stretched their necks as men led them through the sea shallows, and the low booths of vendors and the cotton-clothed crowds wavered in the hot fog; then the ride was over, and Akbar was offering to buy him one of the toys that were sold in the dirty booths along the beach. — "No, thanks," he said, feeling embarrassed at all they had already done for him. "Maybe I'll come back later and buy one."

"You pick it out, we buy for you now," said Akbar implacably.

"No, no, some other time."

"Sure," said Akbar, insulted. It was the first time that the American had not given in.

They took him to the railroad station an hour before the departure time of his train, the Khyber Mail Express. Akbar went and bought them all glasses of *lessee*. The guidebook had said to stay away from *lessee*; it was a health hazard to Westerners. In the vendor's stand he could see the big kettle in which the milk fermented. The surface of the scum was black with dead flies. — "Thank you very much," he said to Akbar, "but maybe—" — "Drink," said Akbar, bringing the glass against the Young Man's lip so hard a tooth chipped. — "Okay," he said. "Thank you very much."

BEGGARS AND CHOOSERS [3]

While they stood there drinking, Akbar had Muhammed Ibrahim buy the Young Man another packet of betel nuts to chew on his journey. The Young Man wanted to refuse, but Akbar took his hand and closed his fingers around the packet. He thanked them both and stood holding it in his hand, drinking his *lessee*. — He felt a touch. A girl in a red sari was standing at his shoulder. She smelled like old vomit. — "She want money," Akbar explained. "She no good." — He shoved her. She took a few listless steps back, and the Young Man forgot her until he smelled her beside him again. She was looking him full in the face, standing there and saying nothing. — "Should I give her a couple of rupees?" he said, trying to make up for the leper. — "No, no," said Akbar, irritated. He slapped the young woman's face and pushed her away again, but without much indignation; it was as if he were brushing a yellowjacket away from a picnic lunch. The girl moved just out of Akbar's reach and began saying something to the Young Man very dreamily, earnestly, but she could not talk, it seemed, and after a while her lips gave up their slow silent fluttering. He turned away, but she was still there. If he took out the pouch with his rupees in it, he knew that Akbar would see and be offended; then, too, no doubt everyone else on the street would see, too, and come running. He would give her the packet of betel nuts in his left hand; maybe she could sell it—it must be worth at least a quarter of a cent. The size and shape and color of the packet reminded him of a sealed condom. He felt disgusted with himself and with her. This Afghanistan project, which he had thought to be such a fine self-assertion, had erased every possibility of existence for him except a waxy passivity. — He held out his left hand slightly. Sipping at his *lessee*, he pretended not to be looking at her. She approached, touched his hand with nervous cunning. He let his fingers begin to open. Akbar was looking at him. He couldn't let the packet drop to the ground; he had to count on her to take it unseen. Her fingers drummed against the back of his hand; the touch of them was loathsome. She did not understand what he wanted her to do. He opened his fingers a little more, but still she did not understand. Finally she let her hand drop resignedly away from his, and she stepped backwards, still looking at him. — He had finished his *lessee*. The hand she had touched smelled like vomit.

HAPPINESS [1]

Akbar and Muhammed Ibrahim were telephone operators. They had gone to school together. Akbar had to start his shift at 7:00 p.m., so Muhammed Ibrahim took the Young Man to his seat on the train. Then they sat looking at each other.

"In Peshawar, people very wicked," said Muhammed Ibrahim. "They rob you, kill you, take everything."

"I'll be careful," the Young Man said.

"On train, very dangerous. You stay in seat three days, until you reach Peshawar. Never leave the seat. You must promise me, never leave the seat. You leave the seat, come back; they take your pack, take your seat, rob you, take everything. You sleep never. You sit like this all the time, with your pack under your feet. You never stand up."

"All right," he said. "I'll be careful. Thank you very much."

"You remember us. You send to us picture. You come back to Karachi, you stay with me. I love you."

"You're my friend," the Young Man replied, a little awkwardly.

"I love you. You come, be my wife. You make me full-fresh. I hate Akbar. You, you are AMERICA. You are my best friend." And Muhammed Ibrahim began to weep.

The American felt bad. "You're my friend," he said again. He let Muhammed Ibrahim take his hand.

"You are so good to me," Muhammed Ibrahim said. "You are my best friend. You make me full-fresh. Please come back to me. Every day I will wait for you. Every day I will keep a room in my house for you. If you call, I come for you. Even to Peshawar I will come for you. If you have trouble, I come to you. I pick you up, take you to my house."

"Thank you very much," he said.

"If you no come back, no write, no telephone, I will kill myself. You have made me full-fresh."

"Thank you very much. You're my friend. You've been very kind to me."

"Do you like me?"

"Very much," said the Young Man. Decency made him say it.

"Thank you. I so happy. I am so happy. I do anything for you. I am your friend."

Muhammed Ibrahim spoke to the passenger whose seat faced the Young Man's. "He take care of you to Lahore," he said finally. "Then he find someone else to help you."

The whistle of the train sounded. Muhammed Ibrahim had to get off the train now. He stood on the track and held the Young Man's hand through the window even after the train began to move. Then he ran alongside, crying. To make him feel better the American stuck his head out the window and waved to him until he could no longer be seen.

HAPPINESS [2]

So when he had to share a bed with the Afghan Brigadier, he soon got used to it. The Brigadier was a good man. He only felt the Young Man's calves in broad daylight, in public, to see if he was strong enough to go into the war zone. Occasionally he held his hand.

"My dear son," he said. "What is your name?"

The American told him.

"If the Amerikis say they *no* can help me, I very happy. I go back to Afghanistan to fight with the *Roos*."★

The Young Man thought of Muhammed Ibrahim's saying: "Thank you. I so happy. I am so happy."

★ Russians.

4

THE BRIGADIER
(1982)

And when your Lord made it known: If you are
grateful, I will give you more, and if you are
ungrateful, My chastisement is truly severe.

Qur'ān, XIII: 14: 7

The Brigadier

Just taking her easy here at the Blue Lagoon Snack Bar
—a ritzy place for Pakistan, to be sure, for it had white lace
tablecloths (full of holes, and so filthy that one touch blackened
his fingers), a dependable fan behind him, and Indian music on
the radio—he sat comfortably, though maintaining good posture.
The waiter, who like his counterpart at King's Restaurant could
tell that this customer hailed from a developed country, brought
him on a plate a real *fork* and *knife* with a paper *napkin* wrapped
around them. At King's he hadn't had a napkin. This was pretty
good. — In front of him stood a blue pitcher of cool *obuh*,★
doubtless full of disease . . . and now he was whisked his dinner
with dismaying speed considering that (a) he was the only customer, (b) they were staring at his every move, and (c) he somehow had to kill two hours waiting for Dr. Tariq. Well, anyhow,
what *was* his dinner actually, let's see, he'd first ordered an onion
steak at fourteen rupees, on the principle that a protracted stay
demanded an expensive purchase, but today was a meatless day,
so he was stuck once again with a chicken roast: mm hm, half-
raw meat given the position it deserved in the middle of the plate,
encircled by okay onions, putrid peppers, merely wilted peppers
and some perfectly acceptable tomatoes . . . Time passed, the meal
passed, and the sick hot evening improved until when Dr. Tariq
came he was in the middle of a conversation with some Jordanians
about how dull the nightlife had been here ever since the impo-
sition of martial law. The Young Man paid his bill, shook hands
all around, and proceeded into the swelter with Dr. Tariq, who
had invited him to stay the night with his family.

The household was headed by Tariq's father, Major General
N., a fine old man who influenced the guest more than anyone
else in Pakistan, for in the end he stayed not a night, but a month.

★ Water.

The General's family gave him food, lodging, clothes and presents. He came to feel love for them.

MY CLOTHES (1987)

I no longer have the plastic scraps of a butterfly mine from Afghanistan, because I gave them to Dr. Tariq's younger brother Zahid (since become a doctor in his own right). One of the yellow glass bangles that the family gave me for my fiancée broke on the trip home; the others left with her when she left me. I do still have a stack of photographs, through which I used to flip with some complacency, the vividness of the color dyes convincing me that I must not have failed in Afghanistan after all, and for a while I busied myself with them, blowing them up into fund-raising posters that cost more than the money they brought in—for I was and still am a most lamentably ludicrous Young Man—but within three or four years I had studied those pictures so many times that not a single image was real. I retain my illegal pen-pistol from Darra, but seldom roll its fat coldness between my fingers. My best aid to memory (for I doubt that I will ever go to Afghanistan again) is the set of clothes that General N.'s family gave me. — They hang in the back of the closet, whose white door is now shut, with its black knob like a sphere of darkness extruded from the darkness inside. — My shirt (which I think once belonged to Zahid) is a baggy affair that hangs down to my knees like an apron. The pants are wide enough around the waist for two people; they tighten with a drawstring. — On hot days, this loose cotton skin of mine feels cool, luxurious.

THE BRIGADIER (1982)

The other guest of the N. household was, of course, the Brigadier, with whom the Young Man shared the double bed. Thirty-six years ago the General and the Brigadier had been pals, back in British days, when the Pakistanis (or Indians, as they then were) had been involved in an insurrection in Kashmir.* — "I was his teacher," said the General, "and I regarded him as an honest man.

---

* Which remains disputed territory.

You think I have picked him up now for no reason? I am convinced he will be of use. He has been with me now for six months. Every day he writes letters. He is the leader of a national party *inside*, you see, and he is trying to obtain weapons. If he had not been of use I would have gotten rid of him long ago. But if your people would just give him weapons, he would be a great thorn in the side of the Russians. When you go back to America, Young Man, you must tell people about him."

The Young Man was given a copy of the letter that the Brigadier had written to President Reagan in October of 1981 (receiving, of course, no reply). It is a remarkable and pathetic document, and is here given as is. (It should be noted again that the Brigadier spoke minimal English; the peculiar spelling and syntax are the fault of the translator employed.)

Oct.29.1981

To his excellency the President of U.S.A.
(Mr. Ronald Reagan) _____

Dear excellency,

I wo-ould like to bring to your kind notice the following facts related to the destiny of Afghanistan.

When the late president Daud went to Moscow to attend the funeral of stalin on behalf of Ex-King Zahir Shah he strength-ened bilatiral relations between the two countries. On returning to Kabul he started his pro-communist activities at the beck and call of Moscow and on 1954 succeeded to the post of Prime Minister.*

Being Brig: in Afghan army I realised his brutel activities. There and then I resolved to lay out all the secrecies and make it public but I could not succeed to overt his false design during my 10 years tenure of service.

On his resigning from the poist of Prime Minister he estab-

---

* Here is one of many examples of the Pakistani and Afghan freedom with dates. In fact, Daoud became Prime Minister in 1953, not 1954. He retained this position until 1962, at which time a commoner succeeded him. In 1973 he ousted Zaher Shah in a coup, and remained in power until he was assassinated by the Taraki coup in 1978. Taraki was killed by Amin in 1979, and Amin was executed by the Soviets upon their invasion later that year. See the Chronology at the end of this book for more details.

lished indirectly of pro-Russian parcham party* on new lines. It was the only alternative to quit my Military services on 1970 to impede their ways independently.

I came to know in Qandahar province in 1973 that Daud succeeded in a Coupe-De-Ta backed by Moscow. Soonafter that I consulted all my Military and companion and various other religious, and Political Co-workers in Ghazni province. It was unanimously decided in that meeting to refer to U.S.A,Embassy in Kabul for the expected friendly co-operation for the solution of our national grievances.

Unfartunately Amirican Embassy was under the Eyes of K.G.B.s and local spies due to which we could not succed to have proper contacts.

Eventually I got an opportunity to contact U.S.-Embassidor through a prominent personality of the Embassy Feroz Mohsin who worked as an interpreter. He was an Afghan National and latter on proved a Rusian detictive. I handed over a list of my fellow Army personnel, Religious Schalor and politicians alongwith other details of national interest to the Ambassador, besides a revolutionary and reactionary plan against then then Daud's regime. He thought over the subject and latter on a states envoy Mr. Edvard Fox Martin came to Kabul and I visited him in Feroz Mohsin lodge. He supported our plan on belhaf of the states Government, which was based on humanitarian and bi-latiral relations. After conversation Mr. Edvard and myself signed on 1976 an Agreement (Known as Ox-Fox plan) bearing the following context that after two months of the agreement we will be helped with the following:

1- 300 Machineguns
2- 240 Bazoka Antitank launchers.
3- 4 Hawan (Marterguns and exessaries)
4- 40 Powerful explosive Bumbs.
5- Numerous Wirless Radio sets.
6- Establishment of Radio Broad-Casting station.
7- 22600000 Afghani money repayable and interest free.
8- 400 Rifles.

---

* The Parcham (Flag) and Khalq (Masses) parties were two rival leftist parties in Afghanistan which found themselves sharing power uneasily after the invasion. Daoud had both Parcham and Khalq backing in his coup. Amin and Taraki were Khalq. Babrak Karmal, their Soviet-installed successor, was Parcham. In 1982 Karmal was still in power.

Soon after the agreement I was chased by the detictives with a consequent imprisoned of 3 years with other four brothers.

On my release from the Jail there was no hope to visit the U.S.-Embassy during the regime of late Taraki. I deputed my companion 1978 Mr. M—— S—— R—— to see the Amirican Embassy in Pakistan and to convey my message to him. He met with the staff of the Embassy in Islamabad but with no result.

Now I have lift the nations behind to fight against the Russian intervention and came to Pakistan with 60 other comrades, who represent all the provinces of Afghanistan, in hope to revive the foresaid agreement.

I visited the 3rd Secretary of states in Islamabad and the Counsellor in Peshawar in this regard but all in vain.

Now I wish to put our problems on your table for a very kind and just favour which is based on share humanitarianism and anti-communistic expansionism ideals. I shall be very much grateful to you in person and on behalf of my nation, if you pay a very kind attention to our matters and affairs and arrange for a possible help and clue.

Thanks and thanks.

Your Sincerely,
(BRIG: — — —)
U.S.A., Counselte, Peshawar
(Pakistan)

In the course of time the Brigadier grew angry at America, for Reagan and the C.I.A. ignored his letters; and the people at the consulate were less and less polite about his coming by. It was clear enough to the Young Man that if the Ox-Fox Agreement had ever been made it would long since have been written off the books by Mr. Fox Marten's organization; for who would want to support a man whose plot had not been airtight? — Then again, Napoleon had made a comeback; so had Lenin. The Young Man, who did not understand very much about political change in Asia, decided to maintain an attitude of genial neutrality until more facts came in.

AT LATEST REPORT (1989)

He is still waiting.

MORNING AND AFTERNOON (1982)

"I was in the jail for three days without food or water, in summer," he told the Young Man in his slow, earnest English.★ "Then three years I was there, and I took up the fight against the *Roos*." — The story went that he had been Zaher Shah's bodyguard, and a jewel dealer on the side. Soon after the invasion, the Russians had napalmed his house and confiscated his jewels—"ten kilos of emeralds, *fif*—fifty kilos rubies, many other—*jools!*" cried the Brigadier fiercely. Some of his fortune remained hidden; this he disposed of by equipping a group of freedom fighters personally loyal to him. Then he set off for Pakistan to obtain the arms due him according to the Ox-Fox Agreement. Here he was. — One of his sons was missing in action; another had been conscripted by the *Roos* and every night supplied the guerrillas with ammunition for their Kalashnikovs. His wife was sick somewhere in Afghanistan, and his daughter (if I understood his pantomime) had a bullet wound in the chest. At intervals he heard from his family. A messenger would come to the General's house and deliver a square of linen, covered with Pushto cursive, which had been sewn into his garments. The Brigadier would read it over and over to himself for hours. When he had not gotten a letter for a long time, the Young Man saw him going through the other bits of cloth which had come to him, and slowly shaking his head.

"What he says, it is a tissue of fictions," said the Young Man's Afghan translator back in California. "I was in Kabul many years and I have never heard of this man. He was no bodyguard; he is no leader; he is nothing." — But perhaps the translator supported a different party.

In the morning and in the afternoon the Brigadier sat working on new letters to various heads of state. He read each draft aloud

---

★ I have not hesitated to edit the interviews in this book in order to make their syntax more readily comprehensible.

to the General, who patiently suggested insertions and modifications. Between his siesta and the evening prayer the Brigadier read his Qur'ān aloud to himself in the low singsong of custom. The Qur'ān was kept wrapped in a bright, supple cloth whenever it was not in use. As the Brigadier picked up the bundle or replaced it on the guest-room table, he kissed it. He prayed outside in the garden with the General, touching head, hands and feet to the prayer mat.

Democracy

"**M**y dear son," said the Brigadier one dizzily hot day, "I am very sorry that I have come to the Pakistan to get help. I want to be back at the fight."

"I hope you can go back soon," the Young Man said. He had a feeling that the Brigadier would still be waiting for arms on his dying day.

Over the course of that afternoon the old Brigadier became more and more agitated. He decided that democracy was the problem. — "*Why* the Amerikis no help in the fight?" he asked over and over. "*Why* they keep me sitting here?" — The Young Man made the mistake of trying to explain checks and balances. (What a theoretical Young Man!) He did not have the heart to tell the Brigadier that the Americans did not want to help him, which fact he knew from the consulate. (And it was even possible that checks and balances had something to do with that.) — He said, "Maybe part of the American government wants to help you, Brigadier. Maybe another part doesn't want to help you. Our government argues with itself before it decides anything." — The Brigadier was astounded and infuriated. If the Amerikis had a dictator like Zaher Shah, he said, there would be no vacillation; the Ox-Fox Agreement would be adhered to with honor. — "Democracy," he cried urgently, "road—to—*Communism!*" — He picked up an embroidered cushion. "Democracy: He want it there"—he touched the cushion and pointed to the bed; "*he* want it *there*"—he pointed to the floor. "Dictatorship: *one* place. Very bad, democracy!"

Well, it was better, the Young Man supposed, that he believe the problem to be one of inefficiency rather than intention. But he felt some revulsion all the same. This was the General's prize candidate, our pro-Western friend, faithful unto death . . . Spitefully, the Young Man told him that he should be happy, that thanks to the *Roos* there was a good solid dictatorship in Afghanistan now. Fortunately the Brigadier did not understand. Later the Young Man was ashamed of himself.

DECIDED OPINIONS

In Peshawar at that time the Mujahideen were divided into six major factions based on tribal antagonisms and on ideological ambitions. They had formed two coalitions, each of which (typically enough) was called the Islamic Unity of Afghan Mujahideen. The first Islamic Unity was composed of the fundamentalists and mullahs: Jamiat-i-Islami, Gulbuddin and Khalis.★ The second was made up of the liberals and social democrats: Hazarat, Mahaz-i-Islami, Herakat. The Brigadier's party, Wahdati-i-Islami, or National Liberation Front, was not officially recognized. Through an interpreter the Brigadier explained that many of the administrators in the liberal parties, and a few in those of the fundamentalists, were working secretly for him and diverting arms to the N.L.F. Naively, the Young Man asked the interpreter why, in that case, the Brigadier needed American weapons. But this made the interpreter angry, and the interview came to an end.

For a time the Young Man paid court to the Jamiat-i-Islami fundamentalists. They were strong in Afghanistan's Panjsher Province, where the fighting was heaviest at that time, and the Young Man wanted very much to go there. But the Jamiat distrusted him. He spent many hot afternoons in their offices, listening to the buzzing of the fans, watching their leader, the famous scholar Dr. Rabbani, talking behind his desk; Dr. Rabbani resembled a saint with his long silver-white beard; and the fans buzzed and the Young Man drank Sprite after Sprite sitting on the carpet

---

★ Each of the latter two parties called itself Hezb-i-Islami.

between Jamiat warriors who teased him and told him that since he was pale-skinned he must pretend to be a Nuristani to fool the *Roos* when he went *inside,* and in his intoxication at the idea of going to Afghanistan the Young Man was not even afraid. — At first the Jamiat said that they could not take him because he did not know the Qur'ān, and so could not represent their point of view to the Amerikis. But the Young Man had learned to bluff his knowledge in school; he quoted a few passages of the Qur'ān back at them. — Next they told him that they could not take him because he was too young; it was too dangerous. He pointed out that many of their Mujahideen were younger than he, and that he could surely help them by taking his pictures.* Then they said they'd let him know if something came up.

"You are not well, Young Man," the General told him. "Why must you go into Afghanistan? You can take pictures of Afghans with guns in Pakistan. The journalists do it. It will be all the same to the Americans. I am concerned about you. You cannot go into the battlefield with a loose tummy; I speak to you as a soldier."

But the Young Man was adamant.

The General was not without influence. General Zia, now the man who ran Pakistan, had once been his subordinate. He arranged many interviews which the Young Man could never have gotten otherwise—for, unlike the Amerikis, the General believed him capable of actually Helping, and so took him seriously.† As a result of these interviews the Young Man was able to string the beads of important men's words into his necklaces of analysis, somewhat as follows:

The major political dichotomy in Pakistan seemed to be liberalism versus Islamization, or (not to beat around the bush) the People's Party of Bhutto versus the established regime of Zia, who had revived Islamic law to such an extent that public floggings were now broadcast on television. At present, the People's Party

---

* "Your gift of help to Afghans is very appreciated," wrote the General in 1984, "but this amount cannot be given to anyone. You could donate the amount to an education institute—if you so desire." — "SORRY," said the rather surprising signs put up by the Berkeley Spartacists in 1983, who vowed to defend bureaucratically deformed workers' states by any means necessary. "AFGHAN SLIDE SHOW CANCELED—will be rescheduled." — "Your show was well received, and, as I believe you would have wished, provoked a goodly amount of reflection afterward," wrote Mr. Scott Swanson in 1985. "Unfortunately, a snowstorm kept all but the most hearty away."
† Or else—what seems more likely to me now—the General had a very kind heart.

was almost impotent, Bhutto having just been hanged in 1979, the invasion year. — "He was executed for *murder*," said the General. "He was a Communist, and all of us in the North-West Frontier were very satisfied to see him replaced by Zia. You see, Young Man, Bhutto was a schemer, but Zia is a just man!" (It was not until half a dozen years after, when Zia was killed in that mysterious plane crash, that Bhutto's charismatic daughter Benazir was able to ride her rallies into power; until then the People's Party barely clung to existence.) The General maintained sufficient relations with a few officials of the Bhutto regime to arrange for the Young Man to speak with them in his presence. One had been jailed several times under Zia. When they visited the man, the General pointed out an automobile parked by his house. — "They keep an eye on him, you see," he said. — They were hospitably entertained. It was Ramazan, and Muslims could not eat or drink until sunset, but the Young Man was brought a Coke on a saucer and many cordialities were exchanged. The Young Man thought that the General and the former official must be friends. Then, as they left, the Young Man's cassette nicely magnetized full of interesting information, the General remarked, "He is a very stupid man, you see. He will be back in jail again, and he should be." The Young Man wondered how he'd ever know who *his* enemies were.

One day they drove to a funeral in a small village to the east, just the three of them: the General, the Young Man and the Brigadier. The village was pro-Bhutto, and the General knew a former minister there who would give the Young Man his recollections. Unfortunately, the man was too busy, although he said hello to the Young Man politely enough and found the time to make a few digs about the postponement of the elections. The General remained calm. — The bier was carried through the mud-walled streets. The Brigadier's deep frown was softened into the expression that he wore when he read his Qur'ān. He strode through the crowd and shouldered a corner of the bier. At the mosque they set the dead man down for the ceremony, uncovering his face for a moment so that the relatives could kiss it. He was an old man, with a long white beard. His mouth was open, his head twisted to one side, like a crawl-stroke swimmer. The next morning the Young Man saw a run-over cat in the same posture, with the same intense, rather scholarly gaze. The man had died that

morning. He was already swelling and yellowing in the heat. —
They drove home in the General's car, with the Young Man in
the back seat. The Brigadier made a remark about the liberals; the
Young Man could not understand the language but he understood
the sneer. — The General laughed and nodded.

The Young Man admired the General in almost every respect.
He was a very moral man who tried to do good. He initiated the
building of a mosque, of a park (the Young Man saw him on the
news once, standing with a group of dignitaries in his new
mosque). He did a considerable amount of social work; the Young
Man was one of his cases. Not only did he give him instruction
in Islam, he also tried to find an appropriate group for him to go
to Afghanistan with. On this subject he had his opinions. Being
a soldier like the Brigadier, he despised the fundamentalists. When
the Young Man asked a guerrilla commander why he belonged
to Herakat and not Jamiat-i-Islami, the General answered for him:
"Because he is not a fool."

BETROTHED

One afternoon they had Mr. Pizzarda, the Secretary-General of
Hazarat, over for a drink (of Sharbet, a sickening syrup of sugared
rose petals). The Brigadier had said that Pizzarda was one of his
men. Was he? It was impossible to tell. — They sat in the patio
chatting about this and that, sometimes, out of politeness to the
Young Man, in English, and sometimes, very fiercely, in Pashto.
The General seemed a little left out of it. But when he sat with
the Young Man later that night, against the soothing roar of the
fan, he said that in ten days the Young Man could go into Afghanistan with the N.L.F.

"But we must be very careful," the General said. "You may
only go if you are completely well. Your parents would never
forgive me if I were responsible for the death of their only son."

The General was big on sons. He treated the Young Man as his
son. When the Young Man expressed interest in photographing
one of the handmade pistols from Darra that were disguised as
ballpoint pens, the General loaned him one, and, seeing his delight
in the toy, smiled and said, "Well, Young Man, if you are so fond
of it I will present it to you." — The Young Man thanked him.

— The General put a hand on his shoulder. "It is nothing. You are an honorary Pathan now: you wear the clothes, we have given you the cap, and now you have the gun."

He was angry when he learned that the Young Man was living with his fiancée in California. He believed that Americans in general had loose morals, particularly in the area of sexual relations. The Young Man wanted to know why the Qur'ān was so hard on sleeping with someone you hadn't married when a Muslim man could legally sleep with up to four women at a time. The General explained that there was always a danger that an unmarried woman would get pregnant. The Young Man assured him that he and his fiancée used birth control, and that his fiancée would be getting sterilized soon anyway.

The General was astounded. "Did you pick her up or did she pick you up?" he said.

The Young Man considered. "She started it, I think," he said.

"Well, then you tell her that you will drop her if she will not bear you sons. What good is a girl who will not have sons? How could your parents die knowing that their only son would have no sons?"

THE MARTYR

In the first few days of the Young Man's stay the General was particularly disgusted with Americans. His son Khalid was a student in California, under a temporary visa, and Khalid's wife had applied for a temporary visa to visit him. The application had been denied on the grounds that it could not be proved that the young woman would not become an immigrant. The General had offered to put up a surety, but this did not affect the case. This hurt the General deeply. He could not understand why his son could have a visa and his daughter-in-law could not. He told the Young Man that America didn't know what friendship was.

"What do you think of Brigadier X?" the Young Man asked at the U.S. consulate.

Thumbs down. "We've passed on his stories, and the consensus seems to be that he's slightly"—finger to forehead. — "He was a Brigadier once, and he isn't now, and he hasn't made the transition."

This might be true, the Young Man thought. Sometimes I myself, watching the monotonous circular motions of his hands, or his talking to himself—or is that just his Muslim devotions? (for I don't speak the language)—sometimes I think that he might be a little mad. — But *how am I to know?* he said to himself angrily.

"It does seem as if he has a following," the Young Man said.

"We're not sure if it's his following or if it's a consequence of the fact that he's staying with General N."

"There are lots of people who claim he's their boss," said the Young Man.

A shrug. "I really have to go to a meeting."

"Well, would you recommend that I go to Afghanistan with him?"

"I'd advise against it."

The Brigadier had told the Young Man to inform the Ambassador and his wife that he sent his *salaam* to them, and to ask when his work would be ready. The Young Man did neither. Returning, he met the Brigadier on the porch.

"What they say?"

"They had no time for me today," the Young Man said.

The Brigadier flew into a rage. — "They Amerikis, but—if they Afghans, I—KILL THEM! They servants—not masters! You—NO help me! Democracy—NO good!"

The Young Man lied, saying that he had done his best,* but the Brigadier would not believe him. At last the Young Man replied curtly. The Brigadier smiled, the way people there smiled to express deep offense.

"They treat me like—DOG!" he said.

Wearily, the Young Man agreed and went in to the toilet. The walk to the consulate and the heat had stirred up his dysentery.

Sitting on the toilet seat, he imagined a dialogue with the General, who had just been lecturing him on the Jewish lobby:

"General," he'd say, "I think the Brigadier's on the brink."

"Because you won't help him," the General would reply sternly. "He's a friend of America, but you're making him an enemy. You won't give my daughter-in-law a visa. If I can't get a visa, no one in Pakistan can get a visa. Zia was my subordinate. If I wanted to, I could go to him, and he would make them give me the visa.

---

* I know now that I could have done no better.

But that's against my principles. I ask no one for favors. I expect nothing from anyone. But now you are supporting Israel, and *lakhs*★ of people are homeless."

And the Young Man, slightly light-headed with fever, suddenly understood his role as an American: to accept responsibility for everything.

The ants

A few nights later, the Brigadier, the Young Man and the General were sitting on the patio. The cement was writhing with winged ants trapped by the house lights, crawling along, hunting in the seamless concrete for a crack in which to lay their eggs and die. Presently came the accustomed stealthy noises from the lawn, and the fat toads appeared. For a moment they stopped short, as if astonished by the profusion of prey. Then they fanned out and began to gobble up the stragglers, avoiding giving alarm to the larger mass. When the stragglers were safely eaten, however, the toads hopped in among the main body of the ants and commenced liquidation in earnest. How the toads flicked their tongues! And how blindly the ants streamed, with the very breath of their predators on them, like philosophers who had forgotten a cause.

The Brigadier was talking about the fundamentalist factions again. — "They—*no* good!" he said. "They very bad. They—*no* true Afghans!"

The reports from Panjsher Valley were bad that day. The Russians were really breaking through. — *"Roos,"* the Young Man said, pointing to the toads. "Mujahideen"—pointing to the confused, decimated ants.

At once the Brigadier got up and shooed and hissed the toads away. He stamped his foot an inch from their heads. They hunched themselves back into the darkness. (But a few minutes later they were back, cautious at first but just as greedy as before. This time the Brigadier ignored them. Soon there were no more ants.)

★ Thousands.

"The Brigadier is a bit of a brute," said the General in his lawn chair. "He's killed over a thousand people."

THE CONSUMMATION

A day before he was due to cross the border, the leader of the N.L.F. band that was going to take him came to the General's house. The General listened carefully. — "They're planning to attack an airfield," he told the Young Man. "Is that acceptable to you?"

"Sure," the Young Man said, a bit uneasily. "That sounds very interesting."

"But they must go to Islamabad to get ammunition. It will be another five days."

On the fourth morning the General put down his paper. "Yesterday in Parachinar they fired at the Tribal Agent," he said.

The Young Man was eating a boiled egg. Everyone else in the household had to be finished eating and drinking shortly after four a.m., when it was light enough to distinguish white thread from black. But the Young Man never got up until seven or even later, and then they prepared for him a breakfast which they could not touch, with their own prized honey for his tea.

"Who fired at him?" he said, not understanding.

The General's good manners forbade him from showing the disgust that this bit of ignorance deserved. "The K.G.B., Young Man. I had best ring up and find out the situation. If there is too much unrest in the border areas it might not be possible for you to go."

He made a phone call. — "Somebody has been killed," he told the Young Man. "We had best put it off."

They put it off for another three days.

The Young Man listened to the sound of the fan, which seemed pitched to remind the user that every second was costing money. The three days passed. So did the fourth. On the fifth day he picked a lime from the General's tree, and squeezed it into a glass of cold water. It tasted so good to him that he did it again after breakfast. He had gotten the idea from the Brigadier, who the day before had walked ten miles in the heat, observing Ramazan the while, searching for the man who should have come back from Islamabad with the ammunition to take the Young Man to the border. But the Brigadier did not know exactly where the man lived, and never found him. He came back silent. As soon as darkness was ruled official that night, the family went in to break their fast, but the Brigadier seemed unable to quench his thirst. He was an old man. An hour later, he came to the guest room and mixed himself a glass of fresh lime water. — "Very thirsty," he said to the Young Man, whom he had adopted as his son. "Ramazan very difficult." — "Yes," said the Young Man. "Very difficult."

The man never came.

"Tomorrow," said the Young Man to the Brigadier, "I will ask the other parties for help."

When he got up in the morning, the Brigadier was wringing his hands. "I no sleep last night," he cried. "He—*no* come. I am party leader, but now you write: 'Brigadier—*wrong*, wrong man.' My party BROKEN, my work here all broken then."

The Young Man felt very sorry for him. On the other hand, what kind of party leader *was* he? — He promised to wait until ten-thirty, when the Brigadier would return from another search for the ammunition man. After that no doubt unsuccessful mission, the Young Man would have the pleasure of going out in the midday heat.

He had come to dread the sun in Pakistan.

The General was very angry with the Brigadier. — "Bloody bastard," he said. "The Afghans don't want to be helped! They just want money. This commander has broken a gentleman's agreement. His father and grandfather come from respectable families, I assure you. And now this fool and the Brigadier have made me lose face with you."*

A little after eleven, the Brigadier came with his man. The next morning, dressed in Afghan clothes, with his cameras and tape recorders in a gunnysack, the Young Man was headed for the border.

---

* Imagine that! This fine old man, who was close to the center of power in his country, was worried about losing face with a twenty-two-year-old boy who got sick in the sun. Why? Because the boy was American.

The statement of the Afghan Brigadier

"**H**ow many people did you kill, Brigadier?" asked the Young Man ingenuously. This would be a good cross-check of what the General had said.

The Brigadier stood straight and tall in the guest room. The curtains were drawn against the afternoon light.

"I killed about a *thousand* and more of *thousand* people in the fight of the Afghanistan," he said in his slow, dignified English.★ "I killed the more people, from Russia. — Russian! In Holy Qur'ān say, 'Don't kill the peoples,' but *who* is peoples? Peoples, he is peoples when he going by the *Holy Books*. Holy Books is four: Qur'ān, Bible, [indecipherable], Torah is the Books.† These people is *people*. Who is don't like the Books, he—*no* people! The *Roos* is wild. Like horses, like donkeys, like cows, they are coming in the Afghanistan here—invasion to Afghan countries! We don't like them. I kill *more* of the Russians in Russian forts. He living in the Afghanistan now. He came, the *Roos*, him, from Russian country to our countries. They are *fighting* with me, they KILLING our little boys—he drinking milk, he hitting, they taking on his shoulder and his small small hand and small feets, they take him away, they kill him; this is not good." — (The Brigadier shook his fist; he cried; I can never forget the anguish with which he said this.) — "Our children they are killing," he said. "Our children, and our girls, and our old mans and young mans . . . In the fight, he taking and putting in the tank, between the tank, the young man and the young girls that are fighting with him; he killing! They are doing the *zillah* with the dead mans.‡ They, they *sexing* the dead girls!★★ They are like donkeys, from another world. I kill them! They kill me! I kill them!"

★ The Brigadier's numbers, like much else about him, are enigmatical. Pakistanis and Afghans seem freer in their use of figures than we. By "a thousand" he might mean "a good number." Then again, he might mean "a thousand." The General's corroboration was important, for I never knew him to make a deliberate misstatement of any kind.
† Indeed, in token of their kinship with us—which we Christians are too provincial to feel with them—Muslims call us "the People of the Book."
‡ Sexually violating.
★★ I have heard many reports of Soviet soldiers' raping Afghan women, but only one other account of sexual violation of corpses.

Old Nick (1983)

Upon his return to San Francisco, the Young Man called the C.I.A. as he had been requested to do. — "When were you in Afghanistan?" the C.I.A. man said. — The Young Man told him. — "What was this Brigadier's full name?" the C.I.A. man said. — The Young Man told him. — "What languages do you speak?" the C.I.A. man said. — The Young Man told him. — "What's your social security number?" the C.I.A. man said. — The Young Man told him. — "Thank you for calling, Mr. Vollmann," the C.I.A. man said. "You can reach me at this number anytime. If you call, please refer to me as 'Nick.' "

Five years later, I still had news of the Brigadier. But if Nick ever rearmed him, I never heard of it.★

★ The Brigadier "is fine and healthy," wrote the General a few months after I left. "All those who matter now realize that we ought to help those who are involved in fighting inside. Masud the hero of Panjsher has contacted him through his father who is also a retired Brigadier General . . . Lord C— B— of U.K. had also contacted him. He will be all right, in spite of no help from his Arab friends . . ." — The General did not even mention the Americans anymore.

II
THE REFUGEES

5
"OR AT LEAST A LONG HALT":
REFUGEES IN THE CITY
(1982)

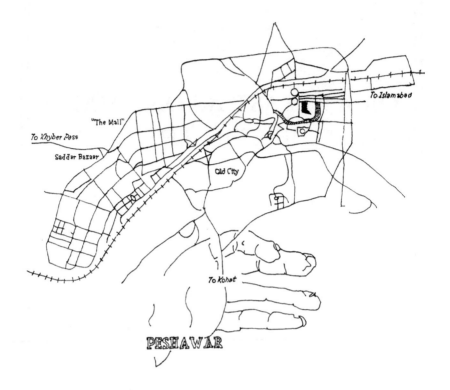

From the Young Man's sketch map

And Peshawar is now, as always, very much a frontier town. The formalities of dress and manner give way here to a free and easy style, as men encounter men with a firm handclasp and a straight but friendly look. Hefty handsome men in baggy trousers and long loose shirts swing along with enormous confidence, wearing bullet-studded bandoliers across their chests or pistols at their sides, as if it were a normal part of their dress. There is just that little touch of excitement and drama in the air that makes for a frontier land. An occasional salvo of gunfire—no, not a tribal raid or a skirmish in the streets, but a lively part of wedding celebrations.

. . . Peshawar is the great Pathan city. And what a city! Hoary with age and the passage of twenty-five centuries; redolent with the smell of luscious fruit and roasted meat and tobacco smoke; placid and relaxed but pulsating with the rhythmic sound of craftsmen's hammers and horse's hooves; unhurried in its pedestrian pace and horse-carriage traffic; darkened with tall houses, narrow lanes and overhanging balconies; intimate, with its freely intermingling crowd of townsmen, tribals, traders and tourists—this is old Peshawar, the journey's end or at least a long halt, for those traveling up north or coming down from the Middle East or Central Asia, now as centuries before when caravans unloaded in the many caravan-serais now lying deserted outside the dismantled city walls or used as garages by the modern caravans of far-ranging buses.

from a brochure by

THE PAKISTAN TOURISM
DEVELOPMENT CORP., LTD.
(ca. 1979)

"Or at least a long halt"

Trying so hard to generalize (why, I really don't remember), the Young Man Who Knew Everything explained to his notebook: "The uncleanliness of American cities is composed of such items as shattered bottles and blowing newspapers, beer cans, chemical spills, styrofoam incubators for hamburgers, and the like. In Pakistan production and distribution are not nearly as advanced; accordingly, the diet of its cities is hardly so rich, and their excretions and lymphatic disorders have an altogether different character. Much that would be thrown away in the U.S.A. is prized here—and of course there are no beer cans." — Peshawar, then, was a city of tumbledown streets and filth; and the Young Man, with his preference for advanced trash, believed it even dirtier than it was. (I confess that I myself would rather die from an industrial cancer than through an amoeba's agency; this is a question of upbringing.) — Then, too, there was the fact of being perpetually observed, accosted and remarked upon; this superfluity of attention was at times somewhat like dirt. Like other cheats, he wanted to study, not to be studied. As the attention was almost always kindly meant, responding to it eventually became a pleasure; but in the meantime the Young Man must also face the city itself: the stands selling rotten mangoes and meat so thick with flies that its own color was a mystery; the gasping men, cooling themselves off in the midst of their labor by sticking hoses down inside their shirts; the shops offering expired medicines, sugar syrup, cooking oil and brand-new fans. In the Saddar district, the sidewalks had buckled and upthrust, as if unsettled by the tunneling of giant moles. Here and there were three-foot pits without apparent purpose: little graves for fruit peels and the hooves of slaughtered cattle, with concrete shards mixed in like bones. When he bought bananas they were soft and black. The gutters stank; the water in them was gray, like the underbelly of a dead snake. Everyone moved slowly in the heat.

The Young Man wrote treatises on the effects of that heat: First
you felt it in your wet forehead, as the sweat began running into
your eyes in the first seconds. Next the sunlight penetrated your
scalp. Your hair warmed uncomfortably. The base of your neck
was sodden like your armpits, and you inhaled steam as though
you were going through the motions of breathing; and soon you
got dizzy and sick to your stomach. Some people (such as Afghan
refugees) might bleed from the nose and ears.

"Yes, it is hot," sighed the proprietor of the hotel. "In Baluchistan, they say, there is a town where in summer the water
comes from the tap hot enough for tea. I have never been there;
I hope I never will, *in sh'Allah!*"★

FREE RIDES

As the Young Man walked along, everyone looked up. They made
the quick hissings used to attract rickshaw drivers, or called out
to him: "Hey!", "What you want?", "Where you going?", or
simply, "Mister!" — To all of these, Mister returned an imper-
turbable and inane *"Asalamu alaykum"*—the traditional Islamic
greeting.† — *"Walaykum asalam,"* they said automatically, becoming more friendly. From there it was only a few steps to the free
soft drink, the tea, the guided tour with the rickshaw to his hotel
paid for at the end of it, the multitude of improbable favors.
Everyone said, surprised that he would even comment: "But you
are a guest of our country!", or, "It's a question of national honor."

Coming back from the Austrian Relief Committee one evening,
he became lost. It was Ramazan, so the General's family had been
without food or water all the long hot day. He did not want to
keep them waiting to break their fast. — But where was Saddar?
If he could find that, he could walk to the General's house. — A
cyclist came up the hill, carrying a great load of fresh-cut tree
boughs. The Young Man asked directions. The other beckoned
to a passing rickshaw. But the Young Man had no rupees left;
they had been stolen at a refugee camp. — "I pay for you!" smiled
the Pakistani. — "No, no," said the Young Man, embarrassed.

★ Allah permitting.
† *Asalamu alaykum:* Peace be upon you. — *Walaykum asalam:* And upon you, peace.

It was not far to a crossroads that he knew; the Pakistani had explained it to him. He could easily walk there. — So then, making certain that the branches were lashed tightly to the rear wheel, the Pakistani set the Young Man sidesaddle just behind the handlebars and began to pedal. — "Allah, Allah!" he cried near the summit of the hill, sweat running down his face. The Young Man, ashamed, tried to dismount, but he shook his head. — "No, no! You friend! I take you there." — In front of the General's house, before the Young Man could thank him, he smiled and turned back the way he had come.

THE RICH FAMILY

The Afghan refugees across the hall at the hotel had been sweet to the point of obsequiousness. They loaned him their soap, rushed to get water when he was thirsty, and even washed his shirt. They made him elaborate Afghan meals. — Every day the "uncle" went to the consulates or the Mujahideen political offices. The boy stayed inside all day. (The Young Man thought of him as a boy even though he had a wife and child.) The Young Man let the boy's brother sleep in his room, on the spare bed, so that he would not have to sleep on the floor with the baby anymore. — One hot night the boy and his brother invited him to go out for a walk. They strolled through Saddar, turned around, went for ice cream . . . All the males his own age seemed like boys to him, because (1) they didn't drink alcohol; (2) they didn't have much money; (3) they deferred to him.

"Why did you come to Pakistan?" he asked the boy.

The boy looked at him with nervous brown eyes. "It was—I was in the Kabul. I was a student of agriculture, and all of my family was investigated. They investigated my father, and they took him in the jail. Afghanistan, it is, it is *all* in the jail."

"He is not my nephew," explained the "uncle," who spoke excellent English. "But I let him call me uncle to show respect. His father, his mother and all his brothers except that one were detained by the Russians and killed one by one. I am all he has now."

The Young Man bought the boy a bunch of bananas, and a

detective novel to help him with his English. — "Why do you never go out?" he asked him. But the boy would not answer.

The "uncle" had three beautiful daughters, who were very shy, but when the Young Man said that he was trying to help they let him take their picture. Standing on the flat roof of the hotel, they smiled sadly. One of them shaded her eyes with her hand. In the evenings they helped him with his Pushto. (It was unfortunate, he reflected, that the word for "sister" sounded like "whore" prefaced by an expectoration, but the moving of one's tonsils among the Pathans would seem to be as much a necessity—here the worms turned over in his intestines—as the moving of one's bowels.) — The girls also practiced their English on him. After he had essayed, with great effort, "I am your . . . friend," or "It is very hot today," they would reward him by smiling, and saying an English sentence that they had memorized: "Brezhnev—is— dog!" Then they burst into giggles. — Once he said, consulting his English-Pushto dictionary at every other word, "I . . . like the Afghan . . . people. I . . . hope . . . I can help you." — They smiled and giggled.—"Dera miraboni."* They made him dinner. They stood and served him while he ate. He was made to sit. They prepared for him curry and meat and vegetables, with plums for dessert. Later he saw them eating old bread.

"There are two kinds of refugee," the hotel proprietor explained to him over green tea. "Rich refugee and poor refugee. Rich refugee, he live in Peshawar, in hotel. Poor, he live in camp. Afghan refugees no good. They wear everything out, break everything. Too many of them."

There were nine people in that family, counting the uncle's old wife. They existed in two rooms. Each room had a table and two single beds. They had been there for two months. They were trying to go to the United States or West Germany, but so far they had found no sponsors. In another month, said the uncle, if they still had no luck they would go to India. They were the rich refugees.

---

* Thank you very much.

HIS POWERS REVEALED

"It is right that they speak sweetly to you," an Iranian told him. "They want your help; you are American; you can do anything for them."*

HOWEVER

"What happens if they go to a camp?" the Young Man asked.

"You don't understand camp," the Iranian said. "In camp they live like animals. They have not enough food; they have not enough water; they are too hot; there is only sickness over there."

THE PROBLEM SOLVED

The Young Man went to the American consulate and asked if he could do anything for the family.

"They need a U.S. sponsor," the woman said.

"What do I have to do to become a sponsor?"

"Can you guarantee their financial security?" said the woman.

"No, I can't."

"Give it up," the woman said. "There are so many cases like this. I see so many cases like this every day. Just give it up."

False impressions

Every day he walked up and down Saddar, interviewing the off-duty Mujahid commanders cleaning their guns in hotel

---

* "Please send me material on Anti-Jamming as well as Electronic Counter measures . . . ," the General wrote him in 1984. But the poor Young Man, try as he would, could find out scarcely anything about this subject. He did not have the right connections.

rooms, talking to miscellaneous Afghans and Pakistanis, buying himself Cokes and Sprites, catching rickshaws to go to the political offices. Peshawar seemed to him a fishy place. Everybody he met wanted to get out or was waiting for something. He was almost the only Westerner. One day he saw a blond, blue-eyed man buying soap. The man started a conversation. He said he was Swiss and he was waiting for a letter from someone who was to meet him there. He asked the Young Man questions in a friendly way. The Young Man saw him again a few days later, in the American Center. This time he was from Rhodesia. — That night he told the uncle about it. — "Be careful," the uncle said. "I have seen him. He is a bad man."

The third time he saw him, the man said, "You want to cross the border, don't you?"

The Young Man did not entirely trust either the Swiss-Rhodesian or the uncle. So he merely said, "Well, that's pretty dangerous, isn't it?"

"Come on with you," the man said. "Why else would you be in this bloody miserable place?"

"No," the Young Man said. "I'm just a tourist."

In the hotel was a fellow from Chitral who was very interested in the Young Man. His brother was the chief of police in Peshawar, he said, and the police were going to come arrest the Young Man as a spy.

"And what will happen then?" said the Young Man, feeling some alarm.

"They will beat you," Yusuf Ali laughed.

"And then what?"

"They will make you sleep with them.★ And they will beat you again. Then you will go to jail."

"Oh," said the Young Man noncommittally.

"They will beat you, you C.I.A.!" Yusuf Ali chuckled, slapping the Young Man's shoulder. "Do you understand? They will *beat* you and *beat* you, you spy!"

"Oh, *I* understand," the Young Man said. He resolved to change his hotel.

"You are very dull, my friend," said Yusuf Ali. "I am just joking."

★ Yusuf Ali was certain that all the boys in America touched each other. "Have you ever touched another boy?" he asked. "No? Very good. You are a pure, gentle boy."

"But your brother is chief of police?"

"Yes."

"And you really think I am a spy?"

"You are C.I.A., yes. But I have no told my brother about you, my friend. But if they find you, they *beat* you, you C.I.A."

His aims and plans seemed to be wandering through alien channels like those narrow, high-walled, white-walled streets of Peshawar, in which men in cotton-white passed white-veiled women. He went out that night to get a fruit drink (which later made him urinate blood). On the way back, a crowd of Pakistanis surrounded him. They had been watching him day after day. They asked where he was going, what he was doing, where he was from. And why didn't he stay in a youth hostel? They could have arranged "a better reception for him there." — The Young Man said that he was happy with his reception here. — Why wasn't he going to India? — He didn't have much money, he said, and anyhow he only wanted to see Pakistan. — Oh, was he applying to his government for assistance in returning home? — No. — Why not? (And, by the way, the youth hostel was cheaper.) — "Don't you want me here?" said the Young Man. — Oh no, it wasn't that at all. But it might be very dangerous for him here, so near the border. — Now the conversation shifted to another topic with which he was already familiar: Could they get visas to the U.S.A.? — The Young Man said that that was very hard; so they had told him at the consulate. — Well, could *he* get them visas to the U.S.A.? — No, he said. — But he was satisfied with his reception here, he'd said? — Yes, thank you; everyone was very kind. — Well, then wasn't he very selfish not to help them? They turned their backs on him. — When he lost his temper, they said that they had only been joking. — "Friend! Friend!" they cried.

. . . Yusuf Ali touched the Young Man's neck and asked him when he would be crossing the border. The Young Man wrote in his diary: "What's so special about me, anyway? Well, if he just wants to scare me, or to try to paw me, I can handle that, but I don't like the idea of arrest and confiscation." — He decided that maybe he should show Yusuf Ali some friendliness, and try to find out what was going on. So he asked him out for a walk the next day. Yusuf Ali rubbed his hands together and agreed. But the next morning, when the Young Man went to knock on his door, there was no answer. The proprietor said that Yusuf Ali had left for good at four that morning. — The Young Man decided to change his hotel. But he never got around to it. The police never came, anyhow. He saw the same people on the street every day. The Swiss-Rhodesian had gone away.

("So what makes you think that I am C.I.A.?" he had once asked Yusuf Ali. "My tapes, my film?" — "No, no," said Yusuf Ali. "My dear friend, it is in the lines of your hand; I can read hands, you see.")

TRUE IMPRESSIONS

In the afternoons he sometimes saw the young soldiers marching and marching along the street. — "It is only a matter of time before the *Roos*, they come here to Pakistan," a man told him. "Then we must be ready with our jihad. Even now they are in Peshawar, the K.G.B., and there is shootings. Their planes, they fly every day over Peshawar."

IN WHICH WE ASYMPTOTICALLY APPROACH AFGHANISTAN

The Young Man now took a trip to the Khyber Pass, so that he could say that he had been there. At the border, they told him, you could wave to the Soviet guard and he would wave back. You could take a picture. Alas, he did not get to the border. The bus took him across the desert and up into the cracked red mountains. Dust blasted in through the open windows and swept through the bus as they went. At one checkpoint there were boys selling water through the windows of the bus. The water came in old motor-oil cans; after you drank you returned the can. The Young Man's seatmate bought him some; it tasted wonderful. They kept going up into the hills. They passed three women in black chadors squatting together under a tree, like resting crows. When the bus entered the tribal area, some of the men began to chew their hashish. The Young Man's neighbor gave him a pinch, and showed him how it was done. At Landi Kotal, an evil little town of ancient, low-roofed houses, he had to change buses. He was five kilometers away from Torkham, the border town. The bus to the border was an old station wagon. All the passengers were nomadic tribespeople: old men with snow-white beards, children carrying chickens, red-robed women with long braids and silver earrings who wore no veils. They could barely understand his Pushtu. — "Kabul?" they said. — The Young Man shook his head. — "Torkham. All you, Kabul?" — "Kabul, yes." — A boy tried to sell him opium, but his father slapped him. — Halfway to Torkham there was a customs check. The officials poked the grain sacks with sticks and looked around. When they saw the Young Man, they stopped dead and began to shout. Then they pulled him off the bus. — The Young Man, feeling as usual that blitheness was his best defense, told the other passengers goodbye with a wave and a smile, but they looked at him in silence. The bus went on to Kabul. — Inside the dugout, they looked at his passport very carefully. He acted like an American, asking them to let him take pictures, and seeming generally friendly but bewildered, until finally they let him go. They put him in the back of a pickup truck and took him back to Landi Kotal. They let him off near the bus station and drove away without speaking to him.

They had many dugouts there on the edge of the mountain. Every now and then, when they were deciding what to do about the Young Man, their attention wandered and they looked up into the rich blue sky, in the direction of Afghanistan. From far away came the noise of a plane.

The man who would have to go to the camps

After another inconclusive interview with Dr. Najib of the Jamiat-i-Islami's political office, he took a rickshaw back to Saddar. The expatriate "Rhodesian" had told him about the joys of the American Center, with its air conditioning and its color portrait of President Reagan, so the Young Man decided to stop there. He wanted to be a recluse for an hour. — They had *Time*, *Newsweek* and even the *Partisan Review*. He took all three. He sat at a clean round table by himself, his happiness alloyed only by the realization that eventually he would have to go outside again and walk past the men in baggy white cotton shirts and trousers who sat cross-legged in small white-painted shops, smiling or staring at him, the sewing machine with which they made their living momentarily idle; they all seemed to have dark faces, dark hair, dark eyes, mustaches and white teeth; they were summer-white like chalk dust or road dust beneath the trees of Peshawar's British cantonment, and their hands were still; then after other ceremonies of mutual appreciation he would find himself back at the hotel; he would enter his room, where every dirty wall was as hot as an oven door, even late at night, and where, in ecological cheer, ants crawled slowly across his bed, and a cricket led him in song from the bathroom, as it had been doing for days; and scorching air came from the fan, which every now and then died for a while along with the lights (electrical power in Peshawar was erratic)—but here at the American Center things couldn't be better. — He picked up *Time* first. Israel had been doing something in Lebanon. He saw an Afghan staring at him from another table. He ignored him. He looked at *Newsweek. Newsweek* appeared to agree with *Time.*

The power went out. At first it was merely dark; within five minutes it was hot and dark. Most people left; the staff brought out dimly flickering lanterns for the rest. The Young Man stayed, hoping that the power would be restored; meanwhile it was impossible to read. He looked up, and the Afghan smiled at him, and he smiled back, and the Afghan came to join him, laughing at the lanterns. — "Like in my father's time," he said.

He was a diplomat's brother. (The diplomat, of course, was now an ex-diplomat.) He hated Pakistan. "Afghanistan once ruled Pakistan and India!" he cried, looking around him wildly. "They are nothing but a nation of money-lovers and slaves! They do not help us!" — He took the Young Man to an ice-cream parlor and bought him a Sprite, which the Young Man drank down thirstily. — "Last month this cost two rupees fifty paisa," the Afghan said. "Now it is three rupees fifty. They make it hard to live."

He took tranquilizers at night, he said. He was thirty, and his hair was going gray. If Afghanistan was free he would have returned there at once. "But also I like America," he said placatingly, "America is a very good country." He had been told that if he went there he could immediately obtain a girlfriend, an apartment,

a Cadillac. He asked the Young Man to call up the consulate and arrange for him to leave tomorrow.

He wouldn't believe that the Young Man couldn't do it. "What is freedom, what is democracy then?" he said.

He said that Pakistani girls were not allowed to meet him, because he was Afghan. He was very lonely. He asked the Young Man if he had a girlfriend. The Young Man told him that he would be getting married soon. — "Very good," the Afghan said in his deep voice. "You are a superpower; you can do anything. Me, I am nothing."

The Young Man could think of nothing to reply.

He implored the Young Man to get him a visa.

"What will happen to you if you cannot get a visa?" said the Young Man, returning his problem to him like a prize package.

"If I cannot, I . . ." The man's voice trailed off uncertainly. "My money will be finished after a few months . . ."

"And then what will you do?"

He laughed. "I—I'm not sure."

He cleared his throat. "But I, also, try a lot to find a job. But I cannot find any job."

"Do you think," pursued the Young Man, "that you'll have to go live in one of the camps when your money is gone?"

"Yah, yah. Yah, I must go."

"And what will happen then?"

"I don't know. But United States is a very good country for me. It's a very big country. If I found someone to send me a visa, I can go there."

"Thank you," the Young Man said, shutting off the tape recorder.

HELPLESSNESS [1]

He never did anything for the Afghan.

It is much nicer to work for the Citizens' Action League, as I subsequently did, than to set out to Help Afghanistan, for all that I had to do in the former case was to get a stoplight built at a dangerous intersection (which also never happened) or fill up ten pages of petitions a day with signatures; but what the Young Man wanted to do is less susceptible to being broken into necessary procedures which can be checked off (and it is certainly an American need to check things off).* I suppose that he would have satisfied that urge had he been a happy part of some worthwhile organization which could require him to inspect so many camps, scrounge so many rounds of ammunition per time period. The only trouble is that committing oneself to any organization requires faith without knowledge, for as long as you are snooping around trying to learn which group, which side is the right one (before going to Afghanistan, as I said, he was willing to entertain the idea that the Soviet Union might be doing something progressive in Afghanistan), all organizations will be like closed clams. And why not? They are as vulnerable as you. — The International Rescue Committee would not hire the Young Man or let him work as a volunteer because it was not his intention to go into relief work for its own sake, but to "help the Afghans" (and, not yet having seen Afghans or relief work, he could not be certain to what extent the two were compatible. If you think this prissy, think again). Understandably, the I.R.C. was not thrilled by his attitude—which perhaps they sensed from his resume, for they canceled the interview—but then of course there were not any positions open even for unpaid work: Pakistan had strict limits on employed foreigners. He was able to visit the camps, in fact, only because Aid For Afghan Refugees (A.F.A.R.), a fine fund-raising organization in San Francisco, sent word that the Young Man belonged to their group. This was generous of them, it not being strictly true, since the Young Man had come to several A.F.A.R.

---

* Probably this is why doctors so often seem callous to those who do not have to do their work. Beset with a flood of suffering and dying, they must accept the fact that they can make almost no difference. Good doctors, of course, only work that much harder.

meetings but neither he nor A.F.A.R. had ever suggested that he become a member. It is my guess that A.F.A.R., like I.R.C., felt slightly uneasy about him. A.F.A.R., like Joan Baez's Humanitas International or Dr. Joseph Pace's Direct Relief in San Jose, could not officially support violence or other forms of politics; and the Young Man was considering going into Afghanistan with the Mujahideen, whom it was important for A.F.A.R. to dissociate itself from. The members of A.F.A.R.—mainly Peace Corps volunteers who had served in Afghanistan—could not quite fathom the Young Man's connection with their issue. Nor were they all that interested. The Young Man was callow, babyfaced, unproven. A.F.A.R.'s president felt sorry for him, though, and very kindly made the telephone call to I.R.C. That made all the difference. So in the end A.F.A.R. committed itself to *him* through a kind of faith without knowledge. — Or rather, A.F.A.R.'s president did. No one helped the Young Man out for any reason connected with what he thought and hoped he was: he was a megalomaniac. Even the Afghanistan National Liberation Front took him into the war zone as their guest only because they respected the General and he asked them to (and because he paid them). Only the desperate Afghans that he met in the streets had any illusions that the Young Man could accomplish anything. After all, what could he have done? — A book, maybe, or a slide show, or a radio show, or sale of his photographs on the street, or mailing campaigns to libraries and churches, or fund-raising booths? — Later, he tried every single one of these.*

And, anyhow, when you're walking among the largest refugee caseload in the world, and here they all are begging you to help them with tears in their eyes, what can you do? First you meet one of them in Peshawar (come to think of it, why not begin counting with the Pakistani beggars in Karachi, or the whores in San Francisco?—the General was always saying that do-gooders must put their own houses in order first), and then you meet a family of them, and then several thousand in a camp (thank God he didn't have the money to go to the Northern Territory, where supposedly it was even worse, with homeless people as far as the

---

* "Professor E— B—, the judge for this year's B— Prize in Political Science, asked me to convey to you his admiration for the work," wrote the administrative assistant. "Although not really 'political science,' as literature it is splendid." — A literary agent thought that it had some good political insights, although it did not stand up as literature.

eye could see along the margins of muddy mountain roads, selling their possessions at bargain prices to rug and curio importers— but he had only *heard* about it; I'm sure it wasn't quite that bad); so you give something to the first person who touches you, and maybe the second if you have more to spare, and then your quota is expended (whenever I hear of a church's sponsoring some starving child in an African village, I, being basically a cheerless fellow, think about the ten others beneath that same roof); and you say to the third person, "I'm sorry, but I can't help you," and he and his three sisters cannot understand why you, who have so much, cannot help them, unless somehow they offended you or did not treat you with sufficient hospitality or else maybe the fact that the sisters put on their best dresses to ask you was unredeeming because the dresses had become shabby, so that they were not worthy of you; but surely once you explain to them what they did wrong they can make amends so that their souls can this time *purely* beseech your soul and then you, being a god, will grant what is after all a *pro forma* gesture on your part?—and you (if you are decent) are cut inside with guilt and pain, so maybe you forget your quota and give them what they need, for it does mean so little to you compared to what it means for them,★ and they all embrace you and go away happy, but now here is case number four, whom you really are going to have to turn away, because the consulate has told you that one can sponsor only so many refugees; and he has in his eyes that same astonished look: *"You are going to let me fall!"*—which is not reproach because you are not reproachable, so how can he reproach you without reproaching the entire world? (and he couldn't possibly be doing that). The Afghans were among the lucky, for their case was one of mere invasion, not genocide, and, as you had already learned, in helping people one has to draw the line somewhere. Of course helping them would be delicious, the line drawn considerately to avoid them, since their distress had been brought about by our international enemy; this was why working with them made more sense to an American of utilitarian bent than aiding Soviet war widows: other Americans would *surely* back you. — Cases number five and six, however, come at you simultaneously with ruthless

---

★ In 1982 someone told me that an American dollar was worth the equivalent of ten dollars to a Pakistani, and a hundred dollars to an Afghan.

aggression; if you gave something to five you'd have to give to six, too, so to hell with them. (The population of Peshawar had doubled since the refugees came.) Here's case number fifty speaking: "But United States is a very good country for me; it's a very big country; if I found someone to send me a visa . . ." — This fellow bears an interesting resemblance to case two, but differs from case seventeen in ways x, y and z; and now, safe on the High Ledge of Generalizations, the Young Man has become me, who is quite satisfied to raise enough money here in Oakland to maybe send the Mujahideen one machine gun,★ and then let's call it quits and go on to some other project.

"A VERY GOOD COUNTRY FOR ME,"
or, HAPPINESS [3]

When the relatives of my friend H. arrived in California, they were kept in custody for several days, and then assigned to a foster family. The parents were treated as servants by the family. The children were made to eat out of dog bowls. When the parents protested, their five-year-old son was placed in an institution. They were not allowed to visit him. (I did not quite believe any of this when H. told me—how could such things happen? Had they entered the country illegally? Was H. exaggerating to get my sympathy? But why would he do that? He had more money than I.) They did not see the boy for six months. H. hired a lawyer

---

★ INTERARMSGram: May 8, 1984

Mr. William T. Vollmann
San Francisco, CA 94122

Dear Mr. Vollmann:

We thank you for your inquiry and request for quotations on anti-aircraft missiles and launchers. We are sorry to inform you that we are unable to be of assistance on these items as we do not handle this type of armament.

Very truly yours,
Carl Ring
Vice President
CR:smc

INTERARMS•NUMBER TEN PRINCE STREET•ALEXANDRIA, VIRGINIA 22313

and filed suit. Eventually they succeeded in getting custody. The boy had become very quiet. They did not know what had happened to him in the institution because he would not talk about it. Meanwhile, the parents awaited a judgment as to whether they would be allowed to stay in the United States. At length the Immigration official assigned to their case summoned them. He put leg irons on their feet. He made them shuffle after him down a long corridor. He told them that he was going to put them on a plane back to Afghanistan. When they landed, the Russians would execute them, he said. It is not hard to imagine how they felt as they walked toward that unseen airplane; they *had* to walk down the hall, just as my friends and acquaintances in Afghanistan must go over the mountains at night to the place where the Russian soldiers had cut their pipeline and stand there selling gasoline or trading it, so much gasoline in a dirty cup for so much hashish, the Russians too stupid to see that they are selling to their enemy one of the things needed to go on killing Russians, and that Russians who use hashish are easier to kill! (Yet I wonder why the Afghans even bothered to pay, why they didn't just go farther down in the moonlight and kneel beneath the leak where the gas came dribbling out; or why they didn't set it afire; — but of course it was their own gas; why should they blow up their own country's gas?) — To H.'s relatives, of course, it did not seem evident that there was anything left to buy or sell or negotiate. — Then the Immigration man smiled and set them free. It was only a joke. They could stay. When I met the family a few days later at a restaurant, they smiled and picked at their food. They spoke hardly any English; they had no money. I gave them two hundred dollars—all I had. They smiled and told me how happy they were to be here. They insisted on paying for the lunch. I think they really were happy. What had happened to them *here* was insignificant.

ANOTHER TWIST OF THE WORM

Let's suppose that the Young Man had been able to give everyone he saw exactly what was asked for; that, being the American that he was said to be, he truly was the genie in the Sprite bottle. After all, their expectations were modest (most of them). They did not want to have EVERYTHING that the Young Man had. By and large, they wanted money and guns. If he gave them those, then the Soviets would feel obliged even more often to violate Pakistani airspace with their low-flying planes that grazed Peshawar so teasingly and then swerved back toward the border to bomb another refugee camp or drop another load of toy-shaped butterfly mines where Afghan children would pick them up; or else another Afghan politician might be murdered in Peshawar and no one would be able to say for sure whether a K.G.B. agent or another Afghan did it. So the Young Man would have to wave his magic wand somewhat more vigorously, to wish the Soviets right out of Afghanistan, which happened eventually, indeed (although few history books will credit the Young Man for it), but until it did his help would not mean a goddamned thing. If he had been the President, would it have meant anything? — Yes. — Then why wasn't he the President? It wasn't fair. If he were President he could do something good that people would respect him for.★ As it was, what was the use?

HELPLESSNESS [2]

At this point, however, the Young Man was still trying, or going through the motions of trying, so he developed a dread of going outside. There were people there who would ask something of him. He often had nightmares. Once he dreamed that he was cutting up a beef carcass on a ranch where he had once worked in California, when suddenly an Afghan or Iranian came up behind him asking for a visa. The Young Man told him that he was busy, for these people never accepted a no and you had to argue with them for half an hour, which was impossible in this case because he was busy fulfilling his own stupid little function. — "I don't think you understand," the refugee's sister said, flashing her eyes winningly. "He's at the top of his class, commended for this and that." — The whole family was here now, sitting down to dinner around that carcass, which belonged to the ranch, not to the Young

---

★ "To Wm. Vollmann the PRESIDENT of Afghanistan Media Committee: We the Revolutionary Community Party of America condemn your rightwing propaganda. We will fight your death propaganda by whatever means necessary."

Man; but traditions of hospitality forbade him from saying anything about that. So he remained his weak self, sneaking around
taking little bits of meat off their plates unobtrusively, trying to
save something for his organization. — The family didn't approve
at all. They ate everything.

PARASITISM

One evening the Young Man was coming back to Saddar along
Hospital Road. A man was looking at him out of the crowd of
people looking at him. — *"Asalamu alaykum,"* said the Young
Man automatically. — *"Walaykum asalam,"* the man said. "Where
you go?" — "I'm just walking," the Young Man replied. "I like
to walk." — The Pakistani bought him a cold Sprite. It was a
very hot evening, and he was dehydrated from dysentery; he
drained the bottle in seconds. The Pakistani bought him another.
— He was an engineer studying at Peshawar University. He also
liked to take walks, he said. — They walked together down past
Balahisar Fort (originally, said the guidebook, built by Babur, first
of the Mughal Dynasty), and along the wide British avenues. The
trees were painted with wide white stripes of lime.
    "You want to see Peshawar Museum?" the man said. — "Very
much," he said. — It was six-thirty. The museum had closed at
five, but the Young Man's benefactor spoke for a long time to
the grumbling old caretaker until finally the wooden doors were
flung back, and the Young Man stepped into the dark. Behind
him, the caretaker turned on the electric lights one at a time, as
they were needed. There were beautiful Qur'āns, in blue and
white, and other colors; a whole room was set aside for them.
There were women's costumes that would have jangled in silver,
had the women still been alive to wear them; and water-skins,
and knives, and muskets; and remote black Buddhas from the
forgotten time. The Pakistani was among friends. He told the
Young Man something about every display that was there, until
the Young Man felt great respect and wonder creeping upon him
like a lovely evening shadow across sunny rooms. Again they
went to look at the room of the Qur'āns, which were so perfectly
made that even now I can still sometimes see them with my eyes

closed, the pure blue and white cursive weave of them, and I hope that I will see them again.

At sunset the Young Man and the Pakistani walked into the old city and its dinner smells of kebab and mutton tika and curry. Entire streets sizzled with frying meat. As twilight came, a weariness settled over the town. In the fabulous garden of Shahi Bagh they stopped beneath the trees, and the Pakistani bought him a Sprite and a 7-Up. Shahi Bagh smelled like flowers. In the fading light, he saw men sprawled in the grass, or sitting with one another talking quietly. — "Who are they?" he asked. — "Afghan refugees," the man said. "They sleep here." — "Where do they sleep if it rains?" — "In the mosque," the man said. "If there is room."

When it was dark the man got him a rickshaw, paid his journey to Saddar for him in advance, and disappeared.

A QUESTION

Did the man do this for refugees, too? If so, for how many? And if not, why not?

ANOTHER QUESTION

Does asking the first question get at something useful, or is it an insult to the man's simple kindness? And this tendency that I now have years later to recall the Young Man's journey as a sort of failed Pilgrim's Progress, does it give me a chance to make practical generalizations about how people ought or ought not to be, or was that my problem in the first place? If these memories were only "travel experiences" for you, the reader, to nibble at, would you like them better? Would that be a more honest presentation of the *understatedness* of life? For as it is, I have excavated and reworked what was once a random if picturesque trail into something resembling one of the freeways in my country, with road signs and billboards writhing with strange secret symbols. — And yet, encrusted though the route may be, I think, I hope it goes somewhere . . .

Statement of the Afghan waiter

In the days before he left his hotel room for the General's, the Young Man spent time with an Iranian student at Peshawar University and his friend, a Jordanian. They were tormented people. The Iranian was effectively an exile, because upon hearing about Khomeini's executions he'd gone to the Iranian consulate and torn up his passport. "Now they will put me in jail, maybe shoot me, if I go back," he said. — The Young Man took a bus out to the Iranian's apartment at Jabbar Flats, and they got a watermelon and the three of them sat on the bed and ate it. The Iranian and the Jordanian were outraged at the condition of the camps. — "Two, maybe three million Afghan refugees are living here!" the Jordanian shouted. "They don't have shoes, they don't have clothes, they don't have food, they don't have books for school; they don't have anything! Every day they become more and more poor, and, you know, they have got only sickness over here." — The Young Man was a little skeptical. For one thing, he recollected that according to both the World Health Organization and the *Great Soviet Encyclopedia*, in Afghanistan in 1965 (around that time the Soviets were offering the Afghans arms against the Pakistanis), thirty percent of the population had tuberculosis, ninety percent had helminthiasis, malaria was ubiquitous, and so was, let's see, typhus . . . There were 1,564 cases of cholera, thirteen percent of the residents of Kabul had trachoma (this figure ascended as high as seventy-five percent in the rural areas); 30,000 people had leprosy; and of course the infant mortality was one out of two—so how could you blame the camps for disease? — On the other hand, with all the overcrowding, conditions were probably worse now. But how much worse? That he never found out.*

They introduced him to a refugee who had once been the editor of a prominent newspaper in Kabul. Now he drove a rickshaw and hauled loads on his back. He was in his sixties. — The Young Man asked him why he did not register as a camp inmate to collect

---

* At that time I thought such distinctions very important, because if disease in the camps was no worse than it had been at home, then I could not blame the Soviet Union for it, so it did not matter. (If this book is only about the effects of the invasion of Afghanistan, then of course that is a fair way of looking at the matter. Fortunately for my soul, it isn't.)

the refugee allowance. The man stared at him; the Iranian had to explain that this Young Man was just an ignorant foreigner who had not seen the camps. "In the camp they must live like animals," the rickshaw driver said in Pushtu. "They have no food, no water." — The Young Man asked Mark Ice, the head of the International Rescue Committee's office in Peshawar, what he thought about that. — "Well, they exaggerate," said Ice. "I've never heard of anything like that. Now, it is true that the administration of the camps is divided up among sixteen voluntary agencies—Saudi Red Crescent, I.R.C. and so on—and some are run by the Pakistanis and are closed to foreigners. Conditions in the various camps do vary."

Meanwhile, the Young Man still had not visited the camps. Every day he took the bus up to Jabbar Flats and talked with the two students in that bare concrete room that was now only patchily white, and the fan whirred and they stood pacing with their shirts off because it was so hot and the clock ticked very loudly. One day they said that the old rickshaw driver wanted the Young Man to meet his son. They went to a restaurant in which the *pukkas* roared futilely against the heat. Sweat rolled off everyone's face onto the table. They ordered a Sprite apiece, and after ten minutes the Young Man had two more. It was a fancy place: with each soft drink the waiter brought salt and lemon.

The waiter was a man in his twenties. He was a very clean and graceful person who was constantly being called for by name among the clattering of teacups; all the patrons knew him, apparently. — *"Abdul, tsalor Fanta!"** Yes, it appeared that he was popular. He was summoned into the kitchen and to a front table and to a back table and into the kitchen. He was very energetic and always smiled as he came quickly to where he had been called. — In two hours, however, business had slackened, and he came over to the Young Man's table to talk.

THE BANDITS

"When I was in Afghanistan my father has a little money, do you know?" began the waiter earnestly. "When we left Afghanistan we sold our furniture and some other things to come here. We

---

* "Abdul, four Fantas!"

walked three days without a stop. Russian soldiers are now living in our home. We came here; now I am working here. I get from here eight hundred rupees monthly.* I am working only for rent, from six o'clock morning until twelve o'clock midnight. We brought a little money with us from Afghanistan. And I think that after two-three months this money will be finished. And I ask myself, what will we do?" — He laughed. — "We cannot live in the camps. By God, we cannot! It is my mother and my sisters —how can she live? She cannot go out; everyone watches when she washes . . . For me it does not matter, but for her—most of the people of Afghanistan is religious. The poor womans, do you know, they don't like the people or the foreign people looking at wife. For this reason we cannot stay in the camp. In the tent there is no water; there is nothing; it is very hot; this is very difficult. It is not safe."

They called him to the kitchen. Apologetically, he laughed. The Young Man shut off the tape recorder and waited. He was almost alone in the restaurant now. The students had left some time ago, and there were only a couple of men at another table, eating kebabs and staring at him. They snapped their fingers and called for Abdul: *Another Coke!* — And now here he came back to the Young Man's table, smiling brightly.

"What do you think the situation is like in Afghanistan now?" the Young Man said. "Is Mr. Karmal† firmly in control?"

Abdul laughed. "Karmal is like a dog; he is like a dog of Russia, do you know? I think sometimes he want to kill himself. If he want to sleep, there is one Russian soldier always watching. They don't have necktie: maybe he will die himself with his necktie." — He laughed. — "In Afghanistan, Russian is everything, Afghanistan is nothing." (How often Afghans said to the Young Man, "You are everything; I am nothing!") "There is only Russian film and Russian dance on television," he said. "In the government they don't like us. But the soldiers don't know. They think they are fighting against Pakistan, because when they came to Afghanistan the captain told them: 'There is attack from Russia and China.' These were Russian soldiers, but they didn't know any-

---

* In 1982, the official rate of exchange was Rs. 11 to the dollar. The black-market rate was eight to ten rupees higher.
† Babrak Karmal was the Soviet puppet in Kabul, later replaced by Najibullah.

thing. He told them: 'There are more than one million China in Afghanistan; they are against the government. They look like this: they have turban, they have beard, they have nose like this.' " (The waiter touched his own nose.) "The captain told them: 'You kill them! You kill the Pakistan people because they want to attack Afghanistan.' And then every person who is bad, who is from religion, they killed them."

The Young Man watched the red light and the steady green light on his tape recorder.

"So they go to village," the waiter said. "They kill the womans. I saw one woman, they kill her, the Russian soldier shoot and she die . . . I was in the village with my grandfather; I was there when the *Roos* attacked. With tanks they attacked our village, and we ran away to the mountains. Another woman there, she started to fight back; she climbed on the roof of the tank, and at last one soldier with Kalashnikov kill her, like that"—he made a machine-gunning noise—"she fall down; she was *young*, and she died in that time. She was a very brave girl. Still she had not married. And she died. — And there was two other old person, do you know, seventy years old, sixty years old; we all us ran away to the mountains, and also the womans, but these two, three old persons, they think the Russians never do anything with them; they are older!" — He laughed. — "One of them carries something with his donkey. But the Russian soldiers came. Before they ask him, 'What are you doing? What do you have?' they kill him, by God, and the other one also.

"And after this time," the waiter said, "we have many problem in the village, because all the womans they cannot run for two, three hours; they are very tired. We make the underground place, and we have a soldier in the first street, and when the Russians attack he run for us and inform to us, 'The Russian soldiers coming!'; then all the girls and womans go underground, and the young boys shooted against the Russian, and they run away; sometimes they kill many Russian soldiers. But one problem was that we did not have many guns and other things.

"At that time my father was in the city, in Kabul, and also my brother and my sisters, and I decided to come here. The village was damaged. I couldn't go back to the city: the policemen was there, and they put my father in jail for two, three weeks for us. They say to him, 'Where is your children; where is your sons?

They are young, so they must be soldier!"* But my father refused
that he didn't know anything, so finally they released him; and I
came here to the Pakistan, and my brother and my father and my
mother and my sisters also came here; and that is the story of my
life."

There was a silence for a moment, and the waiter leaned back,
shredding invisible things in his hands. "Once," he said, "I talk
with Russian soldiers the first time they get off airplane. They told
me, 'We are here to help you, but you *kill* us! I want to fight with
China and Pakistan people.' — I say, 'You didn't come to Afghanistan to help Afghan people; you came to kill them and make
trouble. Go back to your country. Don't fight against people.' —
They say, 'Are you bandit? Why are you talking opposite of your
country?' "

"Abdul!" called the men at the other table. "Fanta, Sprite,
Sprite!"

"I have one uncle, he was twenty-three years old," the waiter
said. "He completed his studies, but he didn't work. They caught
him; they make him soldier. After two, three weeks he die; they
kill him." — He laughed and got up and served the men at the
other table a Fanta and two Sprites, in cool wet bottles. The fans
roared.

A QUESTION

"When I imagine that someone who is laughing is really in pain
I don't imagine any pain-behaviour, for I see just the opposite. So
what do I imagine?"†

HELPLESSNESS [3]

At last the waiter came back and looked at the Young Man ques-
tioningly. So many people had looked at the Young Man full in

---

* The occupation forces found it convenient to conscript Afghans to fight the Mujahideen.
The conscripts were put in the front lines; thus the Mujahideen could usually kill only
other Afghans. Many boys were forcibly inducted at their high school graduation or earlier.
† Wittgenstein, *Philosophical Investigations*, I.393.

the face with pleading glowing in their eyes, so desperate to be saved that they forced themselves to believe in him; but the waiter expected only one thing: that in the space of a few months he must go with his family to the camps. His gaze of questioning was meant only to be courteous—"What else would you like to ask me?"—but to the Young Man it seemed a different kind of question that filled him with fear and sadness.

"What is life like for you here?" said the Young Man, striving instinctively to propitiate that soul that had not been wronged by him, could not be propitiated by him, could not be propitiated by anything that was likely to happen (for six years later, as I wrote this, nine years after the invasion, the Russians were still in Afghanistan, and the year after that there was only chaos).

"Refugee is very bad life," the waiter shrugged.

HAPPINESS [4]

"If you had a message for the Americans, what would it be?"

"All the young boys from the camps," said the waiter, "they are fighting against the *Roos*. There is no difference between Mujahid and refugee; my father and I are refugee and Mujahid . . . * If Americans help us, we want to be helped as Mujahids. It is more important to give ammunition; then we will be able to fight bravely against the Russians. The second is food; food is very important, and medicine."

"And no help specifically for the refugees?"

"Many refugees in America, they have sponsorship and the rich people," the waiter said. "At the embassy in Islamabad they told me, 'Have you a sponsor?' and I told them no. 'Then you don't have a chance,' they say. I asked them, 'Why you help only special people?' "

---

* However, some camp inmates did draw a distinction between Mujahideen (holy warriors in what was primarily seen as a religious war) and Mujahers (people who had become refugees as a result of anti-religious persecution). For the Afghans, the religious nature of events cannot be overemphasized. What they especially despised about the Soviet invaders was that they were atheistic. This helps to explain why they were so perplexed about public inaction toward their cause in the U.S.A. We Americans were also People of the Book, weren't we? Then was it not our religious duty to help the Afghans? — The Afghans had many illusions still to lose about us.

It did not seem to the Young Man that the waiter had answered his question. He sat waiting until for the second time the waiter looked him full in the face and said, "Nothing will help refugees. But send us just one atom bomb and we will be happy forever." And he laughed.

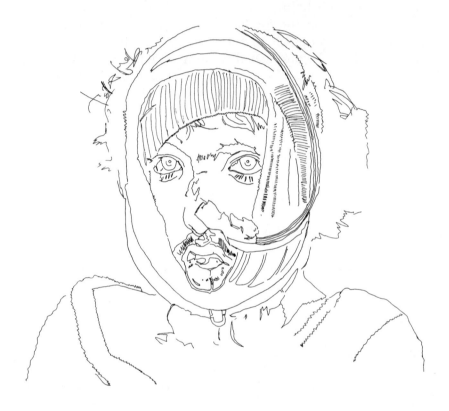

Gunshot wound

6

THE LUCKY ONES: REFUGEES IN CALIFORNIA (1983–87)

One family including women and children found shelter in a cave, but Soviet soldiers killed them with grenades thrown into the entrance.

AFGHAN INFORMATION CENTRE,
Monthly Bulletin No. 11
(March 1982)

Perhaps the most important and widespread issue concerning Afghans resettling in the U.S. is the psychological malaise or depression many experience . . . Though they are grateful for having been able to come to the U.S., Afghans still feel they are strangers in America.

ALLEN K. JONES,
U.S. Committee for Refugees,
Afghan Refugees: Five Years Later
(January 1985)

The hairdresser

"**S**o, we're doing a perm and a cut?" said Anjilla, and Jenny nodded earnestly, her legs crossed; and while Anjilla got her client card Jenny sat looking into the mirror and playing with her hair. She had already put her smock on.

"It's kind of long," Jenny said. "If I cut it I'm going to get it permed anyway, so I might as well perm it."

"It's kind of dry," said Anjilla. "So I'd like to use some lotion on it, if it's okay with you." She took Jenny back to wash her hair.

The hairdressing department was a bright place, bisected into a wide aisle and a series of semiprivate bays angled toward the window. Anjilla's bay was halfway down the room. Her work space was impeccably clear, clean and ordered. Bottles and squeeze tubes stood at the base of the mirror. The cabinet top was white and spotless. The light shone upon it without glare.

Jenny came back wet and smiling, her hair pulled back from her forehead, while Anjilla stood behind her, a handsome brown woman in a blue silk blouse. She had thick black hair, thick black eyebrows and big black eyes. Jenny said she thought that she looked quite Persian. She worked the curlers into Jenny's hair, talking happily about the vacation that she would take when her grandmother came from India next month. Jenny's head was paved with curlers, like the plates of an armadillo. Anjilla tucked a strip of cotton around the circumference of Jenny's head, added the perming solution, and slipped a plastic bag over the curlers.

"So, you like to work?" said Jenny, a little maliciously I thought. Anjilla's family had once been well off.

Anjilla stiffened. "It's fine," she said.

Anjilla and Jenny both wanted to be doctors. They were both Asian immigrants. Jenny became a doctor. When she came to the United States, Anjilla lowered her expectations and hoped to be a nurse. But that didn't work out, either. Her brother was going to be an engineer. He got a job as a mechanic. Her sister had been in dental school. She didn't get a job. And Anjilla, here she was.

When the perm was done, she bent over Jenny. "Any trouble, let me know. Let me give you a dry towel."

HOW TO BECOME A HAIRDRESSER IN ONE EASY STEP

Anjilla's father had had three houses. They lived in Kabul. They had a gardener, and a servant who cleaned, and a servant who washed their clothes. Her uncle got shot in front of his house. After that they came here.

I remember crossing the mountains into Afghanistan when it was around ten in the morning and it was very hot and sunny as we went up among the rocks, and when at last we reached the summit of the ridge and looked down at the green meadow below us and the snow and ice along the shoulder of the next mountain, and mountains going on before us forever, we saw a group coming our way: — a beautiful, proud-looking young woman and her family ascending the divide, leaving Afghanistan; and one of the men led a donkey that clopped along wearily with their possessions on its back. They came up to where we stood, passed us in silence, and went on down into Pakistan to be refugees.

They were going to have to descend the piles of chalk-colored boulders, and clamber down the cliff sides and go down into the trees and cross many streams until they came to Parachinar. Then they would sell their donkey and take a bus or a taxi through the desert to Peshawar, where they would be registered. Next they'd apply for visas and settle into an overcrowded hotel that cost twenty rupees a night (two dollars for me at the current exchange rate, which is to say two hundred dollars for them). Then they would wait. The average waiting time for visas to the United States was two years. Within a few weeks their money would run low. They could try to find work in Pakistan or India, or go to a camp, where it was so hot that their children would bleed from the nose and run high fevers. Because of the crowding in the camps and the dictates of Islamic modesty, that young woman I had seen—and her mother and grandmother—would have to wait until dark to go out and relieve herself. And the canal water that she washed pots in would be the same water that refugees drank from and used as a latrine. ("There is an Afghan proverb," a man told me. " 'Water is clean if it turns over three times.' ") — She would become like the woman in brown and red who sat on the bank of sharp white stones looking at the river that was the color of her clothes, and her family's clothes, the ones that she had just washed, lay wrung out beside her as she sat rocking herself and rubbing the back of her head; she would become like the man who posed for my Afghanistan Picture Show so patiently that he did not even brush a fly from his mouth; like the smiling boy with the growth below his eye; like the man who wore a heart locket around his neck. — Anjilla, however, was among the lucky ones. Her family flew West.

TWO MEMORIES

When Anjilla was little, she wanted to be one of the *puji*.* Her father used to let them come inside the house to drink during Ramazan. When she saw what happened to them after the Russians came, she cried.

One day Anjilla's father saw President Amin on the TV. Amin was talking about loving your country; he was hinting at the need for the U.S. to come in. So he got sick after that, and then they bombarded his castle.

EXPLANATIONS [2]

"Why," the Young Man wanted to know, "did the Soviets invade Afghanistan?"

"To have acted otherwise," said Brezhnev, "would have meant leaving Afghanistan prey to imperialism and allowing the aggressive forces to repeat in that country what they had succeeded in doing, for instance, in Chile, where the people's freedom was drowned in blood. To act otherwise would have meant to watch passively the origination on our southern border of a seat of serious danger to the security of the Soviet state."

---

* Nomads.

A FRIEND OF FRIENDS

Anjilla's family had a friend who they knew was a Communist. He used to bring Lenin's picture to their house. On the night the Russians came, he knew that something was happening, but he said nothing. That night the sky was full of airplanes. In the morning her father said that it was not safe to go anywhere. Her mother wanted the friend out because he was not safe for the family. The friend was up early in the morning. He seemed very excited. He said he had to get cigarettes. When he got to the store, he was shocked. He was expecting that something could happen, but he couldn't believe that the *Roos* had come. The Russian soldiers were looking at him in the store. The friend came running back to Anjilla's house crying, "The *Roos* are here and we are finished!"

That day and the next day the Russians went to all the important places and secured them. On the radio they said that due to U.S. interference they had to get help from our very kind neighbors the Russians. Everyone in Anjilla's family was crying. Anjilla prayed to Allah.

The friend had a brother who was a Mujahid. The Mujahid had said, "If I see him, he's a dead man." But after the invasion the friend became a Mujahid also . . .

Anjilla's family had two guns. When the Russians came, they hid them in the flour. Eventually the Russians began searching the houses with metal detectors. Then they had to give the guns to the Mujahideen.

PRUDENCE

I went to see Anjilla's father at work once. He refused to say anything about himself or his family. His words and thoughts were walled like one of those villages in the North-West Frontier where trees rise randomly from dry terraces, hiding things, and the houses are low and hidden behind the wall, and in the open field below graze bullocks, never looking up at that village, never looking sidelong at the refugee camp beside them where fresh-faced children stare and smile from between the crowd of white tents and everything is open and everybody sees you. — He had relatives in Afghanistan. He was afraid that I would publish his name and then the *Roos* would kill them.

AN AMERICAN GIRL

As for Anjilla, time went on and she got engaged and became less and less inclined to think about the past.

An old yearbook (1984)

And the refugees came year by year.

"I was in an underground press organization," the man said on the phone. He would not meet me; he would not give his name. — "The secret police found out. They put much emphasis on the secret police in Afghanistan today. There is a salary of 8,000 af-ghanis, plus coupons, free medical facilities, and an ID to enter any house at any time. They are entitled to a military rank and title. For many people, this is how they are standing on their feet, actually. The inflation is two hundred percent; and flour, sugar and tea are quite expensive, so one has to live. That is why free-dom-fighter activities in Kabul are—*limited*, let us say. — So they discovered us. Several friends were captured; the rest escaped. I left for this reason, and also because my wife happened to be on Daoud's constitutional committee, and she had training in home economics from Pennsylvania State, so she was an Undesirable Element and assumed to be C.I.A. Amin was president of the ———— ———— Association in the United States in 1965. My wife was the treasurer. (But please change this information; for my safety you must change this information!) Recently in Afghanistan they found an old yearbook of the Association, so they said, 'Ha, ha, ha! We've got another one! Another C.I.A. here!' A friend of mine was in a meeting in which they decided to seize my wife. So we came to Pakistan. My brothers are still in Afghanistan and they are fighting fiercely. My sister is fighting in Panjsher. There are many teams of women fighters there. I am happy to be here. I love you people, really, because you are doing something. Refugee aid is not a solution. The solution is: Give us a gun and we will do the job. God bless you, and I hope we can return the support in kindness."

The waitress

“**W**hen I was in West Germany waiting for my visa,* I was very depressed," Nahid told me, pouring more tea in my cup and then in hers. "I didn't want to go out, 'cause I just left after the demonstrations and I saw some people get killed. Well, I was very depressed in the beginning. What I saw in my country, I thought the whole world would realize it and everybody was thinking about it, but once I left my country everything was normal. It's not that other people don't care, but it's just—you know, it's just the way it is."

We ourselves feel nothing: we do not feel the earth reach up when a stone lands at our feet. But that does not mean there is nothing to feel. The earth *is* moved by the stone. And I hope that it is not a mere conceit of mine that the earth moves when a bomb falls on the far side of the world. But of course it does not move; we are not moved; that is just the way it is.

"What made you decide to leave Afghanistan?" I said.

"Well, almost everything," Nahid said. "The situation, the fighting, the demonstrations, and, uh, those students got killed . . ." She looked down at the floor. "And we couldn't study, you know. Almost the teachers were coming in class and telling us that we should be ashamed of studying because other people were getting killed behind those mountains, because They were bombing everything. And in public you couldn't talk without to be

---

* In Europe the consulates were more willing than in Pakistan to grant visas to the U.S. Lucky Nahid only had to wait for half a year!

afraid of everybody. They didn't like us because They were saying that we were feudals or landowners or whatever, and we were afraid of Them because whoever They were thinking was against the government, They were going to put them in jail and then who knows. They've killed a lot of people. No one asks why. No one can ask."

"Did you consider joining the resistance instead of leaving?"

"Well, it's hard here, you know. We hardly make very much money, you know, to pay our expenses. I do want to help my people and I did, but it's easier to say it than to do it, because if I go to Pakistan right now they won't let me fight, 'cause I have to stay home and cover my face and stuff like that. And when you live, you have to deal with your own problems, too."

A NICE THOUGHT

"What is life like for you here?"

"Well," Nahid said, "the hardest thing is when you think you have lost everything you had behind you. You never know if you'll be able to go back or not. On the other hand, I can go to school here, I can make my living, and people are really nice to us. Maybe it's the nature of America, because it's a country for all refugees."

AN AMERICAN GIRL

Nahid gave a party once, and there was beer and music and dancing. One of the guests got drunk and started shaking his finger in my face, yelling, "You Americans, you don't care about us; you are a *bullshit* people!" and everyone else was shocked and shushed him because he was not being hospitable to me, and Nahid smiled apologetically and sipped her beer, and the musicians played one more song, one more song on their Afghan instruments, until it was three in the morning, and they gave me a bed to sleep in and the next morning they gave me breakfast. But I could not forget that I had seen Nahid drinking beer. She was becoming an American. — "I don't know if the fighting is going to stop or how long it's going to take," she said to me passionately, defensively, "and when you're young you have to *do* something, to *be* something where you are. My grandmother and my mother, they are older and will never be reconciled to living here. They want to go back because it's very hard for them: they don't speak the language, and they're mostly alone because everyone else goes to work or school. But I think if Russians leave my country, then everything will be okay. I think most of us would like to go back. I do." — Her head was down; her voice was very low. — "I would like to go back to help my people, to stay there. But then again, I don't know if . . ." — She stopped. — "I don't want to go back to my country and see that everything has changed so that I can't—*bear* it anymore."

7
"... DESCRIBED FORMALLY AS REFUGEE CAMPS ...": WOMEN
(1982)

Many centers described formally as refugee camps were set up in the territory of Pakistan. Armed groups that are sent into Afghanistan undergo training there. It is in these camps that they sit it out or are being rallied after making raids on populated Afghan localities and communications and other projects. Among instructors training these units are members of the U.S. Secret Services, Chinese experts in so-called "guerrilla operations" and even specialists in subversive operations from Egypt.

TASS STATEMENT, 1979

"... Described formally as refugee camps ..."

The Young Man had expected the refugee centers to look like pictures of concentration camps set in pictures of the Gobi Desert: barbed wire, jaundiced children dying of thirst, work gangs, sentries and corpses in the sand. He can, I think, be forgiven this lack of insight. For an American in 1982, the most practical course was to assume the worst about conditions in Asia. (Now we can fear and hate Asians instead, since they are taking over our markets.) At that time we were sufficiently far away for only the most important news to reach us—and when was the last time that important news was good? Before the Young Man left the United States, a Pakistani doctor had given a talk to an A.F.A.R. meeting. The doctor had worked in the camps. He said that conditions in the camps run by Pakistan alone tended to be worse than in those administered by the U.N. and the voluntary agencies. Some were much worse. But all were bad. Hearing this, the Young Man had felt anguish. It was still four months before he was to leave for Pakistan, and in that time how many more refugees would die? If only he could go tomorrow! Then he could accomplish something that much sooner.★ — Of course the U.N.H.C.R. nutritionist in Peshawar, Marie Sardie, was in the right when she said to him, "I hate typical Western propaganda about Eastern countries: you know, the begging bowls. I hate that. It's this whole attitude that if someone's actually dying, then you help them. But if they look okay, then forget it, Charlie. And this is defeating everything about development." — And yet she was missing a point, because the refugees, being refugees, were by definition not okay. — Can we blame the do-gooder, then, whose urgency planted the camps with imaginary barbed wire?

No, he was right.

★ Consider the simple economics of the project. He spent thousands on transportation and equipment, and raised hundreds.

If I could speak to the Young Man now, what would I say to him? I can't deny that I feel very dull now. There was some excitement and belief that the Young Man had that I don't have. But although my life is flat, it is *content* with its flatness. I am a success. It is only that sometimes, when I read over his words, something brushes against me like a soft garment, and I feel a pang. What have I lost? If I set out to Help Somebody now, I know that I would be more effective, that I would accomplish more, give more, take less. — For a time the Young Man embarrassed me. Now, despite all his ignorance, I admire him a little. I wish that I could be more like him. But when I was him, I got hurt. — What about the saints, and Albert Schweitzer? Their existence proves that it is possible to be inspirational and effective. But did they feel inspired? Is inspiration an indulgence?

Mainly, the Young Man's careful records bore me. He never thought to ask for stories: all he wanted was facts. Those facts are largely meaningless now. All that I have left now are the things that his fact-crusher could not quite digest: debris and colored bric-a-brac, like the old woman with tuberculosis who let him look at her as she sat out on the hard clay ground beside her house, the red shawl flaming about her gray hair, a silver ring on her finger; and her face was almost impossibly lined and wrinkled and beaten but he could not honestly tell her mood or what she was thinking or anything about her except that she was looking back at him, her mouth wrinkled in emotion—but which emotion?— or was it emotion at all?—and the men stood in a line behind, scowling at him as he watched her. — What can she mean or be for me now except another person whom I annoyed or perhaps even tortured with my good intentions? I can't forget her but she isn't alive. But the hand that wrote those records in the battered notebook, those tanned fingers dancing upon the keyboard of my computer now in front of my eyes, that hand fascinates me: it has traveled on a voyage to a place where I have never been.

And yet there is something despicable about it, too.

The do-gooder wanted to do good; he wanted exotic distress to remedy, so he had a sinking feeling on discovering less of that than he had anticipated. To his uneducated eye, it was not always so easy to tell the difference in condition between refugees and locals: *neither* had what he had! (whereas those refugee camps in Thailand really had barbed wire; the Young Man saw it on TV).

The stories—yes, those were sad, but although he thought he believed them, he didn't; that took a few years of bad dreams. The Afghans could go freely in and out of their camps, and while malnutrition was widespread, starvation seemed nonexistent. The men retained their weapons and frequently slipped back across the border to take part in the jihad. To his eye the camps did not seem to be cesspools of misery at all, but rather festive and "ethnic" like one of those big Fords decorated by Pathan truckers until it was more gorgeous than any Karachi bus, the way its pennant pointed grandly down, bearing in its blackness the many-colored wheel-circle, and its paintings of mosques in blue and gold, captioned by Pushtu cursive like white snakes or breakers, ranged all around the top of the cab, framed by golden waves, and sun and dust had bleached these colors to a milky delicacy so that the truck had become a tea-tin from some dream-Persia, and clusters of bright streamers grew down across the windshield and the son and father leaned against the hood squinting at the Young Man; the tiny daughter, already wearing the long strip of flower-patterned cloth over her hair, gaped at the Young Man in pure frankness, clutching at her throat with one hand, holding a ricepot in the other, and the horizon was nothing but a dusty ridge—so too in the camps with the young girls in their bright-patterned garments, the mud houses graced by sunflowers, the extraordinary strength and handsomeness of the people, the sun and the cloudless sky. — Here for once I do not judge the Young Man so harshly. What if Saint George had come all the way across the Mountains of Doom and found no dragon to slay? Of course he'd be happy that everyone was still alive—*wouldn't* he?

Dr. Levi Roque, who headed the International Rescue Committee's field team in Pakistan, pointed out that conditions in Afghanistan were now such that vast increases in the refugee population could well occur. (They have.) — Oh, good, said the Young Man to himself; things will get worse, then. (They have.) He settled into the interview with real enjoyment.

"IT WILL TAKE A LONG, LONG TIME"

"No amount of medicine can cure them," Levi said. "We have to educate them. But how? That remains to be seen; it will take a long, long time. That is why we are starting on this wash-your-hands, cut-your-fingernails business. Why is it important that you wash your hands and cut your fingernails? These are the things that they have to learn right now. We are trying our best to do it."

"How often would you say that refugees ask for medicines that they don't need?"

"They don't ask for things they don't need," said Levi wryly. "They just ask for *everything*, whether they need it or not. 'Give me the white pill. Give me this yellow.' Give me this, give me that. — Oh, I'll give you an example. We're doing family planning. We have these contraceptive pills. So. One of these men got hold of our contraceptive pill, because it comes in pink color. And he's *taking* it, because he loves the color!" — He laughed. — "I hope he don't get pregnant."

The Young Man remembered something that Levi had told him earlier. "Do any of them still hold your medical teams at gunpoint?"

"Well, not anymore," Levi said. "But they always say, 'All of this medicine belong to us anyway; give us all this!' But when we give them proper explanation, they say okay. They are stubborn, but they listen . . . In here, well, the Afghans are lazy. They do not want to help themselves. The Indochinese refugees, they work very hard for themselves. Here," Levi chuckled, "they don't help you. You *pay* them, they help you."

"What do you think the best thing the Americans could do for the refugees would be?"

"I really don't know," Levi said. "Well, the Americans are giving a lot of food, and I think they should keep it up.★ Why? Well, now we are facing so many Afghans already in Pakistan. If we can keep them healthy, that's a very good sign; that's very good. We have to anticipate that those Afghans in Afghanistan, in which, in the long run, there might—who knows?—be an emergency, they will cross Afghanistan like the Kampucheans and be dying of hunger. Then we face only one problem—that one, because we keep the refugees here healthy. So that is why, I hope, a lot of people will give more."

★ They haven't.

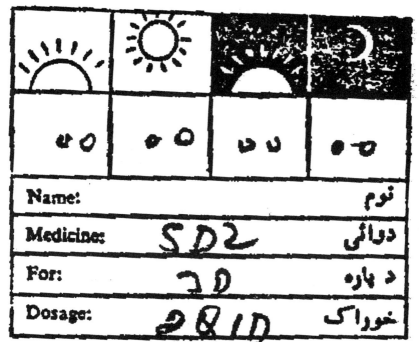

Prescription form for illiterate refugees, the dosage and timing being indicated by the number of pill-symbols blackened and the sun positions.

THE GIVER

Levi was the sort of person that the Young Man had always wanted to be, and never would be. He was quick, brave, effective. During the first outbreak of that disease called Khmer Rouge, he had gone regularly into Cambodia to bring the refugees out. (You knew when you had crossed the border, he said, because suddenly in the jungle you began to see the bodies.) Sometimes he treated the wounded on the spot. He had flown in and out of Phnom Penh under fire. If *anyone* helped people, Levi did. He gave the Young Man medicines for his dysentery, dark beer and prime cut for his homesickness, and even paperback romances in English for the worst of the hot Peshawar afternoons. ("Dirty books!" said the

General.) Everyone got on with Levi, from the pretty girls at the American Embassy to the refugees themselves. And he seemed to run the I.R.C.'s field operation very capably, which meant that he had no illusions about anything.

THE PARABLE OF THE BEER CANS

One morning at around seven they were passing through a bazaar on the way to a checkup of Hangu Camp. It was quite hot already, and they saw a soft-drink stand. — "Pull over there, Hassan," Levi said. "You two want what to drink? Sprite? Coca-Cola?" — The Young Man and Hassan settled on Sprite. Levi got out to buy the drinks. The Young Man stepped out, too. At once he was required to decline a shoeshine, a hat and a live chicken. Then a kid came up to ask Levi for money. He was a skinny, runty-looking little boy, with his hair cut almost bald in the pragmatic Pakistani fashion. He was a Pathan; he might have been either Pakistani or Afghan. He looked like one of the black-and-white magazine pictures of hungry children whom relief organizations invite you to sponsor. — "I—*no* mother," he said. "Please, rupees, please." — Levi laughed, dropping a straw in his drink. — "You don't have a mother? You're very lucky. You do what you want; nobody give you a hard time!" And presently they had all finished their sodas, and Hassan started the engine.

Once the Young Man had worked on a ranch in California with a fellow named Mike. Mike was very idealistic. He even believed in Jerry Rubin. Their truck stalled on them one day six miles from the ranch, so they started the walk back to get another vehicle. After they had taken a few steps, Mike saw a beer can. He picked it up. A few steps later he saw another can. He picked it up. The Young Man looked along the shoulder of the highway where they were walking. As far as he could see there were cans. He pointed this out to Mike. Mike said nothing. Soon his arms were so full of cans that he could not carry any more. They came to the next can. Mike set the cans down and crushed them with his boot; then he gathered them up again. The two of them walked on, Mike always picking up cans, until at last his arms were so full of crushed beer cans that he could not carry any more. The Young Man, who had been anticipating this for some time, waited to see what

Mike would do. Mike stopped for a moment, thinking. Then he put his cans down in a neat stack at the side of the road, walked on, and picked up the next can. When they finally reached the ranch, Mike had left little caches of cans behind them for six miles. The ranch manager bawled them out for taking so long to get back. That Saturday, Mike borrowed a truck, collected all his cans with it, and took them to the dump. For a few days, six miles of one side of the highway was pristine.

Thinking about Mike and the beer cans, the Brigadier and the toads, the Afghans and the Russians, the relief groups and the refugees, the Young Man shrugged a little. He supposed that the boy with no mother was one of those cans on the other side of the road. — Then Levi laughed again. — "You know," he said, "last time I was there, he told me he had no father. I ask him, 'All right, you have no father; where's your mother?' He pointed up the hill and said, 'Up there.' Now he's learning. He's a very bright boy."

GREAT STRIDES FORWARD [1]

The refugees kept coming and coming. Year after year, the ants fled the toads. "They have probably killed a hundred thousand Afghans altogether now," an ex-professor told me in 1984. "Government officials are not killed on the spot; they are given a just trial and sent to jail, but villagers—villagers and freedom fighters—are killed on the spot. This is done regardless of age. If a village is bombed and someone is found alive, even a woman who does not know how to use a machine gun, she is killed on the spot, because her crime is that she helped the Mujahideen. A child is killed on the spot, a child! Even animals like horses are killed so that freedom fighters cannot use them."

VARIOUS SIGHTS

At some of the camps they sat in the sun for hours in front of the signs: **MALARIA DISPENSARY, TUBERCULOSIS CHECK.** There were not enough doctors.

In the I.R.C. camps near Kohat he very often saw the malnourished infants, tightly swaddled in the heat, too weak to disturb the flies that crawled across their faces.

Then for his Afghanistan Picture Show a young boy whose face was spattered with fine birthmarks like a buttermilk pancake stepped forward smiling with mouth and greenish-black eyes and his friend set a watermelon upon his head!

The old ones sat still. They must know that they would die in Pakistan. The little girls tilted their heads at him and ran away coyly, as little girls seem to do almost everywhere. The men took him inside their mud houses and showed him photographs of the martyred ones—large, grainy black-and-white posters on the walls. They showed him their guns and told him that their sons, their uncles, their brothers were in Afghanistan right now killing Russians, and when the others returned they themselves would go. They smiled.

At Kohat the houses were sometimes grass-roofed castles whose ramparts were molded of mud and gravel. These had baked hard in the sun; they were very hot to the touch. Blankets and bedding lay stretched out on them to dry.

At the little soft-drink stands, fruit stands, cigarette stands, sat vendors indistinguishable from those about Peshawar. It was hot in the camps, though, and often there was no ice for the Fantas and orange sodas. — As for the Young Man, he sat in town, drinking his ten Sprites a day.

In the camps people were polite to him. They never asked him for anything.

HELPLESSNESS [4]: STATEMENT OF DR. TARIQ
(Hangu Camp, Kohat—I.R.C.)

Levi's van pulled up by a dispensary tent. It was only about nine in the morning, so it was not too hot yet; and they were up in the hills anyhow. Then tents and mud houses of the camp were widely spaced, but they went on and on. You could walk up the ridge and across the rolling plateau and up the next ridge and along the hill and up the ridge again and still see no end to it.

The dispensary was crowded. A baby cried. Women in chadors—red or green or black—waited silently. They drew back when the Young Man was brought in. Dr. Tariq had stopped his examinations for the moment in Levi's and the Young Man's honor, and his assistant brought them both cups of green *chi*. The baby cried and cried.

"How many people a day do you treat?" said the Young Man, switching on his tape recorder. The Afghans watched in fascination.

"Per day is about three hundred, four hundred patients," said Dr. Tariq.

"What's your greatest need here?"

"Well, we would like funds for the X-rays, because most of the people are having tuberculosis. We would like to screen the patient's immediate family. I mean, like about ten chaps are living in one tent, so when the mother's got it, I think frankly the children must be having it also. They're very crowded.* And another immediate requirement, I should say, is caused by the fact that these people are from a cold climate. They're not used to the Pakistani climate. It's very hot here. And especially for the ladies with this thick garment of theirs." — He pointed to a patient in a chador. — "You see this clothes that she's wearing? It's very thick, and they wear it day and night. We've been having cases of bleeding from the nose."

"Too much heat can do that?"

"Yeah," Dr. Tariq said. "And patients are coming in with a fever of 106°, 107°. We try to cold-sponge them and whatnot, but it takes time. We are hoping that they can have mud houses. In this heat it is too much for them to live in a tent, especially as these tents are nylon, some of them, so the heat is really wicked."

---

* As was already mentioned, by 1982 Peshawar's population had doubled since the invasion. So had that of the Kohat district to the south (178,000 locals, 178,000 refugees), where field teams of the International Rescue Committee operated their mobile medical units. These camps were closed to new arrivals, being already at their carrying capacity. Supplies of hygienic drinking water were a limiting factor: in Kohat there was at least one camp whose only water supply was a filthy trickle that dribbled onto a level space of gravel below the huts. That was also the latrine. Because it was so exposed to view, a refugee said, the women could not relieve themselves at all during the day. More refugees arrived and more were expected. New camps were established in the Northern Territory and down in Baluchistan, but many Afghans chose to remain here even though they could not register for the food allowances: everyone at least spoke their language in the North-West Frontier Province, and the factions had their offices in Peshawar. The cool mountains of the north were only a week's walk for them and their grazing animals, and the Khyber Pass was a couple of hours away by bus. To the east, in the muggy farmland of the Punjab, stood Islamabad, the modern capital, where sometimes imported rocket launchers and cases of bullets could be bought, for increasingly inflated prices.

"Are people suffering from malnutrition?"

Dr. Tariq was surprised. "Oh yeah. About five minutes back I saw a very severely anemic lady, and if there was some hospital I would have taken her . . ."

STATEMENT OF THE INTERNATIONAL COMMITTEE OF THE RED CROSS HOSPITAL ADMINISTRATOR

"We are mainly involved in the surgical field in Peshawar," the man explained. "We have a hospital of one hundred bed capacity, and we treat mostly, uh, victims of war inside Afghanistan. Most of the wounds we have are bullet injury, mines injury and let's say also broken legs from normal accident inside Afghanistan."

It was refreshing to hear his crisp Swiss-French accent. He was very clean, and in fact the hospital was much cleaner than anyone had a right to expect.

A man lay shiny-eyed in the bed, watching the clear liquid drip down from the plastic bag into the first white joint of the plastic tube, then down to the second, not far above his face, then down onto his arm with its white dressings, and his hands were outflung and open, and his chest was etched like a map of islands black upon a sea of tender pinkness. The *Roos* had dropped napalm on him.

"How are the patients referred to you?"

"Well, most of them are coming to our hospital by themselves. I mean they have very often to walk about two, three days from inside Afghanistan to the border, and then they take taxi or private car to the hospital here. The weakest ones die on the road due to the length of the trip. It's more difficult to treat something that is already old, and this is infected sometimes, and they don't have the right thing to treat *inside*, right on the spot where the accident happened."

("Accident" was a quaint term, the Young Man reflected as he came to the man who had taken a bullet in the jaw, so that a bandage went around his head like a bonnet and a plastic thing pulled his lower lip down so that slobber ran down it from his bloody tongue and his mustache was wet with sweat and blood and a tube went up his nose and his red-rimmed eyes stared very wide and still and patient.)

"There is a lot of infections, and a lot of amputations," the man went on, "and we have an artificial-limb workshop for these people after they have been treated, and we help them to walk again after this. And we have a facility for the paraplegics . . ."

The detail that the Young Man most remembered later was a lovely, intricately carved wooden plate. Having nothing else to do, the patients who were still capable of using their hands produced these artifacts. They sold them for next to nothing.

HELPLESSNESS [5]

In his undergraduate years, the Young Man had been very impressed with the way that Wittgenstein would demolish beautiful ontological edifices with taps of a chisel, each tap a vicious, laconic, numbered proposition ("298. The very fact that we should so much like to say: 'This is the important thing'—while we point privately to the sensation—is enough to shew how much we are inclined to say something which gives no information"). As he went about trying to Help the Afghans in the Best Possible Way, his mind composed—effortlessly—a similar set of entries in its ledger of self-torture. At first they were vacuously abstract, like a nightmare brought on by some vague bodily discomfort. As the Young Man's health continued to decline, however, they took on an anecdotal character. The Young Man accepted them, as he did his many free Sprites, with passive courtesy. He knew that they could do him no harm, since he never abandoned a project that he had begun, even if something convinced him that it was wrong. Besides, they tended to contradict each other:

(1)   Being a citizen of the U.S.A., I really don't understand what *anyone* is doing in Afghanistan. This failure of imagination, while not directly relevant, nonetheless vitiates my activities.

(2)   Even if the Afghans get their country back, in the long run it will be invaded again. Whether or not this is a ludicrous argument depends on how long the long run is. It does not make sense to give up brushing my teeth on the grounds that some-

day they will fall out anyway, but it may be intelligent not to rebuild a house of cards in a strong prevailing wind. I suppose that if Afghanistan were left to itself during the rest of my lifetime I would be satisfied. But that would hardly encourage me to live a long time.

(3)   Since I have decided to be "of service," people might well ask me whom I will be of service to, and under what circumstances. — "If I saw a woman being starved by her relatives I would help her." This absurdity can be demolished fairly easily. Afghan women and girls tend to be malnourished. They eat last. Sometimes, a doctor in the camps told me, their families just let them die. If the only evil that had been brought to my attention vis-à-vis Afghanistan were the suffering of women within the family, I'd never have lifted a finger, because I am neither Afghan nor a woman, and so right away I would KNOW that there was nothing that I could do. It might well be that in changing the position of a woman in an Afghan family I would destroy the Afghan family. (Maybe, for that matter, it is better to be an Afghan woman than an American woman. I might prefer to eat last and to be protected from men's eyes by my thick black veil while I sat in my hot tent, than, wearing my fashionable skirt, to eat all I want in some restaurant while enduring comments about my tits. Who am I to say? — How simple, by comparison, is the wrongness of a napalm wound!) — Most likely, if I were an Afghan woman I would have no idea of what it would be like not to be an Afghan woman. As it is, I have no idea how to help any or all Afghan women be Afghan women. Should I marry four refugees, as the Holy Qur'ān allows, and try to make them all happy?

(4)   "If I wanted to help a woman I would not rape her." — This, too, shows a fundamental misunderstanding. I must take photographs of Afghan women. Otherwise, American women might think that Afghans are sexist (wouldn't that be wrong?) and not want to help them. American men would be disappointed at not having the above-mentioned exotic faces and tits to comment on. — Fair enough. — I explain my requirement to the administrator of the camp, a very obliging Pakistani gentleman. — "I understand, sir," he tells me. "I get some women for you." — He turns to the refugees and explains. Voices rise, but he does what he has to do; he yells at them; the voices become more excited and angry than ever; he lifts his arms firmly, shouts the Afghans down, reaches out, pushes away a

boy, and points to a woman, whose baby on her shoulder turns its head, sees me, and starts to cry. The woman crouches miserably in the sand like a dark bird. Her husband comes forward, balling his fists at me, and the administrator puts a hand on his chest and pushes him back. He stands there looking at me. We are surrounded by people—the woman, the administrator and I—all of them standing and looking at me. The administrator speaks to the woman rapidly and fiercely. Everyone is murmuring and watching my face. The woman removes her veil. She will not look at me. I see her cheeks, her mouth. Her unbound hair. I move to one side and raise my camera. I believe I am taking good pictures. — Afterward, the administrator goes to speak with her husband, who finally comes forward. — "*Dera miraboni*," he says to me. Thank you very much. — We shake hands.

(5)   In proposing to help the Afghans, I must accept the postulate that it is better for people to be exploited by their neighbors than by strangers. I cannot prove this.

(6)   Nor is it fair to claim that the atrocities currently committed by the Soviets represent what would be an ongoing situation once the resistance movement was wiped out. Surviving Afghans would probably be forced into a more equitable system of distribution than currently exists. The women would receive as much food (or as little) as the men, we might hope.

(7)   "But this would mean destroying the indigenous culture." — After x years of Soviet rule, it would *be* the indigenous culture. Surely the current culture of Afghanistan displaced an earlier one. There is thus no need for action. Anyway, what does being indigenous have to do with whether a culture is "good" or "bad"?

(8)   "But isn't inaction in situations of human suffering even worse than making the wrong decision?" — Oh, I don't know about that.

(9)   If the Soviets took over the world, humanity would become more homogeneous. It seems that heterogeneity is one of the principal causes of strife: the conclusion must be that every new school of fish that Leviathan swallows extends by so much the dominions of peace. Of course, the process of mastication and digestion is a little painful, but ah! after that, each glob of excrement will be like every other; and Afghanistan, Bulgaria,

Czechoslovakia, and perhaps (if Fate smiles its wide, toothy smile at us) we ourselves will all be one mass of tranquillity and quietude.

(10)   Besides, nobody else is interested in Afghanistan.

HELPLESSNESS [6]

At the far end of the park which the General had arranged to be built was an Afghan camp. On the Young Man's evening walks with the General and the Brigadier, he saw a man bent down, carefully going through the grass to find twigs and thick stalks to burn. A polite distance beyond, women were collecting dung to add to the fuel.

"They would stop it if anyone asked them," the General said. "But they have such a miserable life, poor chaps—nobody would ask them."

There was a lovely purple sunset on the mountains, along which ran the Durand Line dividing Pakistan from Afghanistan.

The next day he walked over to see the camp. It was a hot morning, so hot that he became violently sick. Children were swimming in the big canal, in which, from time to time, excrements came cruising along. The women were washing their pots in that water. As the Young Man walked along the edge of the canal, boys waved at him and begged him to take their picture. He raised his camera. At once they formed two rows, smiling and extending their hands. When the shutter clicked, they bowed to him and hugged each other for happiness.

The camp extended for a long way. A man came up to him and showed him around. Now indeed helplessness was the Young Man's leader, in the person of this man who strode ahead of him along the wall of the canal, brown heels lifting in white sandals; over his head, to keep off the sun, he wore a kerchief that resembled nothing so much as a red-and-white-checked tablecloth, and his baggy shirt and trousers hung limp in the breezeless air as he went on toward the wrinkled dirty tents between which little children toddled silently in the sand, toward the cornfields that did not belong to him, but in the canal a naked girl of three or four stood rubbing her belly and sucking her fingers; seeing the Young Man come, however, she rushed to squat down in the dirty water to cover herself. — Some of the families lived in tents, some in wretched grass-grown houses of earth. They all bowed or nodded to him: He could help them.* It was still Ramazan, and their lips were cracked with the heat and the dryness, but they offered him tea. Guilty and ashamed, the Young Man refused. — Another little girl was running naked along the side of the canal. When she saw the foreigner she jumped into the water. Something gray and bloody floated by her and snagged itself in her hair.

As he came to a great cornfield (owned by Pakistanis), he found a dozing water buffalo blocking his way. He stood there for a minute, wondering what to do. Children ran up and slapped and pulled at the beast until it finally yawned and got up. As he walked on, they followed him. Presently they came to a mullah with sky-blue eyes and a white beard. The children stopped respectfully. The mullah took the Young Man's face in his hands and looked at him for a while, then stepped back. — "Peace be upon you," the Young Man said. — "And upon you, peace," said the mullah. He stood there smiling and nodding after the Young Man . . .

WITH HIS CHARACTERISTIC RESOLVE

So the refugees were not well off. At least, they were not as well off as he was. Well, what should be done about it? (Whether it *could* or *would* be done did not yet concern him, for the Young Man was methodical. Before all else he must draw up his IDEAL PLAN. Then, if he had time, he would implement it.) So he would analyze; he would data-pick and wool-gather; he would take new batteries from their plastic bag in his camera pack; he would insert them plus to minus into his tape recorder in preparation for

---

* On my return, I went to half a dozen radio and TV stations, showing my photographs, carrying my stacks of tapes, but the general consensus was that they just keep breeding and getting massacred over there, and so what? — "The Little Brown People," an American oil executive called them. It was as though he was speaking of sprites and fairies. — "They're like children," he said sadly. "I know. I've spent twenty years in Asia. The Little Brown People are charming really but they can't think beyond today."

The interviews

The first thing to draw in one's IDEAL PLAN is the Overall Picture, the theme, the constellation of significant data points, one, two, three like the three children whose father had been executed by the *Roos*, standing in the coolness between mudstraw walls, a big girl, a little girl and a boy in between. The girls wore red dresses with gorgeous patterns. They stood squinting at the Young Man with slightly averted heads. The youngest girl's face was very dirty. The boy stared straight at the Young Man, his hand, half balled up, thrust before him. In the darkness behind the children, the grandmother was making green *chi* in the Young Man's honor. The children looked at him shyly, curiously; and there was something else in their look as well that he would never understand. It was not hostility or anything like that. It had nothing to do with him. It had to do with something that had happened. — Next you must obtain a few random points that deviate enough from your curve to add the human interest of uniqueness, but not enough to make it look as if the curve was arbitrary. After that, history becomes an organic whole, susceptible to genteel understatements about human suffering and crisp recommendations toward the alleviation of aberrant conditions.

STATEMENT OF REFUGEE IN CAMP (KOHAT)

"Why did you leave Afghanistan?"

"The Russians beat me up because I was not loyal to the Karmal regime," said the man. "And I had not enough firearms—only one rifle for five, six males in the family, so we could not protect our womenfolk and children to be safe."

"Are you happy here?"

"No, we are no happy."

"Do you have any request to make of the Americans?"

"Tell them that we are very grateful for what the Americans are doing, and we say, God be with them."

LOOKING BACK (1987)

Looking back, I am appalled at the unimaginativeness of my questions. I remember that I *wanted* to ask everyone the same things ("Are you happy here in the camps?" — "Why did you leave Afghanistan?" — "How could the United States best help you?"), because I was looking for some underlying structure or other to explain things. Then I could draw a blueprint showing where the refugee money came from, itemized down to the cent; I could draw elegant flow lines showing where it went: to a diamond entitled "**RELIEF**," to a wide thin rectangle called "**CORRUPTION**"—and I could *logically* determine from this exactly how much was needed, and what was needed. (If ninety percent of the Afghans I asked said that they needed guns, I would try to send them guns.*) The next step would be to calculate how efficient the workings of the Mujahideen parties were, and which party was the best to support; from these and related computations I could begin the totaling of broader-based sums to discover who Afghans, Soviets, Pakistanis were . . . when all they were was people.

THE INTERVIEWS (1982)

To get the Overall Picture, you also talk to officials. Through a friend of the General's who worked at the U.N. High Commission for Refugees, the Young Man arranged an interview with Marie Sardie, the U.N.H.C.R. nutritionist. — The Young Man she found slightly bewildering. — "Now, what is your purpose here?" she said at one point. "Is your purpose to increase aid for the refugees, or decrease aid for the refugees, or what?" — The Young Man replied that he wanted only to determine what exactly the refugees needed, and whether they were getting more or less than

---

* In my fund-raising ventures I set out two coffee cans. One said **REFUGEES** and the other said **REBELS**. How thoughtful I was! I remember my first time, when at the end of the evening I found that the refugees were now thirty dollars richer, and the rebels had gained nine dollars. Well, the amounts were modest, but at least, at last, I was accomplishing something! But, as it turned out, U.C. Berkeley charged me forty dollars for the use of the room.

that. If they were getting less, then he would say in his presentation (which you are now reading)★ that more should be sent. If they were getting more, then clearly he need not trouble himself with *that* problem. — This sort of fact-finding is essential to the drafts-men of arbitrary curves. — I for my part am probably even more irresponsible, since in my hesitation to draw arbitrary curves I forget that some curves are not arbitrary, that living, breathing life demands its due, which was hardly what it got when, for instance, I was picking apricots from a tree in Afghanistan with my friend Suleiman and found that I was standing on a human jaw with the flesh still on it, the flesh of a person killed by another person brought specially to kill him by people with their own great dues of state to pay; and I will never forget how blue the sky was. So let me pose a non-arbitrary question for the Young Man to ask Marie Sardie in her pleasant office in Peshawar: Are the Afghan refugees in the camps receiving enough nutrition to sustain life and to keep them—men, women, children—physically and mentally healthy? — Of course, replies the Young Man, if your seemingly straightforward question is broken down into its component atoms and particles, the arbitrariness of it comes to light; you see that, don't you? That must be why your reflection is staring back at me so sadly from the darkness in the window. Yessir, Heisenberg was right, for consider: Whether or not the refugees *receive* enough, what proportion of what we give them goes to them, and what proportion is sold by Pakistanis in the stores at Saddar? How much of what gets to the camps is distrib-uted fairly? — Surely such matters are subject to some ethical calculus, though what the axia of it are would be wretchedly difficult to say. — Is handing out rations year after year a satis-factory method of feeding people? If they don't eat their own food, does something in them go unfed? — And how much from the rations is taken into Afghanistan with the Mujahideen? And is that fair? — Mujahideen are also refugees; many of them are registered

---

★ "We've now had a chance to give careful consideration to your book on Afghanistan," wrote Houghton Mifflin in 1983. "Certainly your journey there was a remarkable one, as was your boldness in making it. Our problems with the manuscript are not so much with the keenness of your perceptions as with what we feel is the nature of your presentation . . . From our point of view . . . though the book might be well regarded by reviewers, we'd have a hard time finding a large enough audience for it to be able to publish in a way that would satisfy either you or us. I am therefore regretfully returning the manuscript to you . . ."

at the camps, and they have as much of a right as any other refugees to the supplies provided—possibly more, since the idea of Afghans as refugees-in-perpetuity is repugnant to all of us who believe that the invasion was wrong, and the Mujahideen are at least trying to use those supplies to regain their homeland, and thus end their dependence on our subsidies. One has to respect them for that; and yet, is it right for the Mujahideen to eat U.N.I.C.E.F. tablets of condensed milk intended for their children? It seems to *me* right, but maybe it wouldn't to U.N.I.C.E.F. — Round and round, round and round went such butterflies in the Young Man's amoeba-ridden stomach; now these questions make me impatient, because, having resolved that the Afghans are in the right, and knowing that waste and corruption exist everywhere, I don't care how many tons of supplies are diverted to uses other than feeding the refugees, as long as the refugees have enough; I cannot be bothered to wish that everything were perfect when all that I wish is that I never had to find that jaw beneath the apricot tree, with the flies on its one black lip; if I had the power, I would send them tons of food and missiles and tanks and airplanes and not worry about where they all went, because here the end justifies the means. It has to. And, so believing, I relinquish that aspect of innocence known as good faith, and my dreams are just a little stained; no doubt that is why the Young Man's reflection is looking so sadly at me in the mirror. (Until he went to Afghanistan, he had scarcely even fired a gun!)

So the Young Man sat in Marie Sardie's office, drinking her tea and asking somewhat hesitant and ill-informed questions, to which she gave entirely reasonable answers. She could not satisfy him, but then no one could, and, being unable to take that leap of faith which is really a fall, he was unable to help anyone.

STATEMENT OF MARIE SARDIE, U.N.H.C.R. NUTRITIONIST

"No one can say what their health is like subclinically," she said, "but clinically it's not too bad. The service they get is much better than the local, and it's far, *far* better than what they get in Afghanistan. They've all got food and schooling and shelter and water supplies—some facilities, anyway—and the medical coverage is at least once a week. Now in Afghanistan they'd be lucky if they saw an orthodox doctor once in their lifetime . . . And this causes a lot of friction between the refugees and the locals. There's no way the U.N.H.C.R. budget would be healthy enough to integrate the local facilities with our own program. But in some cases we've been trying to make the medical dispensaries available to the locals *and* the refugees. But the refugees don't usually like that; and so many times the dispensary tends to be in the center of the camp."

THINGS THAT PEOPLE WOULDN'T SAY ON TAPE [1]

Some Pakistanis didn't actually like the refugees so much. Sometimes they wouldn't even give them water.

STATEMENT OF MARIE SARDIE (continued)

The Young Man edged the tape recorder closer. — "Do you think that equity would dictate that these extras be cut back to the level of the local population?" he asked. He considered himself very precise.

"In the immediate future, no," she replied, "in the long-term future, maybe. Look what's happened with the Tibetan refugees. They get much less than the local population, because who's interested in Tibetan refugees? But at the moment the donor countries are still extremely generous toward the Afghan refugees. But who knows what it's going to be like in five years, ten years? And there are pockets of malnutrition throughout the frontier, but that's not because they're refugees; they have this cultural habit that you don't feed solid foods to the infants until they're around at least two years of age,* so it's survival of the fittest. The strong ones live, and the weak ones"—she shrugged—"just die away."
— The Young Man nodded and gulped his tea. The fan in the office felt very, very nice. — "In some areas we're trying to institute solid feedings to infants six months of age and older; it's

---

* For more on this, see the interview with Mary McMorrow, below.

very difficult," Marie Sardie said. "And the women, some of them, tend to be malnourished because of the repeated pregnancies; and also, as you know, the females in this part of the world have got absolutely no value at all. If the women keep producing female children, the husband doesn't really care if the children die, or if the wife dies; you can always get another wife who hopefully will give you male children."

THE MATTER OF WOMEN

Levi said that men sometimes parked their wives like cars when they went somewhere, eyes facing the wall, and left them there for two hours.

SUCCESS AT LAST

Marie Sardie had her own office and car and chauffeur so that it would be clear to all that she fulfilled the official functions of a man. But Mary McMorrow didn't. Mary was an I.R.C. nurse.

"There was one camp where I was ordered not to return because their women were seeing me," she said. "They were just *seeing* me. They're mostly rural people who've lived in the hills or been out with their sheep all their lives, and this is new: when they see a woman coming in driving a car, when they see a woman telling someone something and they'll do it for her, it causes them a lot of trouble."

At noon the Young Man accompanied Mary to a dispensary tent through whose square sun-choked doorway little brown boys with cropped heads stood staring with dark eyes, frowning or sucking thumbs; behind them old men in white squatted patiently; and inside sat a weary pretty health worker in white, her desk being the white-covered examination table upon which lay her scissors in a steel box of disinfectant, her squeeze bottle of alcohol, her tray jumbled full of cotton and pills; and a refugee, tanned, handsome, unshaven, came before her and was awarded his TB medication, and then came another and another. Only 64 children had been vaccinated since morning. Mary said that in Thailand her team had vaccinated 500 a day. The Pakistani administrator used the phrase "motivation" defensively. A driver was being bawled out for misusing a truck. There was an argument about receipts, which went on and on in the 110° heat. Mary walked up, grabbed two or three children at random, and looked at their arms. All vaccinated; everything was okay. — From the window of the tent could be seen a well, a mosque (which resembled a tin-roofed barn), a dirty mother with her dirty infant, and dirty staring children, one without pants.

"The vaccines aren't being kept cool enough," Mary said.

"It's not my fault!" shouted the immunologist, who was Pakistani. He began barking orders. "Everything here is no good," he said. "We don't have enough of anything! Why won't the Americans give more funds for the refugees?"

"Pakistan refused the aid before," Mary said. "The Americans went ahead and spent the money on something else."

"Well, the U.S. should manage its money better," said the immunologist triumphantly. He stared Mary in the face.

STATEMENT OF MARY McMORROW, I.R.C. NURSE

"The women are the most neglected, the women are the most anemic, the women have the highest level of tuberculosis; the women in general are in pretty bad shape," said Mary. "According to our standards, they're treated pretty bad. According to their standards, they're treated as they expect to be treated. Traditionally, the Afghan men get the best of the food, which is then passed down to the children, and the women eat last, what's left over, if anything. There are certain long-standing taboos: women in some of the tribes won't eat meat or vegetables, because they think they're bad for them. So what they basically live on is sweet bread and green tea.

"A woman's life is really less than an animal's. A camel or a water buffalo is valued more than a woman in this society. You can't get a husband to donate blood for his wife because if you take his blood you take his life, but if she dies he can always get another wife.

"Last week a woman delivered her baby, but retained the placenta for more than twenty-seven hours, which is a very serious

—lethal—problem. You continually bleed. It was just herself and this little old lady who happened to be around. And by the time we found her she was in shock from loss of blood. We had to rehydrate her; we had to give her drugs to stabilize her blood pressure; we had to do a lot of heroics to keep this woman alive. And, you know, we stabilized her and she was on her way to recovery and her husband came in (it was the first time that we had seen him in the five hours that we were in the tent). And the only thing he had to say was, 'How am I going to get water since *she* is useless for me?' "

THE POINT OF IT [1]

But unlike me, Mary accomplished something. She had saved that woman. She taught mothers to breast-feed longer, to mash bananas and feed them to their little children . . .

A SENSE OF ACCOMPLISHMENT

"So maybe attempts to make them more self-reliant haven't been a complete failure?" asked the Young Man so hopefully.

"There have been no real attempts to make them more self-reliant," Marie Sardie said. "Any such attempts have been on the refugees' own initiative. It's very difficult, because in the beginning you're just trying to alleviate your own caseload. You give them goods, like charity. You kill their pride and integrity; you make them professional beggars and parasites. When you give them something for nothing, why should they work for it? But those refugees who are interested in doing their own thing do it. They help out in the dispensaries and with the distributions; they help the staff. Because basically they're bored. They're fed and watered and clothed, so what can they do with their time except look at the empty space? So a lot of them have set up little kitchen gardens and shops where you can buy food and cigarettes, detergents and soap . . ."

HAPPINESS [5]

After his return from Hangu, the Young Man was very sick. Mary
and Levi had him over and fed him. In the middle of the meal he
had to go to the bathroom a couple of times, and Mary said, "You
don't have to eat anything if you don't want to." Then for once
he had a wonderful sense of ease and freedom. He didn't have to
please anybody and do anything, even though the *Roos* were said
to be embarking on much construction now, in Kabul, in Herat,
Mazar-i-Sharif . . . Bases and houses, the Afghans said. At Hai-
raton they were building a city of a hundred thousand people. The
Mujahideen were losing control of many large cities. In Herat they
were still partially in control of the airport, but Shindand was
completely in the hands of the *Roos*. Kailagai was the place where
the Russians built their weapons and bullets. It had been a muddy
and dusty area. Now the whole area is covered with metal! a man
told me in wonder. There are airplanes and tanks there; it had
become a staging area for Soviet troops. The *Roos* had a factory
there; they dug up entire hills to use for their manufacturing,
people said. But he could do nothing; he relaxed and had a bowl
of Mary's soup and drank one of Levi's beers and felt incredibly
happy.

THE POINT OF IT [2]

"There's two hundred schools in our camps," said Marie Sardie.
"There's thirty thousand schoolchildren going to school, and two
thousand are girls."

"That seems a little unbalanced."

"No, response is very high; it's higher than the local response.
There's more refugees who are going to school per total population
than there is per total local population, and very much higher than
in Afghanistan. The literacy rate's extremely high. So we're changing that structure. Many radical changes are now taking place in
two years which would have taken fifty years in Afghanistan.
Exposure to Western influence is very great; it's too great. We've
killed the tradition of Pathan food-gathering; here we *give* it to
them. And we've killed the tradition of male education alone.

Whether that's a good thing or a bad thing, no one's going to give a judgment on that."

STATEMENT OF THE AFGHAN DOCTOR
(HANGU CAMP)

"I think it will take some time to make the Afghan men understand that Afghan women are also human beings," he said, looking out at the women at the well just outside the low baked-clay walls, where a great pale-leaved tree shaded them a little as they pumped water into old petroleum tins and milk tins, and their dresses were blue with orange flowers or red with yellow blossoms or orange or beige but they all wore veils, "and they also have the right to go anywhere they wish to get help, and they need to be educated. It will take the men some time. But a sudden change in their culture will be disastrous, because they will fight with their guns and everything."

8

"... DESCRIBED FORMALLY AS REFUGEE CAMPS ...": CORRUPTION

(1982)

AFGHAN WOMAN: You are a tourist?

YOUNG MAN: No, a fund-raiser.

AFGHAN WOMAN: You raise lots of money,
or only a few thousand dollars?

YOUNG MAN: Probably just a few
thousand dollars.

AFGHAN WOMAN: I think you should either
really help us or not help us at all. You
are not helping us.

An Afghanistan Picture Show [1]

Meanwhile his eyes were blinking, and his Afghanistan Picture Show, with which he would galvanize the world, was staring at him like the two little girls who stared at him between tents. One's hair was combed, and she wore a clean white dress. The other was unkempt, with a dirty face and a faded wrinkled dress; she scratched an insect bite on her knee. Both were beautiful; both were shy. They stared and stared at him; they would never have enough of him. How strange he was! What did he want? Why had he come to them? Why was he so thin and pale and sweating? Something must be wrong with him. The two girls watched him, hoping that he would neither go away nor come closer. His Picture Show was staring at him like the two small boys who squatted down between the tent and the clay box that they lived in; they clasped hands over knees; they smiled, and between them was an empty tin that said: BUTTEROIL 99.8% MILKFAT GIFT OF THE EUROPEAN ECONOMIC COMMUNITY, and another empty tin which had been made into a bucket stood on top of their house and the ground was packed baked cracked clay; it was staring like the square-eyed houses of clay watched him, thatch hanging down over their foreheads like the bangs of the refugee boys, and inside one of them the wide-faced boy who had lost his father to the *Roos* stared at the Young Man through brownish-green eyes, one hand pressed against his temple as if to help him stare even harder, and the Young Man thought: well, maybe I can do some good after all; maybe I can at least be a diversion; and behind the boy, a patterned blanket made a rainbow.

But he could not yet see what these things meant. He was too busy analyzing and solving once and for all (as he had all the other problems) the issue of

CORRUPTION

In effect, Marie Sardie was offering two arguments for the
"extras"—the first being the expedient one that the situation might
reverse itself of its own accord in the future, as with the Tibetan
refugees, in which case hoarded "extras" might be needed; the
second being that even with the "extras" malnutrition still existed,
so the arbitrary curve could be drawn without being arbitrary at
all, and the Young Man's complicated doubts about omniscience
and fairness became irrelevant: either people were malnourished
or they were not.

"Whether you're a one-month-old baby or a forty-year-old man
you get the same ration," Marie Sardie explained, "so there's more
than enough for everybody, which, even without the corruption
of bogus registered families, allows them to have excess food to
sell on the market to get other food and things that they need."

"So," said the Young Man, "you think that between the extra
food and the fifty-rupee-a-month allowance most of the families
do okay?"

She leaned back in her chair. "I don't know about this fifty-
rupee-a-month allowance," she said. "Most of them are lucky to
see it once a year or twice a year. On paper the refugees receive
it, but the experience is that they usually don't get it."

"Where does it go?"

She laughed. "Like most other things here, through other people's hands and pockets!"

THINGS THAT PEOPLE WOULDN'T
SAY ON TAPE [2]

The refugees sold their medicines in the bazaars. (I was *so* shocked
when I first heard this!)

STATEMENT OF THE AFGHAN WAITER
(continued)

"Food and medicine, that is right, some people sell them. I don't
know if they are Afghans. Once I bought the medicine from one

shop and there was written on the medicine: SPECIAL FOR AFGHAN REFUGEES."

HELPLESSNESS [7]

The issue of corruption had begun to occupy the Young Man increasingly. His mind turned to the notion of secret plots. If he could only show that the refugees (like the smiling boy whose skin was just a little redder than cocoa holding his little brother in his arms for the Young Man to see; the little one holding something in a bundle of white cotton cloth that he would not unwrap; he held the twist of it down tight with three brown fingers and his brown face looked at the Young Man so raptly as he almost smiled, his mouth curving in something shy and sweet), if he could only show that the refugees were being cheated, or the Mujahideen were being hindered *systematically*, he would feel much better. That would be a problem whose solutions were theoretically clear. He resisted the parable of the beer cans. He did not want to admit that the shoulder of every road is heaped with waste and wreckage. How much nicer it would be simply to post a sign that said: PENALTY FOR LITTERING Rs. 500. As I reread these interviews years later I feel equally helpless.

STATEMENT OF THE AFGHAN DOCTOR
(continued)

"For example, maybe a medical commander distributes food rations. He makes about four or five rations for himself, and he needs just one; this is one corruption I can tell you about."

STATEMENT OF MARY McMORROW
(continued)

"You give cereal to a mother for one child," Mary said, "and you know the other seven children are going to eat it, as well as the husband."

"So you give her a lot," said the Young Man.

"Well, the more you give her, the more it gets spread out. It's

the extended family, and everything gets extended. A malnourished child is getting, say, two kilos of this stuff a week and he'll
gain half a kilo. And you know that food went somewhere else;
you expect that."

STATEMENT OF THE OLD MAN
(KACHAGARI CAMP)

The question seemed to be, then, how severe those pockets of
malnutrition were. Knowing this, he could construct his *if → then*
conclusions and be on his way to Afghanistan (I remember that
long hot summer so well, when I kept thinking about the border).
Before speaking with Marie Sardie, the Young Man had arranged
with B., a minor guerrilla commander with the Jamiat-i-Islami,
to visit Kachagari Camp on Khyber Road. — Kachagari, he was
given to understand, was administered jointly by Red Crescent
and the government of Pakistan. He would not be officially welcome there; Commissioner Abdullah in the Refugee Office was
unlikely to give him permission to go. So, once he had secured a
note from Dr. Najibula, who controlled the Jamiat's political office, the Young Man passed the note to B.—which gave B. assurance that the Young Man was not believed to be a K.G.B.
agent—and then they set off illegally in a taxi, which happened
to be a big old Packard. The trip cost the Young Man two hundred
and fifty rupees.
    It was a holiday. They were unlikely to meet any of the camp
administrators or staff, and the Young Man had already promised
that he would be the only one in trouble if they were caught, and
that he would bear his punishment gracefully. They rolled cheer-
fully down Khyber Road, raising a persistent narrow trail of dust
behind them as far as they could see. Here was Jabbar Flats and
University Town, and all the sad vending stands, and now, off
to the right, the acres and acres of heat-faded tents and brownish-
yellow walls and streets and houses of some adobe-like stuff. It
was rather hot today; the Young Man promised himself that on
his return to the hotel he would mix up many Mango Squashes
for himself from the bottle of syrup that he had bought. — The
camp seemed to go on and on as they entered it. In its vastness
and seeming lack of people, in the way that it kept to itself, it
reminded him of those old New England cemeteries that stretched

along the side of the road. You held your breath when you drove by a cemetery. The car went slowly down the mud-baked road. — They stopped in a cul-de-sac between cracked walls, and at once the refugees came running out of their homes, the women staying a little back with their water vessels, peering from the rims of deep pits in the baked dirt (were those wells? he never found out), while everyone else rushed up and crowded around the car, children first, putting their heads right up against the windows but maintaining somehow a certain shy distance. They cleared a path when the Young Man and B. and the taxi driver got out and stretched themselves in the heat and looked around them at the dryness and the faded brown tent canvases and the shiny empty tins on the ground which had once held cooking oil (another gift from the European Economic Community); and all the people stood watching, hushing, at the sight of the Young Man. After a moment, the men stepped up closer around him, and the women disappeared again.

B. took him to a tent where an old man sat. — "*Asalamu alaykum,*" said the Young Man as usual, awkwardly. — "*Walaykum asalam,*" the old man answered. He took his guest's hands in his. They all sat down, and the old man poured them water. The people went away.

As the old man and the Young Man could not understand each other's speech, B. interpreted.

"Do you have enough food?" the Young Man asked.

"Yes, enough."

"What kind of food do you eat?"

The old man shrugged. "Sometimes they give it and sometimes they don't give it. We get *chi* and *ghee*★ and sugar and milk. Sometimes for two, three months we don't get nothing, you know. Then we supply for ourself. We didn't get our refugee allowance for two months."

THE MATTER OF FOOD

Of course it was in the old man's interest to say that he was not getting enough food, whether or not he was. That way his "extras" might be increased. The Young Man could afford to be

---

★ Tea and cooking oil.

perfectly sincere in his questions, because he had nothing at stake. But can those with nothing at stake ever *feel* the truth? In the years since I talked with this old man I have talked with many panhandlers and beggars. They always say the same. — Does it mean that you should only listen to what you are not asking them to say?

What the Young Man should have done was to move into Kachagari Camp. Then he would have KNOWN. — But no, he could never have become enough of a part of life there to know. And he would have been a burden. And Abdullah would have caught him. — The truth was that the heat, his illness, and worse yet his purpose, which required so straight and perfect a track to travel in that everything derailed it, had exhausted the assertion in him. He could do nothing new anymore. Through a sad irony he was becoming more and more like his own picture of these people whom he thought to save. It was *he* who was lost, questioning, thirsty, and ever so far from his own land . . .

STATEMENT OF THE OLD MAN (continued)

"What do you do every day?" asked the Young Man. "How do you spend your time?"

It took a moment for the old man to understand this question. — What did he do? What did this American think he did? — "We don't have any, no job to do! Just sitting and reading and losing the time."

"What would you like to do with your time?"

"I am *Mechaniker*, you know. All the time weld. If this job here possible, I will do it. I can do everything. I am ready to do it."

"Do you have a family?"

"Fourteen, sir."

"Many children?"

"Ten."

"And are the children getting any education?"

"There is classes, only for the children, in religion."

The Young Man hesitated. "Are you, uh, *happy* in the camps?"

Both B. and the old man laughed gently. "We have to be here."

"How would you like the Americans to help you? What things do you need?"

The old man answered at once. "What we need, they don't give it to us! We don't need to eat; we don't need money; we need only guns and like this to fight with the Russians, you know!"

THE MATTER OF GUNS [1]

It seemed so simple. It was so simple.

THE MATTER OF GUNS [2]

"From Pakistan they don't give everything to us," B. had said in the hotel room while they waited for the taxi. "I know about guns. We have machine gun, and when the machine gun came here, they took the machine gun away and give us only old guns, you know, from 1861, 1875, like this. This is too bad, too sad for us."

The door creaked. B. stopped abruptly. "But we have good relationship with the Pakistan!" he cried. "They are *helping* us; they are keeping us here; we are very happy happy with the Pakistan!" (The door handle turned slowly.) "This is very hard for the Pakistan, to keep us here," said B. "And the people who are selling the supplies, that is not important—every country has good people and bad people!"

Another Mujahid came in. Sweat was running down B.'s face.

Dr. Najibula had warned the Young Man that B. was considered an unreliable commander.

Snakes and frogs

It was very hot, and the people crowded him. Here it was impossible to do those things which one can check off. Levi had said that for a while the U.S. was sending large quantities of weight-loss syrup for dieters—surely the last thing that a refugee would need. The Afghans very practically sold this stuff. — How useless everything was! How useless he himself was in Pakistan, where he sat around sweating and having diarrhea and passing the time with stupid poems in his head like:

Now, this is a tale fer a ramblin' man, an' not fer a crook or lawyer:
If YOU were a man you'd fan your *nan* in dear old p-Peshawar.

and he thought this was a good start, but it needed a

ROUGHNECKS' CHORUS

Pukka is as pukka does
An' 7-Up is as Bubble-Up was;
So let's send out fer ice, my bros,
In dear old hot Peshawar!

by which time it was obvious to him that it must be a suspenseful narrative poem by R. Kipling and R. W. Service sitting around together thumping the table for ten years in—well, it couldn't be a bar, so let's suppose it was the Jordanian boy's air-conditioned house not far from Jabbar Flats (*he* was rich, it was obvious: imagine that! air conditioning!) and the Jordanian boy, who was very fat, gave the Young Man an ice-cold Orange Crush and put "Seasons in the Sun" and suchlike songs on his cassette player, smiling at him and licking his lips, and he said, "Are you K.G.B.?" and the Young Man thought oh not again and said, "I've got to go," and he walked out into the afternoon furnace and took a rickshaw back to the General's and sat with the Brigadier in the garden, the Brigadier reading and reading from his Qur'ān; and it was ten days and then nine days before he could go to Afghanistan, so he visited the Jamiat-i-Islami again, feeling almost healthy again as the airstreams of his rickshaw fanned him, and the guard was a young boy cleaning his gun; the poster above his head showed a diabolical Russian face above a pool of blood, and everybody was in conference or sleeping or out, so the Young Man went back to the General's and worked on his epic, let's see:

Took a rickshaw to—pshaw!—to dear old p-Peshawar,
Fought the Russkies tooth an' claw fer dear old p-Peshawar,
Then I became a refugee,

Settled down with rice an' ghee,
A girl in the camps an' Qur'ān on my knee
In dear old p-Peshawar.

Got a gun an' took a bead
On another Mujahid
From a rival rebel group
Headed by some Commie dupe
In dear old p-Peshawar.

Must've been in K.G.B.:
'Fore I got him, he got me.
But in jihad that's mighty nice
'Cause you go straight to Paradise,
Which sure ain't dear Peshawar.

The next day he went to Mardan. Since it was so hot there, as
it had been in the I.R.C. camps at Kohat, the Austrian Relief
Committee people began work early in the morning and finished
by noon. He accompanied Hassan Ghulam and his energetic Norwegian assistant on an inspection trip, via Islamabad. The A.R.C.
administered only two camps, but the staff at each was all-Afghan.
The I.R.C. was presumably under pressure from Commissioner
Abdullah not to hire anyone but Pakistanis; the Young Man wondered how Mr. Ghulam had gotten around it, but not too much,
because his diarrhea was back and the nausea got worse every day.
The Norwegian girl was full of energy and good fellowship, playing ball with everyone at the staff house in Mardan, but it was all
that *he* could do to choke down a hunk of the staple (greasy potato
with rice), for after the first swallow his stomach ached at once,
sharply, as if to spank him for giving him more of this oily fly-
infested stuff; then his intestines rumbled and the sweat of his
nausea broke out to refresh him. So his grand empathy with the
Other had failed; the miserable snail pulled in its horns. I cannot
remember exactly what he felt, for my ability to recall my own
humiliation is mercifully limited, but a good way of seeing him
might be the way my friend Jake did a few years later when he
was meeting me in the Long Beach bus station on a hot day after
I had ridden in from Tijuana very hung over on tequila, so I sat
sweating and nauseous in my camouflage shirt in that hot parking
lot, with my head bowed down, and Jake walked right past me
looking for me and thinking: I bet that sad old soldier has some

interesting stories to tell. — The Young Man's diarrhea was now a thin, chalky-brown liquid. In Afghanistan the life expectancy was thirty-five to forty, he had heard; the cause of death was often diarrhea. — Even tea or water made him retch: the conquering hero had a year of pills and proctoscopes ahead of him.

Just lazing around in Mardan, in other words, the Young Man popped rehydration salts. The well at the staff house was full of snakes and frogs. Morbidly, he held his drinking glass up to the light and saw something green in the water. He had begun to look distinctly thin and pale in those days.

"He's going to go *inside* next week," said Mr. Ghulam to the Norwegian girl, who studied him brightly, without sympathy.

"With which group?" she said.

"The N.L.F." said the Young Man.

"The situation in Afghanistan came about because of America's false politics," said Mr. Ghulam. "If America and Russia had not interfered, the Afghans would be living in their homes! And now you seek to solve their problems with this pleasure tour *inside!*"

"Mr. Austrian Relief Committee," said the Young Man, "go take a flying *Anschluss.*" — No, he didn't say anything. He rubbed his aching belly.

Actually it was not a particularly smart idea for him to be going to Afghanistan. He admitted that. The General had said that the way in was very short and easy. All they had to do was go over a hill and they would be there. That did not sound so bad. But he wished that he felt stronger. The Norwegian girl was laughing, calling, playing volleyball . . . They saw no villagers.

In the morning they went out to the camps. Driving through the village, he thought that people were pointing at him and trying to make him look at them.

AN AFGHANISTAN PICTURE SHOW [2]

A refugee camp, it seemed, could be described as a place where two choices were available to the inhabitants: get sick or do nothing. Some children had school of a sort; some men sold soft drinks and fruit; but the keynote was definitely idleness in that sun that he could not long forget because his throat would get dusty and his tongue would get dry and the heat left him dizzy and sick and dreaming of drinking a dozen Sprites. (Could it be that he was not suited for this kind of work?) Here sat the lines of men outside the malaria treatment tent: today was men's day; tomorrow would be women's and children's day. Here two little girls played list-lessly in a wilderness of big blue drums; tents stretched behind them toward the purple mountains. Tawny supply tents, unpleas-antly hot to the touch, sliced off long rectangles of dry shadow unblinking behind eyelashes of guy ropes. Narrow paths (ankle-deep trenches bordered by stones) led between them. The sky was a dusty cloudless blue. But there was one cool place. Sick refugees stood there. The wide dark leaves of the tree behind them caught the sunlight like dust. Men and boys stood leaning around the square waist-high reservoir (which had worms in it), in whose water their faces and the tree were reflected, and they were all looking the Young Man in the face. (Only a mullah in white looked away, smiling tranquilly down at the ground as the Young Man got out his camera.) A dark-eyed young man thrust broad shoul-ders forward to look at the foreigner; beside a diamond-patterned water jug, young boys peeped. Closest to the Young Man was a boy in a silver skullcap. His lips were parted; his eyes were big and sad. Between two fingers he held up a scrap of paper with printed words on it—Pushtu words, though what they were the Young Man would never know. The paper had been torn right through some of the words. Whatever the message said, it was incomplete.

And this would happen again, in Afghanistan where a man stood before him, tall, sad, imposing in vest and cartridge belt, and the clean creek that ran between houses gurgled very quietly (it was early morning), and wide trees roofed that dirt street with shade as the man stood there, not going away because he had something to show him, and he had dark eyes and brows and a rich dark mustache and his eyes were large and there was not a line in his face, and he wore a black cap. In his hand he held a medal, by a little chain. He lifted the medal to his breast and stood there holding it so that the Young Man could see. Beside him stood a young boy, also wearing a black cap. His son? The boy did not look at the medal. He looked only into the Young Man's eyes, as his father did, and the boy's arms fell away from him as if he were almost shrugging, but the expression on his face was so very serious; and this was one of the many frames in the Afghanistan

Picture Show which the Young Man never understood: it belonged
with those other mysteries, such as who the Brigadier was, and
which faction was the best, and how serious corruption was in
the refugee camps, and why the *Roos* had invaded Afghanistan,
and why the Young Man had invaded Afghanistan—but how
strange and sad it was, that the man with the medal wanted him
to understand something, and he would never ever understand it.

STATEMENT OF HASSAN GHULAM, A.R.C.

"Could you tell me a little about your operations?" said that one-
man freakshow, the Young Man, switching on the tape recorder.
The interview was conducted in German.

"We work in two refugee camps," said Mr. Ghulam, "and the
total number of refugees there is around fifty thousand. In each
camp we have a medical team, consisting of a female doctor, a
male doctor, with a sickbed for men and one for women." (The
woman doctor he had seen at work, with the soft white wrappings
about her head, leaning forward, pursing her lips as she brought
the cool stethoscope against the little boy's chest and the boy
turned his face against the shoulder of his father, who, wearing a
cap that glistened like gilded fish scales, seemed to be concentrating
even harder than the doctor; and otherwise, save for a table and
the two chairs that the adults were sitting in, the tent was empty,
and outside there was only whiteness and heat.) "And we distribute
these milk biscuits," said Ghulam, "and we also give instruction
in the schools on basic care and sanitation, and we have maternity
programs as well. We speak a great deal with the refugees, and
tell them that they are not clean, that they are not washing their
clothes, that they are not washing their children, and they ask us:
'why should we wash, and how should we wash?' and we teach
them sanitation. There are many sick people, and especially social
problems, and they come up to us, and we talk to them. We give
the aggressive ones precedence. That is our work."

The Young Man could not admit that it was not these interviews
that were important. Maybe at the time they *were* important.
Maybe the checklists of things done and yet to do were all that
mattered, that good action without poetry. How many sick people
are there? Do we have enough housing? Yes, these are the most

important things, and yet there are new checklists now, and the number of milk biscuits that the Austrian Relief Committee distributed in 1982 carries no more weight now than the Young Man's flock of hopes and aims that dissipated like all the women who so quickly covered their mouths with their veils when they saw the Young Man approaching; they always saw him coming before the menfolk did.

"What can Americans best do for the refugees?" he asked.

"Well, it is hard to say precisely what is entirely good," said Ghulam. "But a general principle that one might state for the Americans is that, as they can imagine, they should do what they can to help. And the help should come either directly to our population or through an intermediary, but the more direct the better. And also, of course, they should not make false politics against Russia, here or in Latin America, because they ought to think of the solidarity of all people, and not help to bring about a war."

STATEMENT OF AFGHAN REFUGEE
COMMISSIONER ABDULLAH (PESHAWAR)

The Young Man's experiences with offices in Pakistan was that the pace of work was not frantic. When he went to the Special Branch of the police station in Peshawar to get the document which he was required to carry as an alien, the police chief and his subordinates all knocked off and had him take snapshot after snapshot of them. They made him promise to send copies. — "We make everybody take pictures, but they never send them to us," the police chief lamented. — The Young Man did not send his snapshots to them either, because in every one the police chief looked quite sinister in his dark sunglasses. — In the post offices in Karachi and Peshawar, they sent you from window to window whenever they could, opened late, closed early, and took long lunches. To transact business at the office of the state tourist bureau in Peshawar, it was necessary to bang on the door for a long time, because the official, a gentle, boyish-looking fellow with dark hair, would lock the door, turn on the air conditioning, and stretch out on the carpet to sleep away the long, happy day.

The Afghan Refugee Office was another matter. It was housed

in a huge building full of guards, waiting rooms and variously stamped passes. True, Commissioner Abdullah did keep the Young Man sitting for three hours after his appointment—but this was due less to a relaxed attitude than to the pressure of more important business. Abdullah was an imposing, brisk man who was not at all impressed with his guest; why, the Young Man felt just as if he were back in his own country! — He was said, this Abdullah, to be a supporter of the Gulbuddin faction, and to direct some of his office's resources toward it (for it was of course impossible to separate refugees from Mujahideen). — The Young Man hoped that he could draw Abdullah out on this with clever and subtle questions. He failed utterly.

The office had a wide wooden desk that was piled with papers. The phone rang several times. Many people needed to see the Commissioner. In the waiting room were racks of brochures about the different camps, almost as if they were summer camps.

"Are you getting everything that you need from the relief organizations?" the Young Man asked.

"Not *everything* that we need," Abdullah frowned, "but we are getting substantial assistance in many sectors. Our basic problem is that our population always exceeds the level of assistance that we receive from outside, from the U.N.H.C.R. or the voluntary organizations. (We have about sixteen of them in our province, including this I.R.C. that you're talking about.) And that complicates the problem of distribution; we have increasingly more people to feed; and it's very difficult to plan when you are dealing with such quantities as appear in the Afghan question. But fortunately in the last two years we have managed to evolve a workable pattern of distribution in planning the requirements of the refugees, particularly in the health sector. So we do get the assistance, and we hope it continues, but it wouldn't be quite correct to say that we get *everything* that we need. We are dealing with a continuing emergency, and the world outside should see it like that."

"So you want a continuation of the same level of aid or an increase?"

"Obviously the level must increase. We have more people to feed, we have more people to heal, we have more people to clothe, to give drinking water to; we have more cattle—and the logistical problems involved are enormous, you know. We had only 300,000 people in 1979; that is our base, that is the benchmark. And in the last one and a half years, we have about 2.2 million people . . ."*

"Do you have much of a problem with dishonesty—refugees reporting larger families than they have, and so forth?"

"No," cried Abdullah, annoyed, "that is a *human* factor; you always find it in all refugee theaters in the world. I don't think it's the kind of factor which should affect our planning or the basic health of this operation. We have been fully cognizant of the situation right from the beginning, and in this last reevaluation operation, which continued more than five months (and even now it is continuing in some areas), we have become very sure of our figures. Those unverifiable families have not been counted."

Commissioner Abdullah, it seemed, spoke on so lofty a level that the Young Man could not relate the words to anything in his experience. For the life of him he could not get a single concrete picture from what the man said.

"How possible do you think it is to separate refugee aid from political aid for the Afghans?" he said, hoping to hear some reference to Gulbuddin.

"Well, that question need not be asked at this forum, for we basically deal with the refugees, not with the politicians. But when you help the refugees, you, in a way, directly or indirectly, are helping their cause also. So, the greatest help for the refugees would be to create conditions where they could go back to their country and live there peacefully and honorably."

"I was under the impression that certain political groups . . . were doing a great deal for the refugees on their own . . ."

". . . Yes, they do . . . ," said Abdullah. "We treat them all alike . . ."†

At the end of the interview, Abdullah made him play the tape back for him, listened very carefully, approved it, and dismissed him.

Going back out, he lost his way and passed through a suite of do-nothing clerks whose desks were clean of papers, pencils, or anything other than their bare feet. They were rolling cigarettes on their knees.

---

* In 1987, there were 3.5 million registered Afghan refugees in Pakistan alone. By 1989, when the Soviet troops left, the number was near 4 million.
† The five deletions here were made by Abdullah.

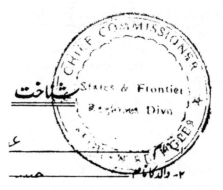

Abdullah's seal, on the ration book of the kidnapped Afghan doctor

A lesson at school (Hangu Camp)

"**S**o the school is closed today?" the Young Man asked.

The administrator nodded earnestly. "It is closed today. They have been given leave."

"Because of the heat?"

"Because of the heat. There were, um, so many illnesses in this school, you see. But the other school is open. The students are studying. We'll take you there."

"How often are the students given leave?"

The administrator sighed. "Only when it is extensive heat, like nowadays. Oh, it is terrible." — He fanned himself. — "For us it is terrible; for them it is, um, killing, you see."

They walked up to the school. The children were reciting aloud, in unison. The nearest one was a tiny boy in blue, leaning over the cloth pages of the book that was almost as big as he was, his hands clasped as he studied the picture of the tent, beneath which were three lines of Pushtu cursive, then the picture of the parasol, and he huddled very close because the tent was dark. The Young Man thought in anguish: so I have seen him, recognized him; but I can never see all the others! — For he could not get over this recurring difficulty. — When the administrator and the Young Man arrived, the schoolteacher stopped the lesson immediately, in order not to waste the Young Man's valuable time.

"What are they taught here?" he asked.

The administrator interpreted.

The schoolteacher stood at attention. "Pushtu, Urdu, English, ABC, and so forth."

"But religion is the most important course?" the Young Man hazarded.

"Yes, it is compulsory, you see."★

"How many students do you have?"

"The total number is about 290. But the smaller ones, they have allowed them not to come, because of the heat."

"What is your biggest need?"

"Books," the schoolmaster said. He was a young, very serious man. "These have been supplied by Hezb-i-Islami. The education department, they have not supplied them to this school."

The children stared up at him from their mats.

"And, you see," the administrator added, "I was feeling very thirsty just now, so I asked them what about these people when they become thirsty and there is no arrangement for water? I have now told one of their watchmen to have a big jug and fill it up."

"I see," said the Young Man. — How odd that no one had thought of this until now! Perhaps by some coincidence the children had never been thirsty before today. That must surely be it.

"Still, this water problem is general," confided the administrator. "In every camp we face this insufficiency of water."

"How do you manage to teach students of different ages all at the same time?"

The administrator did not bother to translate. "But it is all the same class!"

"Could you tell him for me that I'm very sorry to have interrupted his class?"

"No, no, never mind; it is too hot!" the administrator laughed. "They want some diversion. There are very few diversions in their lives, you see."

★ I was told that vocational education was not permitted by the host country, for fear that still more Pakistanis would be displaced in the labor market by Afghans.

A THOUGHT (1987)

Strange as it may seem, I did not understand the nightmare that I was seeing. Partly it was because I was sick that I was sometimes little more than a data collector; partly it was because I was so young that the exoticism of the experience made the greatest impression on me; partly it was because, thanks to my background, I had little understanding of physical suffering. Now, when I reflect upon this school without books, open on a day so hot that the other school was closed;—this school without water, this single class for all students irrespective of age (I saw six-year-olds there, and I saw ten-year-olds, all reciting the same things over and over)—I want to weep—no, to do something—but I don't know what. As for the Young Man, I don't remember precisely what he thought, but the plain of his speculations had already become flat, sandy ground, oval-shaded by a single tree, on which grazed scrawny cattle light and dark. Tents and little stone houses lay along the ridges. It was very hot.

GREAT STRIDES FORWARD [2]

"In education," said my informant in 1985, "the English language was the main foreign language. Now Russian is. But they do not call it a foreign language; they call it 'the language of our big neighbor to the north.' They are gradually eliminating English in Afghanistan. The puppet government is on good terms with the Cuban government, so now Spanish is taught. — This is a new phenomenon on our cultural scene," he said sarcastically. "They still have a German Department, but it is now an East German Department."

Surely thy Lord [2]

In every camp he went they were hospitable to him (except, as I said, when he took pictures of their women). They made him tea and served him bread and meat, always waiting until he had had his fill before they ate. Some of them worked with their trucks and tractors, hauling things. A man laughed and showed him how to plait a rope from grass. The boys played ball. Never did he forget the man laughing so happily ha-ha!, showing all his white teeth, as he braided grass into rope to show the Young Man, and his elder son watched the Young Man with a polite upward-bowing of lips but the younger son stood half behind, resting his head dreamily on his brother's shoulder . . .

The sum of his failures almost, but not quite, confronted him —like the turbaned man who rode his donkey home to the straw-mud-straw house, where he saw the Young Man and stared at him, his two small boys staring at the Young Man also, their arms around each other, and far away, behind the stone wall, a red-veiled woman turned away.

9

ALASKA

(1979)

In order to understand this, we need also to consider the following: suppose B says he knows how to go on—but when he wants to go on he hesitates and can't do it: are we to say that he was wrong when he said he could go on, or rather that he was able to go on then, only now is not? — Clearly we shall say different things in different cases. (Consider both kinds of case.)

WITTGENSTEIN,
I.181

Alaska

While an increasingly desperate Hafizullah Amin was conducting pacification operations in every province, while his superior, Mr. Nur Muhammad Taraki, began the last six weeks of his presidency (and, incidentally, his life), while Babrak Karmal waited in Moscow, while the Soviet Union was bland (for this was still five months before the invasion of Afghanistan stunned and horrified us); in the month of July I first visited Alaska. At that time I had no suspicion that I ever might go to Afghanistan. We were on the ferry from Seattle to Haines, my friend Erica and I. She was older. The inland passage narrowed, and on either side of us evergreen forests ascended mountain shoulders until they met snow, white fogs lying in all the hollows, and we passed rocky grassy beaches and the wind smelled of salt. — When the two shores began to draw away from each other again, the sky to open, we stood on the cabin deck, our hair beating against our faces. We could see for a long way. The windbreakers of the passengers standing at the rail fluttered violently.

Erica pointed down. "If your child fell overboard, would you jump down and save it?"

"If it were a wanted child," I said flippantly.

"If it wasn't, you'd just let it drown?"

"Sure," I said, straight-faced.

When I was growing up, my little sister drowned because I hadn't paid attention.

MY LEADER

"This is the life!" laughed Erica, who had taught at Outward Bound. Her hair was a wild cloud of curls. She had a ruddy, happy face; her skin was so thick, she said, that no mosquitoes could bite it. She was as strong as a bear. How many weaklings had she saved?

Drawn in my notebook by a ten-year-old Afghan girl—parents executed by the Soviets

ABOVE THE RIVER

Tenting in the rain with Erica was always the best part. We were all set up, which was a relief, because I was bad at that and other things; we were resting, going nowhere, and I could feel as though I were in the *Arabian Nights*, the tent covered with tapestries and furs, perhaps, with a brazier of incense between our sleeping bags, and a silver bowl of dates (actually, we ate them from one of Erica's zip-lock plastic bags), and when she slept she kept on smiling, which made me happy, too — the Land of Counterpane was not dangerous at all — we had hours left before I'd have to prove myself again, a good respite to tell each other fantastic stories (the rain being reliable that way); so Erica told me about being married and climbing the mountain in South America that later got named after her, Pico Erica; and being in the Peace Corps and snorting heroin and breaking into people's houses solely to steal ice cream and living with the Navajos and all the other things she had done that left me wide-eyed and determined to do things like that (and at the very end of that year, when I was reading the

Christmas newspapers in Switzerland, and there it was in black
and white and French: *Afghanistan had been invaded!* I suddenly
thought, "Someday I would like to go there," and it was not
because Afghanistan was Afghanistan, but because Afghanistan
was invaded); and my tentmate snuggled her sleeping bag up
against me and asked me to rub her back and I said that I would
and she laid her head on my knee and said, "Go ahead, scratch!
Long, hard strokes, all the way down my back! Harder!"—for
she was from a military family.

"You really want me to *scratch* your back?" I said.

"You got it!"

"All right," I said dubiously.

"What do you mean, 'all right'? My body is different from
yours."

"It must be."

. . . "It's getting monotonous now."

"Sorry."

. . . "Oh, that feels good."

"Thank you."

"That's nice. Could you go just a little lower? And make your
strokes harder. Oh, that's wonderful. Oh, keep doing that."

The rain thundered and thundered.

"Isn't this exciting?" said Erica sleepily.

It was. The tent shuddered and flapped. Water was leaking in.
We had no idea whether or not the evening wind would rip it
apart—a dessert of uncertainty which pleased Erica; Erica loved
to climb mountains because they brought her so close to death.
She'd seen another climber fall a thousand feet; she'd seen a frozen
German couple in the Swiss Alps. Because danger fulfilled Erica
so much, it also fulfilled me—or at least the thought of it did. Or
at least I thought that the thought of it did. I had a crush on Erica.

We were up at McGonagall Pass. To the east were the stony
cones of Ostler Mountain, and the trail that we had come up from
the river. To the west below us was a plain crawling with the
black rivers of glaciers, peaks dolloped with snow and ice everywhere we looked (or at least our maps told us that they were
peaks; *we* could see only massive pillars, some blue, some white,
some gravel-brown, that disappeared into the clouds). That plain
was mainly gravel piles and raw earth so soggy with glacial melt
that it swallowed our boots to the ankle. There were heaps of

loose stones: white granite flecked with black, or rusty shale, or
yellow-tinted crystals that Erica thought were sulphur. We had
both become very quiet; I was almost frightened by everything.
Stones trickled into pools of a strange pale green. The water tasted
sweet and silty. Between the gravel country ("No-Man's-Land,"
Erica called it) and the titanic black-earth mounds of the glaciers
was a river with the same green pallor, too wide to cross, eating
deeper and deeper into a sculpted channel of ice. Not even Erica
dared to go very close to it. What I most remember now is the
still steady trickling of water everywhere, a sound which seemed
uncanny to me because in that vast nature-riddled place everything
should have been roaring and booming, and I kept waiting for
something to happen, for the black mountains to explode, for the
ice to break, for thunder and lightning to come . . .

HAPPINESS [6]★

It was a dark, stifling tent. Flies buzzed outside and inside. The
Young Man felt as if he could barely breathe. The refugees sat in
the hot darkness. The whites of their eyes gleamed. — "Are you
happy here?" he asked the head of the family.

"Oh, you see," explained the Pakistani administrator of the
camp, "we are trying to make them happy, but they have left
their own country, so it is *difficult* for them to be happy! But we
want to make their stay here as comfortable as we can. They are
satisfied with the help that we are giving them and the United
Nations is giving them, and they are appreciating that."

"Do you think they'll stay here for the rest of their lives?"

The Young Man apparently had a knack for surprising the administrator. "Why should they?"

"Because the Russians will not give Afghanistan up."

"No, that is impossible!" cried the administrator. "The whole
world is against them, you see!"

"I hope you're right." — The Young Man turned to the refugees. — "Why did you leave Afghanistan?" he asked.

"Russian . . . attack us," the man said slowly. "Their . . .
airplanes and tanks. Russian came, and they . . . tease our womans,

---

★ Hangu Camp, 1982.

they hurt them . . . and we are very in trouble. Their . . . airplanes come, and . . . bombs *destroy* our places . . ."

"Are you happy living here?"

"No, sir. We are not happy. We are satisfied here, but in summer season, we . . . are in troubles."

"Do you have enough food to eat?"

"Yes, sir. Enough food."

"And enough water?"

"It is hard. We don't have enough drinking water. And the food is not of such good quality, sir. Afterwards we feel ill. And there are giant insects that scare us . . ."

HAPPINESS [7]

"Don't be apprehensive," Erica had said.

"I'll do my best."

"It's really a very trivial crossing."

"Good," I said politely.

We sat down on the moss and picked blueberries into my wool hat. I could not stop thinking about what had happened in the river before. Erica picked about four times more blueberries than I did. The sun was very hot and sweet in our faces.

"Let's go," Erica said at last. We put our packs back on, and I tightened my sweaty straps and hip belt as we went down the incline. The closer I got to the edge of the river, the less I liked it. There were two channels. The first was easy enough: I could see the rocks on the bottom. The second, however, was of the treacherous kind, a wide, deep, smooth stretch of water that might be thigh-deep and slow, or maybe chest-deep and very very fast underneath, and the bottom might be slippery, and that second channel might drown me on this sunny afternoon.

Erica looked at me, scanned the river, and looked at me again. She waded the first channel, stepped onto the sandbar in the middle, peered into the water again, and came back to me. — "Good news," she said, "We're crossing tomorrow."

I felt horribly depressed and ashamed.

"Today's your birthday," Erica said. "You set up the tent and I'll make you a special birthday dinner. I don't want you to help. Just get in your sleeping bag and relax."

"You're so nice to me, Erica," I said.

Erica sat by the stove, singing songs in Navajo and French. The evening was very beautiful. "You know," she said, "one Christmas all my brothers and sisters and I were fighting. My father used to be a brigadier general. All the sudden he lost control and barked out, '*I command you to be happy!*' We kids just burst out laughing."

I smiled.

"So," said Erica, "I command you to be happy!"

ERICA BRIGHT AND ERICA GREEN-EYES

By this time I had separated Erica into two personalities: Erica Bright, who was sweet, playful and girlish (and who liked me), and Erica Green-Eyes, who could best be described as *prowling* and *competent*. Green-Eyes was the one whom I continually offended; and it was Green-Eyes who made my first thoughts so filled with dread as I lay beside her in the small hours of a sunny morning, knowing that in minutes she'd awake and hustle me along to another river crossing, snapping at me, glaring at me, shoving me because I was slow and we had to cross before the glaciers began their morning melt. It maddened Green-Eyes that I continued to lose tent stakes, that I had no sense of balance, that I was a poor map reader. — "Come on!" Erica said as we canoed up Moose River. "*Hard*, deep strokes! Dig into that water! Come on; there's a tribe of hostile Indians behind us and we have to *stroke* for our lives! They're going to catch us at this rate! *Stroke! Stroke! Stroke! Hard*, deep strokes! They're coming closer; they're cocking their bows; let's see you put yourself into your *stroke!* Dig in! *Bend* at the waist, *move* your shoulders; STROKE!" — As we went farther upriver, my stroke actually began to get smoother and better. Erica was happy, believing that maybe I'd actually learned something. I paddled us around for a little while as she lay back and watched the clouds. Presently we felt an impulse to piracy, so we tied up at a private dock, tiptoed into somebody's garden, and stole a handful of strawberries. — "Now stroke . . . ," said Erica very sleepily, laughing and yawning in the sun, and the sunbeams danced on the water and a faint breeze stirred her hair. — Going back downriver, I also stroked creditably. We had a good time until we reached the landing. I jumped out to pull the canoe up onto shore. Still inside, Erica giggled as it wobbled, thinking that I was playing, and as I summoned my energies for a return smile I stumbled, tipping it and her into the water . . . "God *damn* it," she said . . . — In general, no matter whether I did or did not learn things from Green-Eyes (and I do remember a few occasions where she nodded at me in a satisfied way, and once because I had located our position so accurately she gave me the McGonagall Pass topo map for my own), the lessons were neither easy nor pleasant. I would look down at the ground, apologizing for my latest stupidity and feeling a strange tightness in my chest which I thought then was pure self-loathing (but which I now suspect was anger, too); and Erica threw her head back despairingly, reached to me, and cried, *"Think!"* Then she would feel a pitying impulse to rally me, would make herself smile and say, "Your river crossings are a hundred times better than at the start."

"Thank you," I said.

THE KNOT, THE ROBOT AND THE KNIFE

Once when we were hitchhiking, Erica Bright stood on the empty road, ready to play the pretty part (even when it was cold she kept her sweater off so that the drivers would see that she had breasts). She was singing a song by Jacques Brel. Her face was young and clear. She combed her hair, sang a song in Spanish (she knew eight languages); got impatient and sprang upside down, walking on her hands in the middle of the highway, smiling and singing. Then Green-Eyes decided to make me exercise, and she was yelling because I couldn't twist my neck and arms in the way she wanted. — "You move like a robot!" she cried after half an hour. "There's no use trying to get you to do anything, is there? You might as well sit down." — She cheered up, though, a moment later, when I tied a perfect knot (Erica was always making me practice things). — "Good," she said to me. "Very good."

"Thank you," I said.

"You're being sarcastic," said Bright. Her feelings were hurt.

"No, I'm not."

"Yes, you are," said Green-Eyes. "That really bothers me about you, that you'll never admit it when you're being sarcastic."

"What are you doing with your knife?" said Erica.

"Not much."

I got up and started walking. It was my plan at that moment to walk into the woods until I died. Erica called my name, tentatively. I kept walking.

"Come back!" cried Bright.

I stopped.

"Let's just try and enjoy each other," she said. "Okay?"

I didn't say anything.

"What are you thinking?"

"I'm not thinking anything."

CARRYING MY SWEATER

Ten days later we were climbing the side of a steep ravine in the mountains, with a frozen stream below and the dusk-blue wall of a glacier above, and it was snowing but we both felt hot.

"Let me carry your sweater," Erica said.

"No, that's all right."

"Come on, we'll go faster if I have it. Just give it to me."

"All right. Thank you."

"You're welcome," said Erica, smiling at me.

A THOUGHT (1989)

Erica carried my sweater. What did I do for anyone in Afghanistan? Well, once I brought a few armloads of wood for a fire. Somehow this should be worth as much as Erica carrying my sweater, in terms of mass carried over a distance for a Utilitarian purpose; and somehow it seems to me that in Afghanistan I never did a goddamned thing.

RASPBERRIES (1979)

One night we camped in a boggy, grassy place by the highway near Anchorage. It was finally starting to get dark late at night, because we had achieved the month of August, and the tent, which hung loosely on its poles in the soft grass, took on a primeval quality, the walls seeming like shaggy, wrinkled skins in the dusk and the thick grass beneath our bodies feeling like them; and reeds whispered all around us, reddened through the back window of the tent by the alpenglow. Erica's features, hard and shadowy and strong, were in relief as she lay beside me. Her sweater looked like mail. She lay still with her eyes closed. We slept late; there were no more river crossings to make. The next morning was a happy one, a relapse in the progress of Green-Eyes's contempt for me. She talked to me a little, and even smiled at me. She said she'd make breakfast beside the railroad tracks across the highway. When she'd gone I got up and struck camp, shaking the tent fly clean of slugs, pulled my pack on and hiked over. Erica was just fixing my breakfast: a big dish of granola, heaped with brown sugar and beautiful raspberries that she had picked for me.

THE RIVER

It was four-thirty in the morning when we struck the tent and left the wooded sandbar. Green-Eyes hustled me along. It was very warm and sunny; the water level was rising fast. Our boots filled up with cold water and gravel in the first channel. Within a few minutes my feet were completely numb. — "Listen," Green-Eyes told me as we ran through toe-deep streams and gravel beds. "No, don't slow up, just listen. You hear that noise like thunder coming from the east? That's the ice beginning to break up for the day. Look, the water's getting higher! Can you hear how it sounds different?"

We had reached the first of the difficult channels. Green-Eyes tied a bowline around my waist and showed me how to step *into* the rope to pay it out across my hip. — "*Watch* for me as I go across!" she said. "Be ready to pull me in if I fall. If you can't do it, you'll have to throw off your pack and run for me. Give me slack when I call for it."

"Right."

"Now, remember, you have to pay attention!"

"I will."

She undid her hip belt and started across. The gray water was rising very quickly now. The stump on the sandbar behind us, which had been dry a quarter hour before, was now almost entirely underwater.

"Tension!" Erica screamed from the middle of the river channel. I could barely hear her. The water roared.

"All right," I said, pulling in rope.

Erica stumbled in the current. — "No! Slack, goddamnit; give me slack! I tell you to *pay attention* and you pull in rope!"

"Sorry," I said. She couldn't hear me.

I paid out rope, and Erica crossed the channel. — "Come on!" she called. "Hurry!" I started into the water, remembered to un-buckle my hip belt, and crossed slowly, carefully, thinking only *left foot, right foot, left foot, right foot* so that I would not be thinking about where I was, and I did not look around me more than I had to. Green-Eyes pulled in the rope from her side of the channel. The water was waist-deep. It pushed at me, trying to knock me down. I missed my footing for a moment, aborted the step, and reached with the other toe until I found a rock. Carefully, my arms outstretched in proper Outward Bound fashion, I made the crossing and pulled myself up onto Erica's gravel bank. I was numb from the waist down.

"You're going to have to go faster than that," Erica said.

"That's true," I said. "I can see that." — We went to the next channel at a run. I was terrified. The water was somewhat deeper here, and Erica crossed with difficulty. I could see the look of complete concentration on her faraway face.

"Okay—come on!" she called faintly.

I stepped into the water, my open hip belt swinging loose against my thighs. My pack did not feel properly balanced. The current was very strong. I took another step, and another. The bottom dropped away suddenly, and the water was above my belly. The pack twisted on my shoulders as the river shoved me back and forth. — *"Erica!"* I screamed from the middle of the channel. I was falling; I fell; the current was pulling me down, and my heavy pack held me underwater, trapping the back of my head against the hard frame so that I could not reach air. The world sang in my ears. I could not get up, and the cold, cold water was paralyzing me. I thrashed stupidly. Then Erica was pulling the rope tight and calling something to me in a firm voice. I couldn't understand her, but I knew that I had to get up. The water was very cold. My arms and legs still responded somewhat, and I floundered forward, clawing at the rope, until at last the channel was only knee-deep again and I got to my feet.

"Good recovery!" Erica called encouragingly.

"Thank you," I said.

I waded up onto the sandbar, shivering, and stood beside her, looking at the next channel. The water was gray and swollen; it was quick and calm and deep. As soon as I saw it, I knew that I was going to fall.

"Let's go," said Erica. "We've got to get across soon. The water's rising faster."

"All right."

"Watch me! Be ready to run for me! Pay attention!"

"All right."

The water was already up to her hips. As I watched, she staggered and righted herself. Carefully I paid out rope. Then she was across and looking anxiously at me. — "Okay!" she called. "Come on!"

"This doesn't look too bad," I said across the channel to her, knowing that she couldn't hear. I stepped into the water. For the first time that day I allowed myself to look ahead, and saw that the other side of the river was a long distance away. We were less than halfway to it. The bank became a green ridge of tundra that met the horizon, topped by the squat white shape of Mount McKinley thrusting into the blue sky.

"Come on!" Erica called through cupped hands.

I wasn't frightened anymore. I felt doomed. I started stumbling when the water was only calf-deep. Arms spread wide, I kept on. The current pushed at me rhythmically with each step. The cold water was up to my knees. The only noise I could hear was the gravel churning in the water. My legs were numb. I decided to hurry to get it over with. Paying no attention to my footing, I bolted toward Erica. I looked up at her on that distant sandbar ahead of me; she was pulling in rope complacently. She was pleased, no doubt, that I had finally gotten the knack of river crossings and could perform them with all deliberate speed—when actually, of course, I was rushing through the water in a panic. My pack slammed into my back; I felt relief when I finally fell. The river slugged me, chilly, strong and hateful, and ground me into the rocks. I was shooting downstream, scraping across the rocks as I went. I was breathing in water. I didn't even try to raise my head. I considered myself dead.

Then I stopped moving with a jerk. Erica had thrown herself down to the ground and began to haul me in. I felt myself being hauled, but I could not help her. Slowly, slowly she dragged me out of the river. I could hear her grunting with the effort. At last I was lying in only three or four inches of icy water. I tried to get up, but I couldn't. My body was without feeling, and my pack was heavy with water. I undid one shoulder strap, pulled myself slowly out of the other, and dragged myself and my pack very slowly along through the wet stones, as if I were a snail.

"Come on!" Erica was calling. "Get up!"

I tried to keep moving.

"You can do it! You've got to do it! Get up!"

Erica called my name again, breathlessly.

. . . We were on another big sandbar. Erica Bright was pulling off my shoes and my torn, bloody blue jeans; she was unrolling my sleeping bag, which had stayed dry in its double stuff sack; she was holding me tight. My legs and face were bloody. — "Hurry up and get into your bag," Erica Green-Eyes said. "You have hypothermia."

"Erica . . ." I said. It took all my effort to say her name.

"My heart really went out to you, too," she said. "Now get in."

For a long time I shivered in the sun. Erica sat beside me all afternoon. — "You know," she said finally, "I'm starting to get fond of you."

I smiled up at her.

The next day we crossed the McKinley all the way. In the last channel, Erica fell. We were side by side in the water, holding on to each other by my belt. There was a heavy clank as Erica hit the rocks with her pack, and then a grinding. I was pulled down.

"Get up!" I shouted in my best Green-Eyes manner. I pulled her up; she slipped off her pack. We were in calm shallow water. I helped her to her feet, and the two of us dragged her pack onto the final sandbank. She looked at me, wet and smiling, and threw her arms around me and kissed my cheek.

Of course, she hadn't needed my help at all.

THE OTHER SIDE

I will never forget that morning, which was so sunny and joyous, with the river behind us and ahead of us a rolling tundra ridge sparkling with wet blueberries,★ beyond which (although we could not see that yet) was a valley of beautiful little lakes in which we could bathe, and then ankle-deep moss, some red, some green; and then more ecstatic days and terrible days until one morning we woke up in someone's bedroom, she in the double bed, I in my sleeping bag on the floor (for we never slept together), and the shades were down so that the room was so dim that we could hardly see each other; we had woken up at the same time; she reached down from the bed, I reached up, and we gripped each other's wrists in that solid way that gives support on river crossings, and I have not seen Erica again, but I went back and back to the Arctic and crossed rivers by myself because dear Erica showed me how; and as Erica and I came out of the river on that morning in late July I somehow knew all this and was so happy as we ate blueberries out of Erica's enamel cup; and of course within hours came the edge of that mossy plateau, and below waited our next river and I could hear the heavy sound of the water, and the river was just as dreadful as ever; but while we were eating blueberries it was a long way away yet; and the place where we found ourselves was so beautiful, so beautiful, and I was stunned by the sunlight and the sound of the river behind me and the unknown vastness ahead of me; I was stunned by it all.
— I think now that if my purpose in going to Afghanistan was at all good, then it must have been to learn if there was a way to help people get across rivers—as I said, I didn't help them, but they helped me. When I went into Afghanistan, my friend Suleiman carried me across the rivers on his back.

★ When I first read *Purgatorio*, Canto I, it made me feel this way again.

III
THE REBELS

10

A MATTER OF POLITICS:
THE GAME
(1982)

We are just concerned with the receiving
end of the ammunition and the sorts of
facilities to continue our jihad. We are *not*
concerned theoretically with the source,
and we are *not* concerned in this situation
to recognize the intention of the donor.

JUDGE DR. NAJIB SAID

A matter of politics

As long as they grow in the wild, principles of life and meaningful action do quite well, but when they are plucked and brought into our dreary world of imperfect results, they begin to wilt. Happily, our noses are so accustomed to the stink of our enemies' putrefying ideas that when our own give over wilting and commence to decay we can use them nonetheless.★

The Young Man, however, did not yet know this. As yet he had established only the following:

---

1. The suffering that besieged him could not be justified. That put him very definitely on the Afghan side.

2. His belief that he might somehow be of use could not be justified.

3. Being victims did not make the Afghans any better or worse than anybody else.

There did not seem much left to do, then, in those days while he waited for the Brigadier's party to finish its preparations to go *inside*, but to be analytical. That was all that he was really good at. Everything was melting in his hands. But at least the following must be true: I am on the side of the Afghans; *therefore* the Resistance has to be wonderful. (In his mind, the Mujahideen were all storybook de Gaulles; too much reading had relegated him far behind even the zero point of simple ignorance.)

"You really want to know about the parties?" laughed General N. "I can take you around, Young Man. It will be very educational for you."

★ The Qur'ān puts this prettily, remarking what a divine wonder it is that the place from which milk issues is located between the blood and the dung.

Too many puppets, too many strings

Since the man whom I call the Reliable Source was promised that he would not be identified in any way, I will abstain from any description of him or his surroundings. He was hospitable, as everyone was, and gave the Young Man a Sprite. — The difficulties across the border had begun, he said, in 1973. — Yes, it would have been in 1973 that the Soviet Union became especially interested; so the Young Man supposed. That was when Daoud overthrew the monarchy in Afghanistan.* And when the Soviet Union got interested, then Pakistan had better get interested, too. — The Young Man switched on the recorder. "So you started studying the problem in 1973?" he asked.

"Yes," said the Reliable Source, "in '73 our government began to see changes on the horizon—not only in Afghanistan itself but in the entire region. You know, the Chinese leadership was aging, and so *they* would be going out inside some period of time. One had to allow for that." — He was ticking off the falling colossi on his fingers. — "Then the Russian leadership was aging. No one could figure out with certainty who would follow in *their* shoes." — Another finger fell. — "Much closer at home, we saw the Shah of Iran. Now, we knew that he would possibly have to go under to a popular movement at some point in time. There was no organized and organic system which could take over and run the government after him, because there were only court ministers and such." — Another finger. — "Then, closer at home, we saw Afghanistan. With Zaher Shah ousted, we began to have real nightmares—in this sense: that as long as Daoud remained, there was some stability in the country, but once Daoud went out, then unknown people would start emerging. And that is what set us upon a certain plan of action—because we had our own national compulsions, Young Man! — In addition to that, Afghan people had never been friendly to us since '47.† They had also conducted certain activity in this province, and in Punjab, and these areas."

---

* See the entry in the Chronology for that year.
† That is, since the very birth of Pakistan.

"That was because of Pushtunistan?"* the Young Man said.

"Well, that was the racket," laughed the Reliable Source, "but I mean it must have been the other superpower interests who brought it about. Naturally there were proxies who were playing that game, but whether it was at the behest of the Indians, or the Russians, or their own . . ." — He shrugged. To the Young Man he seemed rather lonely. — "But right from the time we joined the United Nations they had opposed our entry, the Afghans. That was the only country that opposed our entrance. — But then we developed a *relationship*. The government of Afghanistan and of Pakistan both knew that if tomorrow, in case one of us or the other of us went out . . ." — The Reliable Source had a trick of not finishing his sentences. Partly, no doubt, that was because English was not his main language, although he spoke it almost fluently; partly it must have been because now everything about the Afghanistan situation seemed so conditional, vanished, wistful. *In case one of us or the other of us went out . . .* — And now, of course, they had both gone out. — "Daoud in 1976 when he came here," said the Reliable Source, "he told Mr. Bhutto, he said, 'if from the north, it is us today; tomorrow it is you. If from the south' (that is, India), 'today it is you; it is us tomorrow.' So they could see the realities. But they had to play a certain chess game that was going on" (and in his mind's ear the Young Man could hear Daoud calling yet again for a plebiscite in the North-West Frontier Province; he could hear the yells and rifle shots of Afridi tribesmen on horseback, come across the border to found the sovereign state of Pushtunistan no matter what the Pakistanis

---

* The ideal or specter (depending on who looked at it) of a separate state for the Pakistani and Afghan Pathans, in Pakistani territory. The inhabitants of the North-West Frontier Province were mainly Pathans, like my friend General N., like his guest the Brigadier, like the refugees that I interviewed. They had more in common with their fellows in eastern Afghanistan, with whom they had traded and intermarried for thousands of years, than with someone from Sind or Baluchistan. It was impossible for a foreigner to understand much of what they thought and what was important to them. The tribespeople on the border passed easily through the Soviet checkpoint on the Durand Line to trade with their counterparts. In those early days before the United States and the Arabs had begun to give much of their so-called covert aid to the Mujahideen, Pathans sold to Pathans. The principal business of the town of Darra, through which I passed in an International Rescue Committee van (it was a tribal area; we were not allowed to stop), was the manufacture of arms, from .38 caliber pistols made to resemble ballpoint pens to antiaircraft guns, all hand-produced. The General said that the people of Darra could copy any weapon so well that external inspection could not determine the original. He also said that those replicas sometimes blew up when fired. The Afghans were faithful patrons in Darra in 1982.

might say; he could hear the border closing, slamming like a door so that the nomads could no longer cross the Durand Line* for their summer grazing in the snowy grassy mountains as they had done for hundreds or thousands of years)—"but the Afghans *never* were against our genuine interest," said the Reliable Source, "in the sense that they never interfered in our communication or our . . ." — Again his voice trailed off. — "In the '65 war† and in the '71 war,‡ if they did not lend us support, at least they did not add to our strains. But then when Zaher Shah went out, we thought that henceforth *that* would be lacking! The royalty gave a continued stability to the system in Afghanistan: — today Zaher Shah, tomorrow it will be his son or someone else; and there was continuity of government in Afghanistan; it remained a stable area. Now, with Daoud's ouster of Zaher Shah, we knew that an element of uncertainty had come into being. And it had to be looked after.

"In addition, as I have said, there were the little bomb blasts and pinpricks in this area. Now, at the same point in time these groups—and they remained as such, as one group, until the fifth of July 1977 . . ." — The Reliable Source was getting something just right in his head. — "Well, first of all came a gentleman by the name of Habib Raman. He was then later captured by the Afghans in '75; he was"—the Reliable Source drummed his fingers—"brutally tortured and finally killed in Kabul Jail. Then, of course, Gulbuddin and those people. Rabbani was brought in later, as he was actually kept in the background because he would not disclose his identity. We kept asking them for some time whether they had a leadership which would meet the situation in Afghanistan, and they kept insisting that they had a man but they would not disclose him. But later on in '74 they brought him, and they said, 'This is Rabbani, and he is our genuine leader.'

"Now, these people had come away—one, against the oppression of Daoud; the other factor was that we wanted to bring home to Daoud's government that two can play that same game with bomb blasts here and things, playing this game across the border.

---

* The Pakistan-Afghanistan border (especially in the North-West Frontier Province). See Chronology, entry for 1893.
† An indecisive skirmish between Pakistan and India.
‡ The war between Pakistan and India, which Pakistan lost.

You see, that is what *we* did in 1975 in Panjsher,★ and we brought home one lesson to Daoud with regard to ending the Pushtunistan problem and getting recognition of the Durand Line and so forth. So that was one of the objectives."

"So Gulbuddin and Rabbani and so forth helped with these bomb blasts?" said the Young Man, trying to conceal his dismay. Somehow he had thought that they were freedom fighters.

"No, they organized, let us say, an uprising; it was not just bomb blasts; it was a *national uprising* against the Daoud regime in the Panjsher Valley."

"Now, what did they want? Did they want Zaher Shah back?"

"They did, yes, because at that time they were all agreed on that, and so was our government—because we thought, you see, that any revolution which came about in Afghanistan at this point in time would not be in the people's interest, in the sense that politically and socially they were not mature enough to take on the responsibilities of a revolution, be it leftist or rightist. So we thought," said the Reliable Source, "that they required more time. And that time could only be forthcoming if Zaher Shah was brought back, and he had given them a few more years for education to start coming up. Now, these groups had also come up, because of the social awakening, like the Parcham and Khalq,† and these elements like the Mujahideen were already here, too. But they needed time."

Clearly the Reliable Source enjoyed the role of mentor. The Young Man felt like a little boy who should have been in bed, being allowed just this once to stay up, raising himself on tiptoe so that he could see where the balls went on the international pool table—and when the Reliable Source had been a man of consequence, in the days before Bhutto's fall, he had let the Afghans stay up late, too, and taught them tricks. He told the Young Man how it had been decided, for instance, to extend the franchise in the tribal areas to include all adult males; formerly only the tribal elders had had it. — "So if you make things better for people *this* side of the Durand Line," he said, "then the Afghans start looking toward Pakistan. So we wanted the elements which were lying

---

★ An attempted putsch against Daoud. See Chronology, entry for 1975.
† The two rival leftist groups in Afghanistan, whom the Russians were to use in their chess game. See Chronology, entry for 1965.

on our borders to be looking toward *us*, to look up to *us* for change. Most of the tribes are so divided that half the elements are on the other side of the Durand Line, *cis*- and *trans*-Durand Line; they have ethnic commonality . . ."

The Young Man wanted to word his question tactfully. — "How did Gulbuddin, Rabbani and so forth feel about the fact that the, uh, main impetus for these changes was coming from Pakistan?"

"They agreed with us," said the Reliable Source blandly, "for they were also, at that time, not quite so militant. They knew that our policy of evolution vis-à-vis the tribal areas had succeeded, and that the Afghans were also looking for these same social reforms. As I said, they were not revolutionaries at that stage. But they wanted a change of two things. One was against the tyranny of Daoud, and the second one was of course what they could see coming in ideologically from across the borders."

"THE TYRANNY OF DAOUD" (1959)

"One of the more important events in modern Afghan history occurred in 1959," writes the historian Louis Dupree. "With no prior public announcement or official proclamation, Prime Minister Mohammad Daoud, Foreign Minister and Deputy Prime Minister Mohammad Naim,* other members of the royal family, the cabinet, and high-ranking army officers appeared on the reviewing stand with their wives and daughters on the second day of *Jeshn* [Independence Week] . . . The women had exposed their faces for all to see. Just thirty years before, the government of King Amanullah fell because (among other reform attempts) he abolished purdah and the *chadri* and established coeducational schools in Kabul.

". . . the large crowd of spectators stared in stunned disbelief.

". . . the inevitable happened. A delegation of religious leaders requested and received an audience with the Prime Minister.

---

* Daoud's brother. Daoud was Prime Minister under Zaher Shah from 1953 to 1963, when he resigned over an imbroglio over the Pushtunistan issue. Daoud and Naim were members of the Royal Family. The Constitution of 1964 prohibited anyone in the Royal Family from holding political office. Daoud seized power on July 17, 1973, when Zaher Shah was on a visit to Italy. Naim was one of his advisers during his five years of power. Both of these men and their families were liquidated in a leftist coup on April 27, 1978 (see Chronology).

The mullahs accused him of being anti-Islamic for permitting atheistic Communist and Christian Westerners to pervert the nation . . . Immediately after leaving the Prime Minister's office the religious leaders began to preach against the regime. Sardar Daoud's efficient secret police arrested and jailed about fifty of the ringleaders . . . Government spokesmen informed the imprisoned religious leaders that removal of the veil was voluntary, which was only partly true, for the government did force officials to attend public functions with unveiled wives in order to set examples for the masses . . . The weight of this logic (plus the fact that Afghan prisons are designed to punish, not rehabilitate) convinced the mullahs of the error of their ways, so the Prime Minister ordered their release after about a week of incarceration. Not all religious leaders accepted the voluntary abolition of the veil and other reforms, however, because each intrusion into their customary power erodes their secular influence."*

EVOLUTION OF THE MUJAHIDEEN (1959–79)

In his pamphlet *What Type of Struggle?* (whose cover bears as its device a shining Qur'ān nested between swords and wreaths), Professor B. Rabbani, the head of Jamiat-i-Islami Afghanistan, writes the following (September 1981): ". . . manners and behaviours should be selected very carefully. For instance; where preaching can be a mean [sic] for invitation (to the Way of Allah), implication of arms is not concordant with the wisdom of Islamic teaching. On the other hand, if expression and persuasion is not able to penetrate through the closed doors of contumacy and deviation or arguments and reasonings do not influence proudness, and if invitation is faced with inimical resistance of vanity, then non-implication of weapons (conduct of armed struggle) is idiocy and ignorance."†

IDIOCY AND IGNORANCE (1987)

Oh, how nice it would have been if the Mujahideen had appeared spontaneously following the Russian invasion! It would still have

---

* Louis Dupree, *Afghanistan*, pp. 530–33.
† P. 9.

been almost perfect if they had come into being after Taraki's coup in 1978, because THAT was probably bad, too, but if Rabbani and Gulbuddin and the rest of them had begun as creatures of the Pakistanis, then they *were* bandits, as the Soviets called them; they *were* terrorists. — It was very difficult for me to accept the tainted origins of necessity.

"IT WAS NOT JUST BOMB BLASTS; IT WAS A NATIONAL UPRISING!" (1975)

The National Uprising that the Reliable Source was paying homage to occurred in July of 1975. It was called the Panjsher Insurgency. Everyone agrees that the rebels were led by the mullahs. And who trained them? Pakistan, of course, denied that it had had anything to do with it. The Afghan population failed to join, and the government helicopters came quickly, shooting the rebels down; they captured ninety-three and found all but sixteen guilty, and then Daoud went on with his business.

THE RIGHT OF IT (1987)

But does what some of the groups *were* matter now? Was the Young Man right to feel that the Afghan Resistance was tainted by its origins? — I think not—not at present. I think that the effects of the Soviet presence in Afghanistan have been appallingly evil. Resistance is justified no matter where it comes from. Then, too, if we do accept the Reliable Source's account, can we say that Daoud was right in his efforts to modernize the country? That (thank God for small favors) is a matter now so laughably academic . . .

THE GAME (1878–1982)

Comparing politics to a chess game, as the Reliable Source loved to do, is, of course, trite in our own mass society, where we expect our politicians to play, and if necessary cheat, for our well-being, while the newspapers glowingly explain the moves for us—for the comparison is trite precisely because it is so valid. The Reliable Source's use of the phrase was equally justified. — It was the British who first began to speak of the "Great Game" between their empire and Russia's; and Afghanistan was at the center of the board.* Every new development was less a willed decision than an inevitable crystallization, for the Game was so Great as to be playing the players rather than the reverse. — "In the natural process of civilized and civilizing Powers which I have already dwelt upon," wrote Lord Lytton on 4 September 1878 (they were invading Afghanistan again that year), "wherever we leave a vacuum, Russia will assuredly fill it up." In the last few years before the Soviets gave Afghanistan their Christmas present, as the Reliable Source saw his anxieties congeal and solidify into real monsters, the Game continued, subject to the same pressures of cosmic law: — Each of the players made his move because the dynamic equilibrium of the Game forced him to; he was only trying to hold his own, you see. More years fell by the wayside; we spoke of the requirements of Containment when we fought Soviet bogeys in Central America; while *they* explained that progression from one social arrangement to another occurs only on a one-way escalator, so that feudalism in Afghanistan MUST give way to socialism as a result of Economic Laws, and all the U.S.S.R. was doing was protecting and implementing and developing. Both players advised their pawns to relax and continue down the slaughter chute. — *"Under the banner of the great April Revolution,† forward along the path toward full unity of all the national and progressive forces, toward the final victory of the national democratic, anti-feudal, anti-imperialist revolution, for the creation of a new proud, free and independent Afghanistan!"* screamed Babrak Karmal after being airlifted into office. (Naturally, it is not in my interest to quote a U.S. counter-example; for if I were so principled as to insist that we help the Afghans for their own sake, not because they are anti-Soviet, whom would I have left to advance their cause with me?) — History shows that the Game has always gone on, no matter who the players are; so if the world must indeed be run in this rotten way we should not blame the Reliable Source, but honor him for his honesty. How ludicrous, how foully ludicrous, when

---

* See the Chronology's entries for 1844–1907.
† I.e., Taraki's coup in 1978.

a player pretends not to be playing (though that is part of the Game, too), as when, for instance, the Soviets insist that they uphold the quaint ethnic strictures of backward countries: In the *Moscow News Weekly* No. 24 (21–28 June 1981), a column entitled "The Home Hearth: From Our Correspondent in Kabul" has the Elder of the Pashtun Tribe say, "The U.S.S.R.'s military help to Afghanistan is in full accord with the code of honor of the Pashtun tribe, the Pashtunwali. It says that if an enemy has attacked your country you can appeal to your neighbors to help oppose the enemy." — As the Persian proverb runs, "If the king says at noonday, 'It is night,' the wise man says, 'Behold the stars.' "

STATEMENT OF THE RELIABLE SOURCE
(continued) (1982)

"Did the Mujahideen groups accept and trust you and President Bhutto?" asked the Young Man.

"They basically trusted us. And that is why they remained with us from when they first came, in October 1973.★ I would say that there were various periods when we were more or less happy or unhappy with each other in the sense that from October '73 until about November '74 they were very happy with us because I was here, and I was looking after them." — The Reliable Source sighed. — "Then, fortunately or unfortunately, my successor who came, he thought he was a soldier, and should not dabble in this political business. So he then deprived us . . . He, let us say, went slow on it. It was a question of policy. It was not a question of personality. The result was that there was a little relaxation in the manner of support."

"It must have been a very tricky job for you," the Young Man said.

"Why?"

"Well, you must have been worried about Mr. Daoud."

"No, at that time they were playing their games with us. So the fact is, when one side is trying to play a game according to

---

★ This would have been a few months after Daoud's coup. He had already begun to send his 1,600 Parcham cadres into the rural areas to preach modernization. The mullahs' hackles were rising.

its own rules, then you also set your own set of rules. We lost Habib Raman, but we brought a very major change to Daoud's mind. He was compelled to come and talk with us.* He was compelled also to understand the nature of those changes, and that is why he requested us, in 1977, 'Please postpone your election on the elder tribal franchise basis, in the tribal area, for one year.' He said, 'You give me some time, so I can bring about a certain amount of reform, so that otherwise, they would rebel against me.' Because you could see people feeling the change over here."

How desperate was Daoud by the time he talked with Bhutto and the Reliable Source? Did he have any suspicion of what his end, what his country's end was going to be? And did the Reliable Source feel less enmity toward him during that meeting, simply by virtue of his precarious position? For however much he disliked Daoud, I imagine that he cared for Taraki somewhat less.

"Now what was the reaction in Afghanistan and in those political groups when Bhutto was replaced by General Zia?" asked the Young Man.

"You see, that is when the split amongst the group came. At the time when they were looked after, they were undoubtedly controlled in a certain manner, in the sense that they remained in one group."

"What form did that control take?"

"By—*understanding,*" said the Reliable Source. "They understood and we understood that we and they had a common program, with the result that we were supporting them to the extent that they required. And they understood, too, that we were using each man according to his ability. Now, this fellow Gulbuddin, he is a militant; Khalis is militant; Nabi† . . . they are all militant. Rabbani, on the other hand, he is one who would like to carry it out through a program of education. He was a preacher in Scandinavian countries. He came to us toward the end of '76.‡ So we told him that he was doing an adequate job in Scandinavia, and he should continue over there; no need for him at the moment,

---

* Which he did the year after the Panjsher Uprising (see Chronology, entry for 1976).
† Here a recapitulation may be useful. Gulbuddin Hekmatyar ran the right-wing group Hezb-i-Islami, Maulvi Mohammad Yunus Khalis controlled a splinter group from Hezb-i called after him, and Maulvi Mohammad Nabi Mohammadi ran Herakat-i-Inqelab-i-Islami, an organization somewhat more to the liberal taste.
‡ This sentence makes it clear that the Reliable Source is not always so reliable in the matter of dates, for earlier (see p. 176) he had said that Rabbani came in 1974.

because all the other groups were here, and they were united
. . . But they were all agreed on wanting Zaher Shah back. That
is why their representatives went and met with him at end of '76,
early '77, and he agreed to come and lead them, because they also
needed a central leadership."

"So why isn't Zaher Shah here coordinating things now?"

"Ah, that is because General Zia got cold feet, I suppose."

"You think all the major factions still want Zaher Shah?"

"Not today. You see, Khomeini had come by then, and that
was one reason; and secondly I told you that after July '77* they
became a rabble; they became a disorganized group for lack of
support. Everyone started looking around. Someone went to Ku-
wait, someone went to Saudi Arabia and so on, because they were
not getting the support they wanted or desired within Pakistan."

"So where are they getting their support now?" asked the Young
Man.

"Now? From the Americans."

"From the C.I.A.?"

"Yes."

"General Zia isn't—?"

"That—that is, my own impression is that, because, uh, there
are so many things one cannot say directly," cried the Reliable
Source. "If you turn this tape recorder off, I will tell you . . ."

The recorder was shut off for ten minutes.†

A SOVIET AMPLIFICATION

"There is an obvious connection," says the Tass statement on
Afghanistan of December 1979, "between visits of American
emissaries to Pakistan, their visits to some areas in Afghanistan
and the operations of the rebel forces. It is not a chance coincidence that the mutiny in Herat to which Afghan reaction
Washington and Peking were establishing special significance
was started immediately after one of the ringleaders of Afghan

---

* I.e., after Zia displaced Bhutto.
† In June 1982, when this interview was given, the United States had not yet admitted
that it was supporting the Mujahideen via Pakistan. Therefore this was interesting news
to me at the time. Five years later, it seemed only vaguely sad and sordid, like the Panjsher
"Uprising"—and sadder and more sordid still because I support overt and covert aid to
the Mujahideen. How true, alas, that there are so many things that one cannot say directly!

counterrevolutionaries was received at the U.S. Department of State. There is data about the attempts of U.S. representatives to get from the Pakistani leadership a consent to still wider use of Pakistani territory for sending armed groups into Afghanistan. Even wider participation in aggressive actions against Afghanistan was being demanded of Pakistan.

"There is no need for special insight to be able to see through the motives of the United States's actions. There are figures in Washington who persistently look for replacements for the positions which were lost as a result of the fall of the Shah's regime in Iran. Cracks appeared in the notorious 'strategic arc' that Americans have been building for decades close to the southern borders of the Soviet Union, and in order to mend these cracks it was sought to bring under the Afghan people and also peoples of other regions.

". . . External imperialist reaction is working constantly to undermine the organs of state power and disorganize the ranks of the People's Democratic Party of Afghanistan."

I imagine that every word of this is true.

A THOUGHT (1987)

Well, perhaps it was no wonder that almost every Afghan or Pakistani I talked to believed that I was some omnipotent C.I.A. manipulator;—that almost every Afghan or Pakistani thought that he was controlled;—that in Peshawar they kept saying that a secret deal had been made whereby the Soviets would be allowed to hold onto Afghanistan and the Americans were to take over the Middle East. — What would these people have thought if they could have been, say, in San Francisco on 12 February 1987 (a rainy day), watching an anti-Asian rally in front of the Korean Embassy, the workmen with their heavy slickers, the good old boys twirling unbrellas, waving American flags and yelling, "*Flag! Flag! Flag! Flag!*"* — The young men looked serious and stupid. The older ones were smiling. Everyone was tremendously excited. The iron-workers' union was there, saying that Korea was exporting un-

---

* Or, as they must say in Afghanistan: *"Parcham! Parcham! Parcham! Parcham!"*

employment. — *"GET THE GOOKS OUT OF AMERICA!"*
— For the Americans also believed that they were controlled.

And yet the situation was not entirely symmetrical. For when
the Young Man learned that so many Mujahideen groups had
come into play long before the final change of government, as
maliciously twiddling and poking fingers of Pakistani *Realpolitik*,
he felt a deep sense of shock—and yet he ought to have known
how matters stood as soon as he saw the Brigadier's letter!

> . . . that after two months of the agreement we will
> be helped with the following: . . . 40 Powerful explosive
> Bumbs . . .

Somehow when his own government did it, it did not seem
either surprising or bad. Why was this?

STATEMENT OF THE RELIABLE SOURCE
(continued)

"How do you think we can best help the Mujahideen groups
now?" the Young Man said.

"The problem is still the same as it was," said the Reliable
Source. "It requires a central leadership; it requires a central figure
who enjoys the confidence of all the elements of the Mujahideen,
and that is the only way you can bring about unity amongst them.
It is first amongst themselves, and then between them and the
tribal elders, but first of all a program must be chopped out, about
what is the best form of government that should come about
initially in Afghanistan."

"And who can that figure be if it isn't Zaher Shah?"

"Well, it has to be someone by consensus. In tribal society that
is always simple. But the mullahs—Gulbuddin and Rabbani—they
will not accept that. The tribes will accept that, yes, but not the
mullahs. So again you are at cross-purposes. The fact was, in 1973
to '77, though we voted that we wanted Zaher Shah and we did
not get him, the fact is that they remained an effective group,
because there was effective coordination. And that could be
brought about even today. — Now, the history of Afghanistan is
that the kingmakers have been the tribesmen of Pakistan. What is

the kingdom of Afghanistan? It's a grouping of tribal groups brought about by Ahmad Shah in 1747. It is a medieval age there still, a tribal society, and this is what the Russians miscalculated, and this is why there are uprisings always. Now, what was Ahmad Shah doing? If there was uprising in Kabul you use Kandahar. If an uprising in Kandahar you play off Kabul. So these two elements were always made to balance each other. Or the Pushtuns were made to balance the rest. And so this sort of thing carried on. And this was how we operated as well. This was part of our program: *that the groups of Gulbuddin and all were just to raise the issue*, or bring it to the focus in case something happened. Our own tribesmen, of ethnic commonality, would also move in such large numbers that they would then have their effect and bring about that change. That was the program. Now, this government again miscalculated and lost an opportunity between April of '78 and December of '79*—this could have been successfully achieved."

"Given this tribal predominance and the fact that the tribes move back and forth across the Durand Line, can the Soviet Union digest Afghanistan without also digesting Pakistan?" asked the Young Man.

"It depends, you see," said the Reliable Source. "They have, let us say, already digested Afghanistan to all intents and purposes. Now with the Geneva talks I think they are just going to give the situation *de facto* or *de jure* recognition. I do not think the Russians will enjoy any additional advantage by taking Pakistan. Now, Afghanistan was important from our point of view in the old times, when their objective was Delhi, and the army must move through the N.W.F.P. and those regions. But with that violently left movement in 1971, the Treaty of Friendship and things, the Russians and the Indians have a common axis, a common interest. So the objective is not Delhi anymore. If it is the Gulf, or denial of the Gulf oil to the West, then the next objective will automatically be Iran; it will not be us. If the goal is Baluchistan, then it will be us."

"So you don't think the Russians will care that they won't have entirely subdued the tribes in eastern Afghanistan?"

"The point is, if the Pakistan government is not willing to interfere in Afghan affairs, then these tribesmen will be neutralized,

---

* I.e., the civil convulsions in Afghanistan just before the invasion.

as they are today. With all these events taking place in Afghanistan, the tribesmen on our side remain neutral. But if the government had motivated these tribes, then of course the question would have come about."

"What would you say the chances are of the Russians being pushed out of Afghanistan?"

"None whatever."

COMMON SENSE

Well, and so the Reliable Source was wrong, for the Soviets did, of course, leave Afghanistan in 1989, and yet the Great Game may not be over.

11

A MATTER OF POLITICS: FRIENDLY ENEMIES (1982)

It is not important whether an Afghan is Shia or Sunni. We are all brothers . . . All those who lead the present resistance and fight against the Russians are patriotic and great personalities. Professor Rabbani is both Shia and Sunni. I am both Shia and Sunni. Everybody is both Shia and Sunni in Afghanistan, and the one who is not is not Muslim.

(Young Man: Is Gulbuddin your brother?)

Yes, of course he is my brother. He has very courageously fought against the Russian invaders. It is a matter of politics which causes disunity among the parties. There are Russian agents who make mischief and cause disagreement and difficulties among the leaders. They are all great men of their time.

SHIA MUJAHIDEEN
COMMANDER

Friendly enemies

Of course the Afghans were unified now. The Young Man knew they must be; he had read it in the papers over and over. They had even formed a common organization called Islamic Unity of Afghan Mujahideen. — Well, no. Actually there were two rival organizations by this name, and they hated each other. But everyone told him that until recently there had been some trouble, but now the factions were as tight as the Three Musketeers. (In his notebook he wrote: "Need to know how often they kill each other before I know whether I can countenance supporting them."*)

"So now the Mujahideen never fight each other?" the Young Man inquired.

"That is very much exaggerated, you see," said the refugee camp administrator quickly. "That news item is very much exaggerated now. There might have been some very few cases, but not the thing it has become in Western media. It was individual enmity that developed. That was one case. Another case was the soldiers of the Karmal regime, you see. They wanted to surrender to one party of the Mujahideen. While they were on the way, Jamiat-i-Islami people caught them. And they were going to shoot them. And the other party, Hezb-i-Islami, told them that you shouldn't. And a fight developed . . . There *was* a fight, a long, long time ago. But now it has finished."

"So everyone is unified now?"

The administrator nodded. They were drinking *lessee* in a guest tent, and the administrator finished his cup and held it up until an old man gave him more.

"Everyone is united and quite satisfied," he said. "And if some-

---

* "Thank you for submitting the manuscript," wrote the literary agent, "and my apologies for my slowness. I hope your intestinal parasites are a thing of the past. I do appreciate the chance to read *An Afghanistan Picture Show*. I only wish that I could get someone to buy it . . ."

Secretary-General Pizzarda, holding the helmet of a Soviet soldier

body wants to surrender, he surrenders to the whole organization, you see."

STATEMENT OF PROFESSOR S. SHAMSUDDIN MAJROOH, AFGHAN INFORMATION OFFICE

The General took the Young Man to see Professor Majrooh. Everyone meant well in this interview: the General in bringing them together, the Young Man in wishing to determine whether U.S. covert aid was effective and sufficient (imagine the laughable scene! imagine this Young Man who was about as well suited to deal with spy matters as a grasshopper!), Majrooh in aiming to help his fellow Afghans; but because the Young Man's role was so confusingly pure, differences soon began to swarm like midges, and the usual ambiguity of these affairs dizzied the Young Man far more than the heat.

The Young Man considered that if he were going to send his nickels to a Mujahideen organization (the misunderstanding might be succinctly put by saying that Majrooh must have thought: "If the boy has come all the way over here, then surely he must at least have dimes!"), then he ought to make sure that said nickels went to the group that devoted the greatest proportion of its resources to killing Soviet soldiers *inside* as opposed to killing members of other factions in the Resistance.

And Professor Majrooh—who can blame him for responding as he did? In his mind, factionalism was unfortunate but it did not *ethically* prejudice the whole. And in this he was correct.

"I was a professor at Kabul University," he said. "I was also Dean of the Faculty. I left Afghanistan at the beginning of the Soviet invasion, at the beginning of '80, and came to help here, in my way, the war of liberation. And we are here; we have a small office. We receive information from *inside* and pass it on to the outside world."

"And you are not aligned with any particular group?" asked the Young Man.

"No, we are not. The Afghan Information Office is independent and we try to be impartial, though of course we *are* on the side of the Resistance, but we try to have good relations with all the groups."

"That must be very difficult," said the Young Man politely, while on the sofa the General smiled wearily.

"A difficult task, of course," said Majrooh brightly, "not to present the picture of one side or group, and to tell the situation as it really is: the serious burden of most refugees in Pakistan today, you know; and then we have the refugees who could not cross the border. These people must be helped. We must find a way— I don't know how—to reach the people *inside*. The French are doing this, but their means are limited; the problem is too big for them."

And he looked at the Young Man hopefully.

"How well would you say the officially recognized parties here in Pakistan represent the people in Afghanistan?"

"All are present on the fighting front *inside*," said Professor Majrooh. "But they do not represent the whole. There are lots of population there who are just fighting for themselves—the Civil Defense system. Anyway, they are representing an important part of the fighting."

"What percentage of the people in Afghanistan would you say are supporters of one or more of these officially recognized groups?"

"They make up fifty percent of the fighting forces."

"What about the other fifty percent?"

"They have their own weapons which they captured from the *Roos*, and they have their own region, and they are not moving from there. And an important part inside is free; the *Roos* have only the big cities."

"What would be the most practical means of distributing arms?" asked the Young Man. "If I were to give arms to Gulbuddin, say, he might use these arms to, oh, for instance, kidnap someone from the National Islamic Front."

Professor Majrooh laughed politely. (It was here, I would say, that a shadow began to creep over the interview.)

"So can we give them directly to the people who need them," the Young Man persisted, "or is there some party which is relatively more appealing than the others?"

"First people must agree to *give* arms to the Mujahideen," replied Majrooh drily, "and secondly there is the question of what type of arms, and only thirdly the question will be this, and I think we will be led to discuss and study this with the professionals, the experts. And I think there are ways. But it cannot be answered like that."

"Well, I don't represent anyone," said the Young Man, "but so far I don't have anyone I'd want to give arms to. Can we start this process? Can we propose a favorite candidate?"

"No, no," said Majrooh, much as a senator might say, "No comment." "I would not propose it. That would be premature."

"You have no suggestions as to whom I might go to, to find someone who could use these arms in an effective way against the Russians? And not against others?"

"No, no, they don't do that," said Majrooh. "If you study— if you have time—you will understand that all the groups who are here, they are quite efficiently fighting. A small proportion, of course, and there are always in a situation like this internal problems and problems of organization, but it is not the whole picture. And now, as you have heard, they are fighting in Panjsher quite effectively, and the fifth Soviet offensive was just checked there . . ."

"That's mainly the Jamiat group, Rabbani's group?"

"No, I have told you, there are many others who have come to help, as for instance from Ghazni. It's not a serious problem, as you seem to think. They're not just fighting each other. There are some, but it's not the general rule."

"So you think that the United States should arm the Resistance."

"Absolutely."

"Well, if you could give me a proposal as to how that ought to be done . . ."

Majrooh fitted his fingertips together. "I think that we . . . we are in Pakistan, you know. And we try to have good relations with the official authorities, and I think that all this help must come through the official authorities."

How pleased the Reliable Source would have been to hear these words! Evidently the puppet masters yet held the strings.

"So we should give arms to the government of Pakistan and let them decide how to distribute them?" asked the Young Man.

"No, I would not make a recommendation like that. Only when they decide, the Americans, they should discuss it with the authorities in Pakistan."

From the sofa the General said, "I know there is a firm in London that can deliver arms anywhere in the world, including Pakistan."

"The Americans, they know how to do it," said Majrooh. "With the Pakistani authorities. They know the problem."

"If you had those weapons," said the Young Man, "it would just depend on the circumstances who you gave them to?"

"I'd not accept them personally," said Professor Majrooh. "I'd tell you where to go, but I would not take this military responsibility. But when the question is there, I think I could give you some advice—practical advice."

STATEMENT OF JUDGE DR. NAJIB SAID, ISLAMIC UNITY (LIBERAL COALITION)

The offices of the factions were scattered about Peshawar. You took a rickshaw. If the driver was Pakistani he might have to stop and ask directions a few times, but an Afghan would know. The metal trim of Pakistani-driven rickshaws was decorated with pictures of sexy Indian movie stars, whereas the Afghans preferred pictures of men with machine guns.

The "liberal" coalition known as Islamic Unity of Afghan Mujahideen was neither close to nor far from the fundamentalist Islamic Unity of Afghan Mujahideen. It was in a tan cement building several stories high. There were no guards, but then everyone seemed to be a guard. Big, well-built men lounged around in the courtyard and on the terraces, chatting, cradling their guns. Pizzarda,* the Secretary-General, had work to do, so he took the Young Man to his office, told him to be comfortable, and sat behind his desk. Everyone had stood up at his arrival except for a fat man in a turban who slumbered on the bench, head forward, hands on lap, as the fan droned slowly. — Pizzarda slipped a second pair of glasses over his first, for reading, and began to sign papers.

This Pizzarda was a hospitable man. The General knew him well. Pizzarda had taken the Young Man personally to see the Hazarat Museum, which was a flat in a private apartment building where bits of rocket bombs and captured helicopter parts were mounted on a heavy brown pasteboard, along with gunship helicopter bullets, shrapnel fragments, a dead Ivan's dogtag, a metal plaque that said something in Russian about what to do before you charged the accumulators; and from the corner Pizzarda took a Soviet helmet with a bullet hole going in and going out, and he grinned. They sat on the floor and had green tea, and later the Young Man took pictures, so that there stood Pizzarda forever, wearing his silver spectacles, unsmiling now with thin lips when the Young Man raised his camera for the Afghanistan Picture Show, and his beard was silver and gray and his wristwatch glittered and the helmet glittered and there was a bloodstain around the hole.

Watching him at work, the Young Man looked interestedly round the office, and it was at that time that Judge Dr. Said came in. Seeing that Pizzarda would be occupied for a few minutes longer, he agreed to talk with the Young Man. He was a tall, handsome, Semitic-looking man with a thick dark beard. He spoke an Oxford-accented English.

---

* I never saw his name transliterated, and am spelling it exactly as it sounds.

"In your belief, are there many Communists in the other factions of the Mujahideen?" asked the Young Man. (It had been the General's shrewd advice to ask about Communists. Anyone considered dangerous was called a Communist.)

Smiling, Dr. Said put an arm around the Young Man's shoulder. "That is a *very* difficult question, my dear friend," said he. "Nobody graphically understands how to put a graph on the *heart* of the people and the *totality* of the people, to know what faith they have got. But by political charter framework of the Mujahideen, by our *efforts,* by our *endeavors,* by our doctrine and our way of life, nobody is entitled to join who is thought to be pro-Communist."

"So what do you do when you find a Communist?"

"Then we search to find the Communist people; when we find them it is *difficult* for the Communist people! It is difficult for *us* to find who is Communist. The Russians are not only fighting us by weapon; they are fighting us by K.G.B.; they are fighting us by *any* available type of means."

"So, suppose that I were a member of your group, and you discovered conclusive evidence that I was a Communist. What would happen to me?"

"You should receive your tort, your punishment."

"What would that be? Would you kill me?"

"Yeah."

"How often does this happen?"

"Where?" said Dr. Said. "In Peshawar, or abroad?"

"In Peshawar."

"This is difficult, because some of these questions should not be divulged, but our effort is continuously being—done, to find such people, and to give them punishment. This is our understanding—our law, and our charter. Those who are Communist by their nature, now they can realize that they can never *ever* divert this thing from Islamic roots. Do you understand my point?"

"Yes," said the Young Man dutifully. He gathered his courage. "Just a few days ago," he said, "if I'm not mistaken, uh, someone, um, a doctor was kidnapped by the Gulbuddin group, uh, because he was believed to be a Communist. Do you know anything about that?"

"No," said Dr. Said firmly. "Just only as a *rumor* I have heard

Identification page from the ration book of the kidnapped doctor

that. And there is *no evidence*, and I do *not* base my judgment on hearsay evidence!"

"Maybe you could tell me about an actual incident?" suggested the Young Man brightly.

"There is no evidence available to me."

"I won't press you."

"Thank you."

A few minutes later, when the interview had been concluded, Dr. Said picked up a dogeared letter from his desk. It was in English. He had evidently forgotten about the young American snooping behind him. The letter was a plea to Afghan Refugee Commissioner Abdullah—who was said to be a partisan of Gulbuddin*—for clemency and help in regard to this very same kidnapped doctor. Dr. Said wrote something on the letter in Pushtu, stamped it with his seal, and gestured to one of his men, who took it off somewhere.

---

* See Chapter 8, in which Abdullah is interviewed.

THE OCCUPATION OF DR. SAID

"What do you do from day to day?" asked the Young Man.

"My actual job, according to the law, and the procedure, and the charter, comes to enforcement. This alliance consists of thirteen different committees. Each committee does its own job. For instance, Secretariat. What do they do? They do their *own* job. Political Committee does perform its *own* job. Research and Inspection Committee performs its *own* job. And I am the president of the Research and Inspection Committee. Because I studied law, I was a judge in Afghanistan in the Supreme Court. In various cases, I do investigation. There is interrogation of the people, clashes, offenses—minor offense, major offense—felony, misdemeanor . . ."

"So what do you do in the course of an interrogation?"

"Ah, interrogation is, as far as we are concerned, a very great major crime. To do the research, this is a police function—to find the criminal, to bring him in for interrogation, and when they are brought for interrogation, then as a prosecution I determine my own vote on these people, and I send the vote and interrogate these people, in a very *human* way. After the completion of the case according to the realm of international law, we send the case to the Commissary. Whatever they like, they may perform in conjunction with the case. — I personally from the very beginning up to the last find this interesting, but if you have specific questions as far as you are concerned, please come up to my office and ask this question and I will show you the type of work: how we interrogate the people, how the accusation is delivered to the people and how their denial is accepted."

"When can I come?"

"Anytime. Do come, and do ask for Dr. Judge Najib Said, the President of Investigation and Research."

SEMANTICS (1987)

At the time I thought Dr. Said to be a very cruel man. Nowadays, I am happy or sad to say, if I were to meet Dr. Said I would scarcely give the possible cruelty of his occupation a thought. If

there are Soviet informants among the Mujahideen, then they must
be identified and killed. (But what if the Communists are not
Communists at all? — Well, everyone makes mistakes.)

EPITAPH FOR THE YOUNG MAN

"Here it is difficult as it were to keep our heads up," says Wittgenstein (I.106), "—to see that we must stick to the objects
of our every-day thinking and not go astray and imagine that
we have to describe extreme subtleties, which in turn we are
quite unable to describe with the means at our disposal. We
feel as if we had to repair a torn spider's web with our fingers."

EXTREME SUBTLETIES

"So Gulbuddin kidnaps people?" the Young Man asked ingenuously.

"Yes, he kidnaps so many peoples here in Peshawar!" the man
cried. — They were in Secretary-General Pizzarda's office. Judge
Dr. Said was there, too, but he was talking to someone else, so
he did not take note of the interview. Both the Young Man and
his informant kept turning to watch Dr. Said to make sure that
he was still occupied. None of the other Mujahideen said anything.
— "He kidnap last year one person in ——— Tribal Agency,"
said the man quickly, "and last month he kidnap another person,
then he killed him. Last month, he kidnap my brother, Dr. Abdul
Sumad Durani; he was my brother! Now he—*refuse* him; he say,
'I didn't kidnap him,' but we have some document: he kidnap, he
catch . . . Police catch his vehicle in driveway."

"Gulbuddin thought he was Communist?"

"No! He was not Communist; he was Muslim; he was Mujahid!" The man was weeping quietly. None of the other Mujahideen in the office said anything.

The Young Man tried again. "Why was he kidnapped?"

"He don't like so many social person; he don't like educated
person here in Pakistan. You know? He don't like."

STATEMENT OF THE KIDNAPPED
DOCTOR'S FATHER

"My name is Habib Shah Alaquadar," said the old man, standing straight and tall.★ "I am married. I am from Sayed Karam, in Paktiya Province. When Taraki came to power we started our jihad. At this time, my son, Dr. Abdul Sumad Durani, worked among the freedom fighters as a medical doctor. He took care of wounded people . . . After we came to Peshawar, he founded the doctors' union here. This union represented other medical unions from Italy, Germany, America and France. He was the representative and director of this medical union. He received medicine and other humanitarian help from America and other countries and took them inside Afghanistan for distribution among the people. But now Gulbuddin has kidnapped him! On May 25, at 12 p.m., he was taken away by Gulbuddin party members. We don't know where he is now. He must be in one of Gulbuddin's prisons. We have reported this incident to different authorities. We have told the Commissioner, and the police. But Abdullah, the Commissioner, is a supporter of Gulbuddin."

As he talked, the old man unbuttoned his shirt and reached inside to show the Young Man his cartridge belt. His voice was firm and calm. "Dr. Sumad was not an ordinary man," he said. "He was a leader. We Afghans have a custom of taking revenge. Gulbuddin has killed a leader of ours. We must kill one of their leaders. The leader that we must kill could be Gulbuddin himself, or Sayaf or another leader. About eighty percent of the freedom fighters in Pakistan belong to our party, and we are stronger than Gulbuddin."

STATEMENT OF DR. NAJIBULA,
JAMIAT-I-ISLAMI (FUNDAMENTALIST)

The Jamiat-i-Islami had two separate offices. The Young Man was always directed to the Political Office, which was right around

---

★ This interview, like many others, was conducted in Pushto. I am indebted to my Afghan translator in California (who does not wish to be identified).

the corner from the street by whose low white-brick wall a vendor of little red plums stood watching the Young Man, smiling without really smiling, a red cloth around his head; and his sons big and small stood holding plums and staring at the Young Man, and the vendor looked youngish except that his stubble on chin and chest was gray; and the Young Man bought a handful of plums, which were delicious, and then he turned that corner and strode into the central courtyard, where the young boy with the AK-47 would stop him. Then the Young Man had to wait until someone could identify him. Meanwhile the guard smiled, puffed out his chest, and gestured that he wanted a photograph taken of him for the Afghanistan Picture Show. When the Young Man obliged, he beamed in delight. This happened every time.

Dr. Najibula* (or Najib, as the Mujahideen called him) was a young-looking man with a black beard, piercing eyes and a high, clear voice. He had the Young Man over for supper several times. There were always young Mujahideen present at those occasions, sitting cross-legged on the carpet, polishing their Kalashnikovs (those who had them) and talking earnestly about the Panjsher situation. The *Roos* were trying to crush Masoud's army that summer. They bombed clockwise, round and round the ring road; but always they singled out Panjsher Valley.

Jamiat-i-Islami had a strong presence in Panjsher.

At the end of the afternoon, when it came time to break fast, the Mujahideen washed themselves and prayed. Then they sat on the carpet and ate their vegetables and rice. There was one dish for every three or four men. You took your *dordai* and tore off a piece to scoop up food from the dish. (When the Young Man tried it, he usually spilled a little onto the floor.) After dinner everyone listened to Radio Afghanistan, the free station, and the only word that the Young Man could understand was Panjsher, Panjsher, Panjsher.

Sometimes when the Young Man was at the Jamiat-i-Islami he sat and listened to Professor Rabbani speak. Rabbani was a grave mullah with an iron-gray beard. He sat at a table and talked, and his followers sat motionless on the carpet and listened. The Young Man understood nothing. When there was a break, the Mujahideen

---

* I have transliterated his name thus to avoid confusion with Babrak Karmal's successor, Najibullah.

smiled at the Young Man and teased him. They touched his shoulder. — "Afghanistan?" they said. — "Yes, yes," the Young Man replied in Pushtu. "I go there, see Mujahideen fight the *Roos.*" — "You are white," they laughed, "too white! When the *Roos* see you, you must say: '*Ya Nooristani; Pukhto na pwaygum.*' "* And they all laughed. — But they did not really want him to accompany them. They thought him too young.

In his notebook he wrote such entries as:

> Went to Najib at Jamiat again. He said take as little as possible *inside*—but must bring passport, Afghan clothes.

> Sat around for a long time. Asked Najib what they'd set up for me. Nothing. Group leaving early this week if passes open (blocked by tribal fighting). "If you are lucky you can go with one of these groups."

> "Otherwise how long will I have to wait?"

> He spread his hands.

But at least the Young Man could *interview* the Mujahideen to his heart's content. He turned on his tape recorder in Dr. Najib's office. — "I've met a number of people who seem to think that the Mujahideen are much less unified than they claim . . ."

Dr. Najib had the office cleared of other people. "First of all," he said, "it is unfortunately true that there is not as much unity as we would like, but you might know that efforts are being brought about to make a new organization called Islamic Unity of Afghan Mujahideen."

"Is there one organization by that name or two?"

There was a pause. — "Two," said Najib finally. "But I'm talking about the *main* one, you see; and we are working together, and in a month or two this problem of unity will have been solved. About the other group, it is true that they have established propaganda against our organizations. It must be kept in mind also that the Russians have puppets and agents in this area, and they exaggerate our disunity."

---

* "I am Nuristani and understand no Pushtu." (Nuristanis are often light-skinned.)

THINGS THAT PEOPLE WOULDN'T
SAY ON TAPE [3]

If a man were to switch political parties, he'd be killed. If my informant's party were to find out that he told me this, he'd be killed.

The General's statement

The two of them were sitting out on the patio in lawn chairs. It was hot that day, and the General had turned on a large fan that at least moved the hot air around. Not even a grasshopper stirred.

"So you think their problem is that they're not willing to compromise?" asked the Young Man.

"Well, they say they must get together. That is one of the first principles of Islam: *towhee,* oneness. Yet here they are. And there are nine of them, ten of them—all these groups! They ought to be making common cause to kick the Russians out. They are doing it, but individually."

"Do you think it's possible for them to stop kidnapping each other and so forth?"

"Traditionally we have a system," the General said. "You and I are at daggers drawn, and our common well-wisher decides to intervene between us. He says: 'All right, for two, three months there will be no killing, no kidnapping, no cursing.' And it is honored. So the differences could be done away with for a limited period—up to six months."

The Young Man shifted in his chair. "Well, will it happen in this case?"

"The saner elements are not there," said the General. "The young fellows . . . Well, the saner elements are *inside.* Ninety percent of the fighting is going on inside Afghanistan by the people who are there. And those chaps who are over here, they are all very ambitious; they all want the chair. And as they are ambitious, they will probably not get together. I feel we should help the majority, the ones *inside*. They are starving. And they are fighting your war, my war, the war of the free world. And that help should be extended materially, economically, medically. Most of the fighting takes place May to September. The rest, Afghanistan is under all this snow. Afghanistan was never self-sufficient. And with the present circumstances, the Russians are there; they can't do any cultivations. These winters are very hard. These winters are *very* hard. The Russians are so bloody stupid—or clever—that they bombed their harvest and compelled them to beg food from them. So far, the common man has been rejecting these things from the Russians. Well, how long will he go on rejecting it?

"In Panjsher, the person who is fighting there, Masoud, he is paying his own men. He has a full-fledged army of two thousand people of his own. He's a gemstone dealer: he sells his emeralds and rubies in the United States. You see, fighting inside has to be either on a tribal basis, with individual khanates, or else with those who can afford to wage the war. We must help them, not these bloody parties."★

★ In comparison with their occupiers, the Afghans did quite well, for any *person* will always come off more favorably than the *soldier* who has come to dispossess him. Since by the time I wrote this book my sympathies in this matter had come to lie wholly with the refugees and the Mujahideen, I considered hiding or denying what is blighted on their leaf. However, that is not only a bad way to begin (and I am not certain, anyhow, that I would be capable of doing so suavely), but—more to the point—I think it is both unnecessary and inexpedient: unnecessary, because from *our* viewpoint the stench is hardly noxious, we being, in all respects, on the other side of the world, and because these things that the Afghans do are not of significant harm to anyone but themselves; and inexpedient, because pointing them out will not be "of aid and comfort to the enemy," the enemy having been clever enough to play on them already. Anyhow, the war is over for the moment.

12

THE RED HILL

(1982)

I think it is like Vietnam. We will have to be
here fighting the Russians for five years,
ten years, twenty years, fifty years. But
finally we will regain our country.

HERAKAT COMMANDER

The red hill [4]

The five of them were in a fine, spacious house in a wooded village. The Young Man could hear the river outside the window. To get up here you crossed a number of tiny makeshift bridges, said *"Sta ray machay"* to the boys standing seriously under the trees, ignored the girls, who were loaded down with water and firewood, and ascended a ladder. The village was made up of tall, narrowly spaced two-story buildings. The first floor was stables and fodder sheds. Above their cattle the people lived, in houses of wood whose doors were carved in whorled patterns. The malik's guest chamber was cool, thanks to its thick mud walls, and sluggish with shadows. From the wooden beams hung paper decorations in various colors, which reminded the Young Man of the Christmas tree ornaments he had made in elementary school. Along the length of the far wall ran two lines of pictures: — dim family portraits (he supposed, not knowing, not asking) of stern Pathan men; and color prints of mosques in Afghanistan. The wall behind the guests' heads, however, had been papered from the floor up to the height of a sitting man, for cleanliness. They all stretched out on the floor there, on thick rugs of red, green, white and yellow, with big embroidered pillows against the wall for their heads. In the back of the room were three *charpoys,* or rope beds.

His four companions slept beside him, their rugs thrown over their faces to keep off the flies. The Young Man was not sleepy. So, squatting at his side, the malik entertained him. He was an old man with two rifles—one Chinese and one Indian; each was kept loaded with a clip of thirty bullets.

"You are Mujahid?" said the malik. They spoke in Pushtu, which required the Young Man to go to the grammatical heart of things every time.

"No," he said. "I Ameriki. I want to help Afghan Mujahideen. I come, take photos, bring photos to other Amerikis, and they

see, they understand Mujahideen, understand refugees, maybe send rupees for Kalashnikovs, bullets, Ameriki guns, *owuh dazai.*"

An *owuh dazai* was a seven-shooter, a Lee-Enfield rifle. He had learned the word from a century-old manual for soldiers of the British Empire. It was probably hard to find an *owuh dazai* these days, but the Young Man had to do what he could with his vocabulary.

"You go to shoot at the *Roos?*" said the malik slyly.

The Young Man had hardly fired a gun in his life. "If *Roos* shoot at me, and Mujahideen give me *topak,* I shoot at *Roos.* But I am no good shot."

The malik grinned. "I also no good shot. My father, he come from Afghanistan; he can kill. I am like you, just C.I.A., just tourist." — He took the Young Man to the window. A thousand yards away, a goat was grazing among the rocks. The old man fired two shots almost simultaneously. Two puffs of dust appeared, one on either side of the goat. The goat leaped and ran.

"Very good," said the Young Man, feeling it incumbent on him to say something. "Very good."

The malik radiated delight. He got up and brought his guest some very good bread, made of thin, crackly, buttery layers. You rolled it in sugar and broke off pieces to dip in your *chi*. They offered him tea constantly. He was the only one who could legitimately eat and drink during the day. At least (fortunately for those who kept Ramazan) it was cool. The valley was at about 4500 feet. Its sides were terraced with green rice paddies. Through the window he could see the snow on the mountains they would have to go through to cross into Afghanistan.

He had diarrhea as usual, his eyes hurt, and nobody would leave him alone.

"Sind chi wushka?" they asked him. Do you want river tea?

"Nuskam," he replied. Don't want. He went out and walked up to the cemetery, which was where everybody relieved himself, and had diarrhea.

THE FOREIGN LINGUISTS

The children understood his Pushtu the best, perhaps because they had not adopted one accent forever. It seemed that a man from one village might have trouble understanding a man from a village twenty miles away. The General's son Zahid once told the Young Man that his family missed one word in five of the Brigadier's speech. It must have been even more difficult to understand the Young Man, who had gotten his Pushtu only out of an old book.★ — The children were willing to make an effort with the Young Man because he was a novelty momentarily eclipsing their other recreations, which consisted (I am of course speaking of the male children, for I never saw the other kind doing anything but hard work) of spitting, gathering apricots, listening to the men talk beneath the trees, and punching each other. The men watched and laughed. The more impudent the boys were, the more the men liked it. The boys would gather around the circle of men at the

---

★ A manual for soldiers of the British Empire, with such helpful pattern sentences as "Silence!" or "Bring me at once five hundred coolies," or "You are now under Government rule." One of the most humiliating things that happened to me on this journey occurred when I was still on the plane, and I proudly told the man in the seat beside me that I had studied some Pushtu, and he said something that I could not understand, and I said, "What?" and he said, "I asked you how your Pushtu was."

end of the afternoon and begin spitting. They would spit closer
and closer to the men's feet. Finally they would just miss someone's feet, and the men would scold them sternly. The one who
had been scolded would be punched by the others. The men
deigned to chuckle.

The four Mujahids with the Young Man believed that if he
couldn't understand something they'd said, all they had to do was
yell it loud enough. When that didn't work, they were angry and
dismayed. One of them, Muhammad, could read. In Peshawar
the Young Man had bought an English-Pushto dictionary. When
they had something to communicate to him that he could not
understand, Muhammad scanned the pages until he found a very
rough equivalent for what he wanted to say (a procedure which,
since the words were arranged entirely according to their counterparts in the Young Man's alphabet, took Muhammad a long
time), and put his finger on it. The Young Man, who could not
read Pushto, would say the corresponding English word aloud,
as if Muhammad could somehow tell him whether this was the
one right word out of millions; and Muhammad always nodded.
— They thought he wasn't happy. After flipping through the
English-Pushto *kitab* for a quarter of an hour, Muhammad pointed
to a word at last. — "Tragic," the Young Man interpreted aloud.
— Muhammad smiled at him like a psychiatrist. *"Tuh* [you]
tragic," he said sympathetically. "Do you understand my speak,
Mr. William?" — *"Na,"* dissented the Young Man heartily.
"Kushkal, kushkal." — Happy, happy. Of course he would be
even more *kushkal* if they ever crossed the border, if they came
back alive, if his rehydration salts held out, which they
wouldn't—oh, he was an unhappy, even tragic Young Man, he
was! They had been here for days, waiting for Poor Man, the
guerrilla leader, to show up with the ammunition.*

One afternoon the Young Man wanted to go out and take pic-

---

* The General told me that ammunition was hard to get, and when it was in good supply,
the Peshawar-based organizations distributed it stingily, so as to keep the individual bands
from becoming too independent. So it was like everything else. If their parties helped them
too much they hurt themselves. So Commissioner Abdullah had thought, not wanting to
give vocational training to the refugees because that took work away from Pakistanis, so
he left them as beggars, as a burden. So our C.I.A. might have thought—why should
they be in a hurry for this embarrassment to the Soviets to come to an end? So the Young
Man undoubtedly thought; otherwise he would have given away all his money and let
them feed upon his flesh.

tures of the mountains. They told him he couldn't do that. Muhammad borrowed his English-Pushto *kitab* again and went off into a corner with a new arrival who knew a little English. Finally, beaming, they brought him back a note:

> *Not* — *the chawkar*
> *becose this pipol is jahil*
> *you is DAY Doyuo my*
> *spieke M.R.* — *Uuiliam* —
> *becose this pipaeli is not*
> *have ajoucatan* —
> *because this pipole is impolite*
> *he spieke cam say topak.*

In other words, said the Young Man to himself, interpreting the text like the student of comparative literature that he was, "Not the hills, because this people is ignorant. You is DIE. Do you understand my speak, Mr. William? Because this people is not have education; because this people is impolite; they say that your camera is a gun." — Well, it was certainly nothing to DIE over, so he stayed indoors. It was all getting on his nerves.

The two men of the house kept picking up their rifles every day, taking them outside into the town and returning half an hour later with expressions of deep contentment. The Young Man looked up the word for "hunt" and asked Muhammad if that was what they were doing. — Muhammad laughed, pointed at the Young Man, and said, *"Jahil."* — Ignorant. — Then he pointed at the malik and his gun. He perused the English-Pushto *kitab* and pointed to a word. — "Hostile," the Young Man read.

(Surely they didn't kill people for half an hour every afternoon? He never found out what they did. Maybe it was like one of those American Civil War parades.)

THE SECRET OF OUR SUPERIORITY

On the morning of the next day, ten Mujahideen came in, and the Young Man packed up quickly, but they only stretched out to sleep. That afternoon they pulled some refugee medicines from their baggage and asked the Young Man to explain the labels. The

Young Man did his best, and they noted down his words beside the English names. One of the Mujahideen took a capsule of oral tetracycline, opened it, and poured its yellow powder onto a blister, which he had first prepared for treatment by rubbing it with a matchhead. They went through all the medicines, opening tins and packets which should have been kept sealed until use, and doling them out — a handful of painkillers, antibiotics and B vitamins per man, all tossed together in a length of previously sterile bandage. They asked the Young Man if there was anything to make them strong. One of the doctors in the camps had told him, "Every Afghan believes American medicines will turn him into a superman." — The Young Man knew that they would hold it against him if he refused to disclose the secret. Reflecting on the diet of the traveling fighter—a piece of bread, a raw onion, a lump of hardened sugar and a cup of tea—he decided that it was ethical to point to the B vitamins, which he did. They were all happy. They asked him how many to take. Fancying himself a great social liberator, he said one a day for them, and two a day for the women and children. All the men immediately took two.

TRIUMPHAL RETURN

At *pindzuh*★ o'clock in the evening, there was big excitement. — "Poor Man, Poor Man!" they all said. The Young Man didn't see the guerrilla leader, but he was willing to accept the idea that smoke signals or something had been perceived. A moment later a new man rushed in and cried in English, *"No go Afghanistan!"*—smiling and spreading his hands. — The Young Man, at whom this was evidently directed, smiled back and said, "Okay." — What the hell.

The next day Muhammad stayed under his sleeping rug, only poking his head out every now and then like an aquatic mammal surveying the surface of things as it refills its lungs; then Muhammad dove back into his own unconscious.

Whenever the Young Man wrote in his notebook, men came up to him and looked over his shoulder. When they could, they sounded out the words to everyone else, who nodded approvingly.

★ Five.

The Mujahideen grew concerned about their guest's restlessness. In the early afternoons of those days, they would invite him to go up the river with them. Just out of sight of the village, near a shed they called "the schoolhouse" (it was always shut), was a pleasant slope of alpine meadow, studded with smooth warm boulders. On these rocks the Mujahideen would stretch out for hours, eyes closed in bliss. At first the Young Man accompanied them. But he got bored quickly. So he remained inside the malik's house; he preferred to be bored indoors.

One morning at around eleven a youngish fellow showed up and wanted to take the Young Man somewhere. The Mujahideen had gone out early. — "You from what party?" said the Young Man in his cautious Pushtu. — The other smiled, hesitated. "Gulbuddin," he said at last. — "Where you go?" said the Young Man. "What you want?" He knew that Gulbuddin and the N.L.F. were at loggerheads. — But the man just smiled and touched his sleeve. — "I stay here," the Young Man said. — The Gulbuddin man lay in the next *charpoy*, staring at him. He stared at him for half the day. — To hell with him. To hell with the Afghans. Stupid idea to come here. — When the Mujahideen came back, the Gulbuddin man got up and left.

A great anger was swelling inside the Young Man—the righteous fury of the spoiled child. He said to the Mujahideen, as he said this time every day, "I only want to help you; this is for *you*, not for me; I've been waiting a long time here; my time will soon be up, and then I won't be able to help you, to send you rupees. Mujahideen—*thoughtless, disorganized;* maybe they don't *want* me to help them!"★ — It had taken hours to learn to say all this (he had had to look up almost every word), but, after all, the Young Man had all the time in the world, and he had been practicing every day. — "Tomorrow," they soothed him. — "Tomorrow no good," he replied as usual, "every day you say 'tomorrow.' I must go to Afghanistan *today* or I won't be able to help you."

He'd *scored* this time, though; that he could see. The Mujahideen conferred. Finally Abdullah, the one who knew a little English, said: "Sit down, please." They all went off.

He waited until his dysentery called him. When he returned from the cemetery, Muhammad was packing the Young Man's

---

★ Probably they didn't.

things and telling him to hurry. Evidently, the Young Man reflected, this sort of continual quiet insistence had been what was
required all along. Maybe a positively dictatorial European manner, like that of any Great White Man, could even arrange him a
skirmish at the appropriate hour . . . Then the Young Man noticed
that they were heading back down the valley toward Parachinar.

"Peshawar?" he said.

"Peshawar."

They were sorry for him. They kept asking how he was and
picking apricots for him to eat. Muhammad carried his pack. When
they got to town they told him that the bus was "broken"; he'd
have to spend the night in the N.L.F. office; but, as for Peshawar,
"tomorrow!", they told him confidently. At the N.L.F. office they
left him.

He sat in the courtyard of the office, surrounded by heroic
posters and cartons of biscuits marked for Afghan refugees. The
green flag of Islam blew above his head. He was stunned and
despondent. An old man came up to him to display his prosthetic
arm. The Young Man interrupted, explaining why it was so desperately important for him to go to Afghanistan that day. The old
man replied that he was at the American's service, which meant,
no doubt, nothing. — It was very hot now that they were out of
the mountains, and the Young Man's intestinal parasites churned
nauseously. There was no bathroom in sight, and no word for it
in his English-Pushto *kitab*. He longed to go home.

POOR MAN

Then Poor Man strode in, smiling. — "You angry?" he said.
"Pindzuh minuta." Five minutes. — His men carried cases of bullets
and rocket-launcher shells into the storeroom. Then Poor Man
snapped his fingers for the American to get up, and everyone
climbed into the back of a covered van. All the other Mujahideen
were sitting there. They smiled at him. The van went up the dirt
road toward the mountains. It began to rain. Cool rain dripped
in through the canopy, refreshing everyone's face. The Young
Man was exhilarated. Around him sat the Mujahideen—twenty
of them now—laughing at each other, smoking, cleaning their
topaks. The van was full of the pleasant smell of gun oil.

At six that evening they reached the village again. The malik welcomed the Young Man back and embraced him. All the other men were sitting out in the middle of the village, watching the Mujahideen. They were cooking kebabs for the children who were too young to observe Ramazan. The Young Man's mouth watered. Suleiman, a Mujahid with whom he was especially friendly, offered to buy him one, but the Young Man smiled nobly and said, "You no eat, I no eat." (It sounded very funny in Pushtu.) — The children of the village surrounded him; he was a novelty again, having been gone for half the day. They wanted him to take pictures of them for the Afghanistan Picture Show. But he said no. He was only taking pictures of the jihad. He was afraid that his film would run out.

The malik invited the Young Man into his house, where, out of sight of the others, he was given a meal. It had not occurred to them that he wanted to be strong like them; how could they know? And if he refused the meal he would give offense. It was lukewarm tea and bread with a bite taken out of it. The malik explained proudly that the Young Man was receiving Poor Man's own leavings. They tasted good. — An hour later the Mujahideen broke fast together in a grand meal. Poor Man had the Young Man sit at his right side, and spoke to him in his minimal English, to honor him. They were to leave for Afghanistan at 3 a.m.

The Young Man lay awake all night, bitten by bedbugs, excited and terrified. He had been given a *charpoy*. Beside him, in the next bed, Poor Man coughed and coughed.

POOR MAN'S STATEMENT

"My name is ———— ———— ————. I come from Ningrahar. I am the son of ———— and the grandson of ————.* I command a group of Afghan Mujahideen. In a recent battle I succeeded in getting some small souvenirs, including the uniform of a Russian brigadier general, which I brought to Peshawar and had sent to Islamabad. This battle took place at a Russian base with a hospital and landing facilities. The fighting lasted for eighteen days, in which period I killed the Russian general and several other people."

---

* Why should I give the enemy anything?

"What tactics have you found to be most successful against the Russians?" the Young Man asked.

"Last year, when we were weaker from a military point of view, we used to perform night operations. Now we have Russian weapons, such as Kalashnikovs, and the battles can take place in the daytime. We can inflict heavy casualties now. We still cannot give them a pitched battle, especially in the daytime, but in our hilly terrain we can dig in with trenches and give them a good fight."

"Which Soviet tactics cause you the greatest problems?"

"There are four stages," Poor Man said. — He was sitting out with the General and the Young Man at the General's house in Peshawar, and a bird was hopping in the lime tree. — "First they come with gunship helicopters, and they know our locations; they bombard us. After that, the gunships having marked the place for them, come the MiG bombers. Third comes heavy artillery fire —mortars and rockets. And then the fourth is the Soviet infantry. We have to fight directly with them in this fourth stage, because the infantry comes up against us head-on. All of this is difficult."

"What arms and other aid would you most appreciate?"

"The first thing we want is anti-gunship weapons, to shoot down the helicopters, because they are the most damaging thing. And secondly, we want weapons that we can give to the people, so that we can raise troops."

"Are the Afghans getting tired of fighting now? Do they fight less strongly?"

"We have a high morale," Poor Man smiled. "We like to fight, and we will keep on fighting."

The red hill [5]

They walked for thirty-six hours. What the Young Man hated the most were the river crossings in the dark, when you could vaguely see the rocks and foaming water, but well enough to be gambling with each jump from stone to stone. The Muja-hideen did everything they could for him. They carried his pack,

held him by the hand, and let him lean his weight on them as they
made their way up and down the mountains. They even carried
him piggyback where the fordings were especially difficult. Even
so, the Young Man quickly became exhausted. One thing that
forced him to go on, however (the other was the impossibility of
returning alone), was a sense of shame, for his body was no less
well-made than theirs; and in appurtenances he was better
equipped, having his comfortable Italian hiking boots while *they*
wore sandals and slippers, and as they walked their feet were
sometimes bleeding on the rocks. Their limbs, like his, swelled
up and purpled with the altitude and the great exertion. Like him,
they licked their lips with thirst. They went up into the snow and
the fog of the mountain peaks, and across a terrifying green
meadow where it hailed continually—hailstones half as big as a
fist. Then they were in Afghanistan, and it was not safe to slacken
their steps, even, for fear that a helicopter would see them.* They
descended through the mists again, the trail down the cliffsides
being nothing but loose, wobbling rocks (for all the easy paths
had been mined by the Soviets). Then they slipped down kilometer
after kilometer of snow-covered, rotten summer glacier, the snow
sometimes covering huge pits where a boulder had broken through
to the water ten feet beneath. The Young Man was exhausted and
terrified. He stumbled along, leaning on their shoulders. — What
a burden he was! As I recall this, you cannot imagine a tenth of
the shame I still feel. — At one point he tripped in the unfamiliar
baggy trousers and ripped them halfway up the length of a leg.
They all chuckled. They sat him down; a Mujahid pulled out
needle and thread and sewed them up again. (If a plane had come
then, not a one could have survived.) They were unfailingly cheer-
ful, praying and singing and smiling as they went. No one lagged
or complained but the Young Man. Once he was so tired that
they carried him half a kilometer. Then his shame overcame his
exhaustion again, and he kept on. Early in the second morning,
when it was still dark, he thought he couldn't go on. Then one
of them finally lost patience and gave him a prod in the back,
yelling at him to go faster. Another one pinched him in the arm

---

* In April 1987 I read with great pleasure that Pakistan had shot down a plane of the
"Afghan" Air Force over this terrain, not far, said the paper, from Parachinar. The plane
had violated Pakistani airspace a day or two after two other bombings by "Afghan" planes
which had killed about a hundred people.

and hand. This made him angry. — "Don't treat me like that!" he said to the Mujahid who had shoved him. "I Ameriki, not Mujahid." The Young Man meant: I don't belong to you. He shook the Mujahid by the shoulder. The man snarled and shook him back, much harder, and dug his rifle butt into the Young Man's back. This was real; this made him keep going. His slowness was endangering their lives. Without him they could have made the journey in one long day.

When they came up to the top of a bluff, Poor Man told him to be careful where he stepped. The trail had many little bombs, he said.

A little after sunrise, as they came into the main war zone, they stopped for tea. They fed him unripe plums, which tasted delicious in his dry mouth, and lumps of *gura,* or hardened sugar. Gradually the way grew easier and shadier. As they walked they reached up and plucked fruits and nuts. At all times his friend Suleiman stood at his shoulder supporting him.

"You go slow-slow," Poor Man told him. "What takes us fifteen minutes takes you ten days, ten years."

The Young Man apologized.

"Ah, Ouilliam, Ouilliam!" they said indulgently, and carried his heaviest camera for him.★

RUINS

They took him past a deserted village and a bombed-out village. An old woman in black came hobbling through the ruins, shaking her fist at him, but he said, "Ameriki!" and then she smiled.

[NOTE: I saw on this journey a very ingenious procedure employed by the Mujahideen for dealing with the mines, but will not reveal it here for fear that it might possibly be of aid to those who have dropped them. These mines are quite diabolical. They are small and hard to see, especially

---

★ "Then we have the problem of the journalists going inside Afghanistan. Even if they can smuggle [themselves] out the Pakistan checkpoints, it is difficult for them to walk for several days and weeks in the mountain terrain of the country. Moreover, danger awaits them in every step they take. Very few exceptional journalists can work under such conditions. Most of those who go inside limit their trips to areas near the border and write superficial reports." —*Mirror of Jehad: The Voice of the Afghan Mujahideen* (Jamiat-i-Islami publication), January–February 1982

at night. They can blow an arm or leg off. When detonated, they leave behind a little twisted lump of green or blue plastic. It is said that some are made to resemble pens or toys, so that people will pick them up. I saw a little toy hashish pipe lying on a rock once. The commander I was with told me that it was a mine. I did not see it detonated, so I cannot confirm this (we went very carefully around it), but no detail of the Soviets' foreign policy in Afghanistan would surprise me.]

POOR MAN'S STATEMENT:
CHEMICAL WARFARE★

"The day we killed the Russian general, it was the next day. They are very reluctant to use this chemical warfare, or they don't do it with the winds, but that day, it was the next day the general was killed. They attacked us. They used this gas about thirty yards away from where we were. When the battle is on, these birds, on account of the sound, get frightened and they fly. We saw the pigeons being killed. They came down; we saw them coming down, so we thought probably the enemy has used this gas. They fired the rocket, and it hit the ground. It didn't make much noise. After thirty, forty seconds, a streak went up—a white streak. Up to forty feet it spread, on all sides. Then the wind took it from one side to the other, and whatever came in the way of that gas had got killed. All the animals. And we lost in the process only three. Three from my band, they got killed in the process. The gas passed over there, or near them, and they died.

"The [first] two died spontaneously. When we discovered them, to see if they were hit by the gas or otherwise, we took their clothes off to check to see if they were hit by a bullet. We saw no—nothing, no injury, nothing at all . . . The third one, who was slightly poisoned, he lived for a day or two; we did our best for him, with the medicine and so on, but nothing happened, and he also died."

★ This portion of Poor Man's statement was translated by a different person than the other, which explains the syntactical differences. For more information on the use of C.B.W. agents in Afghanistan, see the Haig Report cited in the Sources section at the end of this book.

WITTGENSTEIN'S STATEMENT

"If I see someone writhing in pain with evident cause I do not think: all the same, his feelings are hidden from me."*

THE NEW COUNTRY

So they came into Afghanistan with its chalky ridge-shoulders from which shade trees grew like miracles, leaf-crowned, fruit-crowned, with great dark root-knees for tired men to sit upon, but they scarcely ever sat, being anxious now to get home to war, so, steady in baggy pants, with bulging canvas sacks slung over their backs, they descended into steep green valleys whose terraces of fields were cool and wet; they followed the river down to the lower mountains. — His thoughts rolled down ahead of him like the men with guns winding down the trail between rockheaps and purple sand ridges and rust-red ground whose barrenness left the widespread grass clumps pale. Here and there you might see a shade bush, but the farther down into Afghanistan you went, the drier it seemed to become. What was he going to see? What would he find? But after a while he was too weary to ask anything.

Two pairs of hands

He made himself a refreshing drink of water and sour grape squeezings, only he had forgotten how bad the water tasted (it came from the muddy ditch) and how much worse it tasted in that corroded, dirty tin cup, to say nothing of the fact that the grapes actually weren't so good, either.

As they walked along the mountain trail, butterflies settled and rose in the sand, fanning their wings like helicopters. The guerrilla

---

* *Philosophical Investigations*, IIxi, p. 223e.

beside the Young Man took his hand, the palm of it, the soft flesh of it, between two fingers, pinching it and working it. — "Why . . . like this?" he said. "You not strong." — The Afghan's hand was dark and hard, like a new walking shoe that hadn't been broken in. — The Young Man was not ashamed. "I do different things in America," he said. "I read, write, push buttons. You dig, plow, shoot." — The guerrilla said nothing.

An Afghanistan Picture Show [3]

Seizing the charred stump of a rocket bomb, a Mujahid raised it high above his head and turned to face the Young Man, his eyes shining fiercely as if to say: This is why you came! Now look, look! Your business here is to see! See this, and understand it; never forget it! and the Young Man stood looking at the man's leathery reddish-brown face, the cheeks drawn up in effort as he held the bomb high, the parted lips, the even white teeth, the graying hairline just below the double-lipped prayer cap, the shadow of the bomb falling from shoulder to shoulder, those upraised arms in which the bomb casing lay khaki and black and orange-rusted, rusted through in places so that the Young Man could see the skeleton grid beneath the shell (it must have been a dud), and the bomb hung eternally in the air and the Mujahid's cotton shirt hung down and the river flowed clear and shallow behind him, leaving undisturbed the white rocks that lined it, and the hills were tan with dry grass, green-spotted here and there with a bush or a tree, and the other Mujahideen had also turned and were staring at the Young Man as the bomb stared at him and he stared back and said to himself: whether or not I can do anything useful, at least I will remember.

In so many frames of my Afghanistan Picture Show I see the men in wildly various caps grinning at their guns and cradling them, uplifting them among the tree-pocked mountains, loving them, pointing them, holding them like guitars, the bullets long and gold and heavy together in cartridge belts sweeping down shoulder and chest; each laughing at the sight the others made, each looking at his Kalashnikov or Lee-Enfield or Springfield with shy fondness because the weapon was a dream like a son was a dream;★ the weapon was a dream of revenge.

And I also see those Pakistanis and Afghans leaning forward into the tape recorder, talking and talking emphatically, some hoping, some desperate, some without expectations, just helping me to understand. — What a daunting thing RECOGNITION is.

The red hill [6]

It rained there every day at a little past twelve. The result was to raise more dust. It always stank of dust there, a metallic, choking, dirty taste in the throat like you might expect to get after

---

★ And here I see the slide of the boy who stood on a high green Afghan hillside, pointing at the sun the wooden toy gun that his father had carved for him (had he already crossed the river also, so young?), and his little sister's hair was falling out in patches from some disease but she wore a necklace of heavy squares of pure silver carved with signs, gladdened with jewels or colored glass beads (how would I ever know which?).

kissing someone who'd worked for twenty years in a tombstone company or a cement factory. Everybody coughed all the time. It was no wonder, the Young Man thought, that Pushtu speech has so many *t*'s and *s*'s and *kh*'s; if you are going to hack, why not make use of it? Maybe people with the same disease ought to get together to communicate with their spots.

Every time it rained the rooster crowed.

The men sat around in their baggy white shirts and trousers, spitting.

The Young Man hated the flies. There were always dozens of them on him, with at least two or three on his lips and eyes.

To console him, Poor Man went and got him some peaches. — "Go back to Peshawar," he said. "Tell them, send strong American."

"You want I go to Peshawar?" said the Young Man angrily.

"I want you see the fight. I want you go to city, see dead *Roos*. But you"—he pointed to the Young Man's legs—"no good."

Across the river gorge, a few clouds lay over a grubby reddish hill. There were trees on the hill; there was agricultural terracing; there were flies there, and a smell of dust, bomb debris and one tiny spring. There was a wide and easy path up the hill, but the guerrillas told him that an *alootooka*★ had flown over it and dropped butterfly mines there. So to climb the hill you had to ascend a steep slope of loose rock. On the summit of the hill were many trees, and empty Russian food tins. It was here that the war zone really began. Looking discreetly through the tree branches, you could see Afghanistan ahead, a desert dream of sand dunes and hazy dunes spread out far below, for this was the edge of the mountains. It was like a map that kept unrolling in the sun, with its bright baked canyons and oases and villages showing forth on the plains as if they had been painted there.

To the left of where the Young Man stood, the hill continued onto a ridge that made a right angle and ended in a spur, like an arm and fist extended from a man's shoulder. The ridge was bare. It was very dangerous to go out on it. It had been torn by rocket shells. It was explained to the Young Man that if you went out on it the *Roos* could see you.

Just on the horizon were six black dots in the middle of a village.

★ Airplane.

Suleiman guided the Young Man's eyes to them. — *"Roos,"* he
said. The Young Man peered through his telephoto at 600 mm.
— Sure enough. Six tanks. — He looked at them for a while.
Later he and Suleiman went down to the spring, and Suleiman
gathered for him little sour yellow peaches and the *tutan* fruits,
although it was still Ramazan and Suleiman could not eat. Suleiman smiled happily to see him eat. — *"Malgurae,"* the Young
Man said. — Friend. — *"Malgurae,"* Suleiman said, and gripped
his hand.

He had finally gotten to like the food. The morning after they
had arrived, Poor Man had made him breakfast with his own
hands: two eggs fried for a few seconds in very hot oil (so what
he had, then, was a glass bowl full of hot oil, with the eggs diffused
through it in curds of greater or lesser size) and a hunk of bread
to eat it with, salted cucumber slices and tea saturated with sugar.
It all tasted good. He was very hungry.

Every day a boy sneaked him dried apricots and *tutans* beneath

his armload of kitchen onions. The Young Man took himself off to eat them. In midafternoon the Commander in Blue, Poor Man's lieutenant, would fix him beef kebab and sweet green tea. An old man brought him a double handful of almonds. Later he found out that they were not almonds after all, but the nutlike kernel of the *zwardailoo*.★

"Much rain tomorrow?" he asked the Commander in Blue. Poor Man had gone into the *chakar* to meditate and pray.

"*Kum-kum,*" said the Commander in Blue. "*Leg-leg.* Fifty-fifty."

He went up to the top of the red hill again. The tanks were still there. From nowhere he felt a hand on his shoulder. A Mujahid smiled at him. There was always someone on watch here. — The Mujahid asked him to take his picture. When he obliged, the Mujahid was very happy and honored. It did not matter that he would never see the picture. He stood there with his Kalashnikov and smiled. Later he gathered a bunch of wild grapes for the Young Man. The Mujahid's lips were chapped with dry dusty thirst, for it was still Ramazan, but he insisted that the Young Man eat the grapes there. (If he ate them, he would not be as good as the Mujahideen were. If he did not eat them, friendship would be insulted.) They tasted so sweet, so refreshing; he ate them and was ashamed.

On the safe side of the hill, just below the crest, was a line of shallow pits. Against the tanks a semicircular wall of stones had been constructed in each pit. In the event of an attack, Poor Man told him, the men would get into these pits and begin to shoot. A single gunship helicopter could probably have killed everyone in the pits. But they were all the Mujahideen had.

PREPARATIONS

One morning the air of laziness disappeared from the camp. All morning the men cleaned their weapons and loaded them, soberly, but in good spirits.† There was no wasteful shooting off of cartridges.

★ Small sweet apricot.
† This may sound like propaganda. It is not. Never have I seen people so serene, yet so full of a great considered purpose.

Down by the Young Man's *charpoy*, Poor Man and the Commander in Blue sat on a mat in a circle with some new arrivals who had brought cases of bombs. With them also was a commander with whom the Young Man had eaten dinner in the treehouse the previous night. He wore flashy rings and bird ornaments; his face was made up. He carried with him little balls of colored sugar, in a hashish box. He gave the Young Man a handful of them. When he posed for a picture, the Commander in Blue made him put his ornaments aside, which made him crestfallen. Later, when the Commander in Blue was gone, the Flashy Commander winked at the Young Man and posed for another picture.

Poor Man was talking slowly, fiddling with a rocket launcher. The Commander in Blue, who had just thumbprinted some new recruits, was studying a letter which one of them had given him. Poor Man seemed abstracted. His round face looked up smiling sometimes, but then his eyes flickered down again to the rifle he was cleaning, or to the message that he'd already read. He was a pudgy man, graying a little, who, unlike the grandly gesturing Mujahideen commanders whom the Young Man had met at the General's, did not seem impressive. Poor Man had been sick to his stomach during the journey from Pakistan. Every hour or two he stopped to vomit, but that had never kept him from returning to the head of his line of men (who never waited for him), leading them at a steady, rapid walk, with his arms serenely folded across his chest. Within a few minutes he would be so far ahead as to be out of sight, and they caught up with him only when he paused impatiently for them, or when he was sick again. He said very little. His men honored him. They carried a bottle of rose-petal Sharbet syrup which only he could drink. In the high passes, he poured a little of the syrup into a snowball and ate it, smiling. Sometimes in the morning Poor Man looked very pale, and then the Mujahids massaged his back. But when it came time to go, he was never anywhere but in front. — The sunshine was white and brown as Poor Man and the Commander in Blue sat in state, and Poor Man flexed his toes, turning a cartridge slowly round and round in his hand, and the cursive on the green N.L.F. banner above his head was like swords, crowns, wriggling snakes, crossed ribbons, and the Commander in Blue sat dreamily in the half-darkness of the doorway, and the books shone snowy white in the sun.

Elias, the malik of the village nearby, came up the trail to the camp, leaning on his staff. He took his cap off, brushed away the flies from his baldness, put his cap on again, picked up his staff, and put it down . . . He sat on the mat with the others. He leaned forward and spoke. Now several men were speaking excitedly at once. Old Elias shook his head. — "Qur'ān," he said. — Poor Man's eyes flicked back and forth slowly.

Poor Man signed a book slowly, carefully, as yesterday he had done with the new party membership cards. A young boy leaned on a gun sternly, then rose as Poor Man reached to take his hand, put his hand on the stamp pad, and entered his fingerprint in the register book. The boy looked proud. Every man smiled at him; every man was like the man in the white skullcap whose cheeks were wrinkled into long laugh lines as he stood cleaning his rifle, the stock braced against his belly with one hand, oil can in the other, and the stained awning covered the others who sat talking quietly on their mats and Poor Man sat against the wall, watching with eyes that gave and took.

Poor Man seemed more relaxed now. The talk was slow—and then abruptly he ordered away the Mujahids sitting by the Young Man's side on the *charpoy*.

The Flashy Commander stretched, got up, and put his sandals on. He winked at the Young Man and chewed a ball of sugar.

Poor Man said something about guns, and everyone laughed. He and Malik Elias gripped a Kalashnikov from opposite ends, inspecting it, and then he entered a note in his book. Someone handed him another gun. He looked it up and down very slowly, and then fingerprinted the next recruit.

It was half past seven in the morning now. The flies were coming out strongly. The battle was set for nine.

Poor Man took a cartridge and straightened it with a pair of pliers. — Was that safe? the Young Man wondered. He knew nothing about guns. It reminded him of the way the Mujahideen used hair tonic as lip balm, because it smelled like peaches and was thick and yellow. They wouldn't believe him when he translated the label for them.

Poor Man checked over and rendered fit each of their weapons, attaching straps, loading bullets, with the same peaceful, unhurried spirit as when the Commander in Blue cooked kebabs and wetted down the mud floors every morning. — Sighing, Poor Man inserted a fuse in a grenade.

Elias borrowed the key from Poor Man. He went to the storeroom and brought a sack of dried *tutans*. (So preserved, these fruits taste like very sweet raisins gone slightly bad. Fresh on the tree they resemble white, pink or black raspberries without seeds; then they taste like sweet grapes gone slightly bad.) Poor Man ran a few of them through his fingers and made a note in the book.

The toy airplane

The council of war went on. Near the Young Man's bed, suspended by two ropes so that it hung over the steep riverbank, a little wooden airplane twirled in the faint morning breeze. Beside it, three pairs of soldiers' trousers swayed like hanged men.

Because the Young Man had never seen a battle, the associations he tended to make were with boyhood's summer games. The Commander in Blue, for instance, slept in a tree fort, complete with real machine guns and a plate full of peaches that he could snack on at midnight, if he chose, spitting the seeds into the river below. To the right of the Young Man's *charpoy*, a twin-log bridge led to a watch post in another tree. Down the riverbank and over the next rise was a real enemy somewhere in the dreamy distances of desert—namely, a division or two (what exactly was a division?) of the Soviet Army—but that had nothing to do with him. The exploded bombs and the downed helicopter that he'd been walked past were also toys, like the wooden *alootooka*. Seeing Poor Man counting shells brought him a sensation of thrilling delight. Once again, I do not think the Young Man can be blamed for this.

The plane was really an ironic touch. He wondered which of the guerrillas had made it. In his imagination it had overflown a thousand English children's gardens, the pilot bailing out every now and then as a flung stone or a division of scarecrows necessitated. Then, wandering for hours behind the enemy lines, ducking spiders' webs and hungry moles in the shadows of the cornstalks, he was finally rescued by a little girl, who found him wedged in a tree root by a stream.

"Poor soldier," she said. "Poor dear soldier. You've tried so hard, haven't you, and it's all come to nothing."

And she rocked him in her arms, but he could not cry, being made of wood.

He knew that eventually he'd rot or burn or get lost among her worn-out stuffed animals (those other refugees from the Land of Counterpane, lovestained and tearstained, gaping at the world through scratched glass eyes); or the girl would grow up, nervous at first because the training wheels were off the bicycle, but the day she stopped being afraid of falling was the day she'd be too big to listen to the reading of *Just So Stories,* and that was when she'd get tired of him, because he could never be anything new. So he had the certainty of a negative future. He decided, therefore, to make the best of the present. Maybe she'd buy him clothes, or a toy gun . . .

But as the days went like clock-hands crossing, he began to miss the wooden airplane. The view at the window seemed the same, even though the leaves turned red and yellow and then curled and dropped off, and the children came back from school with their books in their arms, going around the corner until they were lost in gold leaf-shimmers; and while it was very nice to sit by the fireplace, the heat soon began to dry him out and warp him. Yes, her bed was lovely, but sometimes he'd get thrust under one of the pillows where he could scarcely breathe; or she'd jog him carelessly with her elbow. Even wood can feel, although his thoughts were empty like bombed-out villages with crossbeams of shadow resembling gallowses, rubble and emptiness inside the roofless rooms whose cracked walls were still strangely straight-topped; and through doors and window frames he could see the mountains to which the survivors must have fled. — One day he said that he had to be going. (At least he would have said that if his mouth was anything more than painted on.) He went out into the rain and found his downed craft in a stubbly field. With leaf and rubber band he made emergency repairs; then he took off again on his mission, which was to get from Point A to Point B. He skimmed his way through the backyard airspace of white houses, glimpsing sometimes the children at piano practice, or the families out together in their colorful automobiles . . .

Now, which do you think would be a sadder fate—to be rescued time and time again by the same person, and find that the accu-

mulating separations were making her simultaneously more distant and more stale, or to travel forever through an afternoon
above the many gardens, being rescued by different girls (that is
every Young Man's dream), for him the familiarity of an unfamiliar elbow in bed, the knowledge that the afternoon would go
on and on like this until he broke? — At least in the latter case
he'd be going Somewhere; whereas to be rescued by his first love
again and again he'd have to fly in circles around her house, its
field and brook. (Not that this is objectionable in principle: a kite
is not unhappy for being attached to a string.)

The airplane beside the Young Man's *charpoy* had no pilot.
Something must have happened to him. Either he'd gotten killed
or he'd gotten permanently rescued. Of course, everyone gets
permanently rescued eventually (when one gets killed). But isn't
it better to get an early start on death, so as to at least *taste* per-
manence on one's own terms?

The airplane still twirls and twirls there above the guerrilla
camp, every afternoon, but for its pilot there must have finally
come an hour when the lights came on, and the children were
getting ready for bed, and there was time for only one more
emergency landing.

HELPLESSNESS [8]

The day passed. The battle was postponed. A skirmish with some
Gulbuddin men had occurred, Poor Man said; someone had been
injured. The Commander in Blue prepared for the Young Man a
marvelous dish of tomatoes, cucumbers, onions and peppers, all
sliced thin and covered with salt.

Shadows began to stain the red hill across the valley. The Young
Man's own afternoon was ending. Flying finally on his night mission through the clouds of sleep, he sat among the red lights of
the cockpit, bomb-bay switches in hand to deal with any nightmare, but as he flew on and on, he understood that anyone who
might have been able to rescue him, should he need it, was long
since in bed; that the fields and gardens had grown in the dark,
widening and drying and crinkling into vast mountains, the entire
Hindu Kush; and sand and snow and icy, filthy streams all around
him, no moon in sight, and the *Roos* picking up the tenor of his

night thoughts on their electronic gear—and he realized that he had succeeded in his objective of several years, which was to get himself in deep trouble.

He imagined being caught with the Mujahideen in some sandy gulley by a patrol of the *Roos*. They must surrender; they were disarmed. Then, one by one, the prisoners ahead of him were machine-gunned. Did he say, "Ameriki!"—at first softly, out of shame, then in a shout, so that everyone heard, and the Mujahideen, the doomed ones, turned their backs on him contemptuously, the guards understanding him at last, pulling him away, offering him water before his first beating, priming him for his television appearance as a spy, as meanwhile the Mujahideen, muttering earnestly, "Allah, Allah," were shot behind him? — Or did he loudly insist, "Yah—Afghan!" as the guards led him up for execution, and as he hid his glasses to hide his foreignness, the fanatic Gholam Sayed, who had not permitted the Young Man to give Suleiman medicine when he was sick,* because it was Ramazan, cried to the guards, "Mr. Ouilliam—Kaffir, *na* Muslim!"† so that he would not even have the satisfaction of that stand? Which, oh which would have been worse?

HELPLESSNESS [9]

The Commander in Blue invited him to accompany them on the raid. He lay in his *charpoy*, trying to ignore the flies, waiting for the sun to come up, the ordeal to begin. At 4:30 a.m. he had tea and eggs in the treehouse while the Commander in Blue stared into the foliage. At 6:45, old Elias came to him. — *"Alootooka— chakar!"* he cried. — Right, he thought skeptically, but the old man kept grabbing his arm and yelling, so he put on his shoes, took a camera, and ascended the red hill. As always, there was nothing but a group of Mujahideen practicing with their guns. They were astonishingly good marksmen. Maybe he had been too slow to see the plane.

---

* The Qur'ān in fact states that sick people, travelers and warriors on jihad may break their fast and make it up later. Suleiman, therefore, would have been triply justified in taking the medicine.

† Mr. William is an unbeliever, not a Muslim.

HELPLESSNESS [10]

They were to leave for the battle at ten. At twenty of eleven the whole camp was asleep. The Commander in Blue, that source of kebabs and consolation, lay wrapped in a cloth in his loft. No tours for the Young Man today, no viewing of the anti-aircraft gun, no U.N.I.C.E.F. tablets of condensed milk with sugar glaze to cheer him, no Poor Man for him to pester. At least some new guests were here, travelers carrying grenades to Herat, who distracted most of his flies. The sky was cloudless. In an hour and a half it would be time for the pathetic dusty rain.

THE RED HILL [7]

The hill was not that red, actually, but more of an ocher color. It was a series of nondescript curves with local exceptions, such as the Russian and Bulgarian food tins, the spring, the stone walls, the shooting pits, the dead bombs. On the whole, the hill still interested him because he was careful not to look at it too much. He had a feeling that if he ever became bored with it, that is, really bored with it, there would be difficulties for him. Every day, Suleiman and Elias sat up there behind the dusty trees, watching for the *Roos* with their binoculars, and their Kalashnikovs gleamed in the sunshine, every curving groove of the banana magazines outlined in precious silver, and the wooden stocks gleamed and glowed, and the sun was white on the two men's caps and noses and foreheads, and it seemed that the world ended just behind them because they sat at the very tip of the ridge, beyond which the mountains fell into a distant sun-dusted wrinkle of bluish-gray dunes far below like waves of infinity; in this sea the *Roos* trolled. And so Suleiman and Elias trolled for the *Roos*.

He lay in bed dodging the flies, whose angry whining voices reminded him to kill them. The songbirds emitted sounds lethargically from their wicker cages. Gholam Sayed sat reading his Qur'ān in a semiliterate stammer. From the far side of the red hill came a gunshot—certainly another Mujahid practicing late. A breeze began to blow through the sour grapes, and the wooden airplane stirred. Soon it would be afternoon.

The man in the bed beside him stirred, pulled a canvas shirt away from his face, scratched his mustache and went back to sleep.

He thought about getting up quietly to ascend the red hill one last time, and continuing down into the desert where the cities were, and the tanks. What were the *Roos* doing right now? What would it be like when he met them? — Then again, suppose they came to meet him; suppose that right now something shiny were to poke itself over the crest of the red hill: a gun barrel, a turret, a tank with a big red star on it . . . ?

"Mister," said Poor Man, striding over to him, "Russian soldiers coming this way. Five hundred tanks. Tomorrow we fight."

"Oh," the Young Man said.

"You ready? Your legs good now?"

"Very good."

"We go early."

The Young Man lay back in his *charpoy*. All around him, the men slept the afternoon away. He could not sleep. When the breeze picked up, he climbed aboard the wooden *alootooka* and soared over the red hill. He flew for a long time. Finally an interceptor beam got him, and the plane fell into splinters. They picked him up a few yards from the wreckage, ushered him into a black jeep, and brought him into the presence of the Commander in Red, who was the Commander in Blue's counterpart, and had sworn to destroy him. Within a twinkle of a Slavic eye, he'd poured the Young Man a shot of vodka, or whatever the Russians drank in Afghanistan. (The General had said that many of the *Roos* were addicted to hashish.) Then it was time to talk business.

"Now, where exactly is this rebel base you came from?" the Commander in Red would say.

"If I tell you, you'll destroy it."

The Commander in Red shrugged. "Destroy it, pacify it, save it from feudalism," he said, "make it safe, let us say, for us to visit."

"And if I don't tell you?"

"We're both clever—no need to even answer that."

"Well, you see," the Young Man explained, "I have good friends there."

"Friends? What did they ever do for you that we can't? Why, I bet they made you *walk* all the way there!"

Now this was in fact a sensitive point with the Young Man,

for the Brigadier had promised him that he would be given a horse, and when he told that to Poor Man, gasping his way up the mountain, Poor Man gave him a piece of snow to slake his thirst, and then called the Brigadier a son of a dog. "He lies!" Poor Man continued; "he told me nothing! He is nothing; he is no leader; he is C.I.A.; he is K.G.B.!" So evidently it was all the Brigadier's fault. Or his own. Or someone else's. When he got more tired still and asked the Mujahideen how far it was, they said, "*Tsalor* kilometer!" and when he walked four kilometers and asked them how far it was, they said, "*Pindzuh* kilometer!" and when he walked those five more kilometers and asked them how far it was, they said two, then six, then one, then another, then seven . . . — Nonetheless, the Young Man was no Benedict Brezhnev. He hoped that he wasn't, anyhow.

During the evening meal, which he ate with the Commander in Blue, the red hill turned slowly orange, like a photo of the surface of Mars.

No, it was really impossible to imagine what it was like in Afghanistan.

The red hill [8]

Then they were going into battle, over the red hill. But it turned out that there was actually not one red hill, but a whole series of them, and they went over them for hours without seeing a *Roos*. Once they had to be very quiet, and tiptoe along the base of a dour red bluff, in a place where the river echoed. There were supposed to be enemy tanks on the other side. But they never heard a sound, except for a faint hum, which was either the Young Man's imagination or the change in altitude. Going over red hill and red hill with the guerrillas, he looked up at the sky, but never saw a helicopter or even a cloud. Maybe they weren't in Afghanistan after all. Maybe the *Roos* had long since died of some disease, like Wells's Martians, and the Mujahideen were having a great time swaggering around their wasteland and firing Chinese candles at each other.

Then he saw his first *alootooka*.

They walked along down the river. After a while, they saw pomegranates and ripe red figs all around, and grapes so good that the village dogs stood up on their hind legs to eat them. Near the town of ———, where the Soviet garrison was, they stopped under the trees, unrolled their mats, and prayed beside their machine guns, each in his time. They kept asking the Young Man how he was. Elias and Suleiman embraced him. Poor Man looked for a long time through binoculars at an ancient clay fort in which nothing moved. They all sat there behind the trees, waiting for the hot daylight to go away. — *"Roos,"* whispered Suleiman, pointing over the ridge. Elias was praying again on his blanket, his head touching the stock of his Kalashnikov, and the grenade launcher also prayed like a mantis, a single grenade pointing upwards toward the sky, and the other fighters sat patiently. — Now at last the country began to darken, and the men to tense themselves for what was about to come. They prayed again. Poor Man led them into the village, stepping only on the boundary stones of the fields so as not to damage the crop. The village dreamed under wide fig trees. The houses were made of clay. The Mujahideen bowed to the village malik, and he brought them fermented milk and beans cooked in oil. Then they sat there waiting. Presently it was completely dark, and through the sky passed a silent, eerie swarm of winking lights. Planes. They waited. In front of them rose a red hill (now a gentle black solidity in the moonlight). They walked along the edges of the rice fields, trying not to damage the crops. Crickets chirred around them.

POOR MAN'S STATEMENT (continued)

"Why are you fighting?"

"I am not fighting for myself; I am not fighting for Afghanistan; I am fighting only for the God."

THE RED HILL [9]

Ahead of them, at the summit of the red hill, there was a flash. Poor Man had begun to fire. The boy who carried the rocket launcher ran up to Poor Man, smiling happily. A Soviet shell exploded loudly somewhere near them. The Young Man felt cold. He looked around him. All his companions were happy. Another shell landed, flinging stones. While the boy prepared the rocket launcher, the other Mujahideen began to fire. They shot beyond themselves like the snap of the slide projector in darkness as he advanced the carousel, letting image after image tumble down into the abyss of light (more than ten seconds' exposure is said to put the transparency at risk of fading, and now it has been eleven years!), and the Mujahideen fired in this long moment that was the reason that I came; I don't want or need to say much more about it; they were fighting and I was not; they were accomplishing the purpose of their lives in those endless night moments of happiness near death, no fear in them as I honestly believe; they had crossed their river so long ago that I could not really comprehend them as anything except heroes shining like Erica on the far side of the water; they were over the red hill and nothing else mattered.

STATEMENT OF JAMIAT-I-ISLAMI MUJAHIDEEN COMMANDER

"What weapons do you most need?"

"Anti-aircraft guns. And if we get anti-air missiles, you will see what a lesson we can give the Soviet invaders!"

"How is the food situation in your part of Afghanistan?"

"Very bad."

"What will you do if you cannot get what you need?"

"Why, perhaps we will kill ourselves, but we will certainly never surrender."

13

ON THE TRAIN

(1982)

Hail Red Army in Afghanistan! Down with
Islamic reaction! No to the veil! Extend gains of
October Revolution to the Afghan peoples!

SPARTACIST CAMPAIGN
LEAFLET, U.S.A.

On the train

$\mathbf{A}$t the end of his voyage he took the Khyber Mail back to Karachi—second class this time, for financial reasons (cost: about Rs. 103). It brought back to mind his nightmares of the Karachi railway station, City and Cantt: — the wild-eyed woman holding out a hand and bringing it slowly to her mouth, then stretching it out again, saying, "Give me only for food—only for food!"; the soft, persistent "Hello, mister? Hello? Hey, mister!" gradually increasing in volume as the Young Man walked past until it became a desperate shout, the faces of the red-uniformed coolies contorting with rage when he clung to his pack, and always people staring, staring at him, moving in like flies if he so much as slackened his step, old men bellowing offers of hotels and rides and hashish, filthy kids standing there with waiting palms, and all of them crying out to him to help them, until for frustration he could have killed them.

The Khyber Mail, anyhow, was packed even worse than usual, it being the Eid holiday at the close of Ramazan. Second class was just wooden benches. Men slept braced between seat tops and the luggage rack, the rest of their bodies entirely in space; or piled on the floor, pushing at each other in their sleep. To go to the latrine you had to step on heads or fingers. (There was no toilet paper; the doorknob was slippery with shit.) If you were lucky enough to be sitting on a bench, two or three heads were heavy against your ankles like cannonballs; someone else casually slung his legs up on your shoulders; a third had his head on your thigh—and stretched full-length on the bench was another sleeper, anyhow, so that everyone else on it, including you, had to sit an inch from the edge. When the Young Man couldn't stand it anymore he got down on the floor with the others. A man pressed up against him fiercely in sleep, pushing him at a slant against the faces of other sleepers. He slept for half an hour. Then finally when he couldn't stand it anymore there, either, he sat up on the floor. Above him, in the little space where he had been sitting, was a stack of feet originating from all directions—five or six pairs of feet, each on top of the others.

An acquaintance invited him into an upper berth. He accepted with alacrity, for there were little army-green fans up there, on the ceiling. He discovered immediately, however, that they did nothing. When he put his hand right against the grille he could barely feel any disturbance in the air.

"Are you married?" his companion asked shyly.

"Soon," he said.

This evidently excited the fellow, for the Young Man felt his hand poking slyly in his ribs. It was 3:00 a.m. He reached out to push the hand away and found it to be the foot of another aerial slumberer.

The instant he had gotten on the train (the General's son Zahid had driven him to the station and found his coach for him), sweat began to run down his face, as with everyone else's, so humid with bodies it was in there. During the two nights of the journey it only got worse. Every time the train stopped, the fans stopped and the lights faded to red-eyed bulbs. It was an express train, so, unlike the Yugoslavian trains of that appellation, it didn't stop at every single station—it stopped at every station but two. He got desperately thirsty. Few pleasures of beauty or love, or any other, are as wonderful as the satisfaction of thirst; few needs are more tormenting. At those midnight stops, sometimes he'd see (in the larger towns of the Punjab) a man presiding like a bartender over Fanta and Coca-Cola, the bottles not even cold the way they were in the daytime when musclebound old men with sad faces walked up and down the trains, carrying buckets filled with drinks in ice and crying: — *"Bottali! Bottali! Soda! Yaukh!"** (*"bottali"* sounding to him like beetles or insects)—no, now there was just the filthy, hazy, soggy night as they trundled on and on through the farmland province, and the man seated behind the counter with his bottles would refuse to come to the train window—and there was no predicting how long they might stay at any one station—fifteen minutes? half a minute?—so climbing out the window was very risky and he never did it.

On his trip back to the base from the raid, the Young Man

---

* "Bottles! Bottles! Soda! Cold!"

traveled with four friends who had given up their jihad for his sake. (In every respect, it seemed, he was a burden.) The way was very steep for the last two hours; it was *der möskel,* very difficult. When he began to fall behind, he told them to go on; presently he was all alone, and walking among unfamiliar hills. He thought: oh, God, I'm lost in Afghanistan, and with no water. But he kept on walking; and after a while he recognized a landmark, a view he'd stared at through his telephoto for days as he looked toward the tanks, so he kept going until the angle of vision was right, and he saw the beginning of the forested mountains and knew that he had made it. — *China, china,* he kept saying to himself, licking his lips: — spring, spring.

Suddenly he saw two of his companions a hundred feet below him. It was almost sunset. — *"Asalamu alaykum,"* he said. They had been wandering all over the hills looking for him. — "Ouilliam, Ouilliam," they sighed tolerantly. — He expressed his apologies. — One of his friends helped him down the last hill with his strong hand. The Young Man was in an agony of thirst. He kissed the Mujahid's hand with his bloody lips. At the *china* he drank a quart of *obuh,* then settled back for serious and attentive consumption. As he walked the last hundred yards to the spring, he had kept thinking: I'm so happy, I'm so happy, I'm so happy.

Now on the train he was not as thirsty as that, but still he was thirsty, and it was hard to think of anything else in the world. They stopped at a little station, and a banana seller came by. The Young Man hissed, the way the Pakistanis did.

"Hello," the banana seller said in English.

Bananas were safe; you could peel them. And they would be moist inside. There was a great cracking lump in his throat.

"Bananas," he croaked, not knowing the Punjabi word.

The vendor went back to his cart and pushed it away, walking down the tracks to the next car. The Young Man hissed and hissed, without any luck. Finally the train began to move slowly away from the station, and he passed the man again. He held out a five-rupee note pathetically. The banana seller stared at him, said something, and thrust a giant bunch of bananas into his hand—it must have been forty or so. The train went on. Evidently most people used a one-rupee note for that transaction.

A few of his compartment mates had woken up, and they

laughed at him and his many bananas good-humoredly. "Okay," they said to him delightedly. "Okay."

The bananas were juicy and sweet. He ate about twenty of them right away to satisfy his thirst, and gave most of the remainder away over the hours.

One man had a flute. He played sitting on a seat top. The flute was gorgeously carved and painted with rings of color.

"You like?" the flute player said when he found that the Young Man could speak a little Pushtu.

"Very much. Very good. How long you play?"

"Ten years. For you. Gift. Take to Am-rika."

"But I cannot use. No understand flute."

They tried to show him how to play. For half an hour they tried. He couldn't blow a note. They laughed and laughed; it was a game. He laughed, too. After a while another man tried to learn. He couldn't do it, either. They all laughed.

They bought him sodas all day, and dinner (*dordai* with onion, a few tomato slices and, for the main dish, lumps of corn flour fried in curry oil). When he thanked them, they looked a little hurt, and said, "But it's our duty!"

On hospitality:

---

1. If you extend it to everyone, does it mean less because you don't care about the particular person involved, or more because you genuinely care about everyone?

2. If you exclude Russians, Kaffirs, etcetera, does that make hospitality mean more or less? (Sartre says two people make a community by excluding a third.)

You cannot love as thoroughly as you ought to, and you cannot love those who aim to destroy you, but you can love (maybe, the Young Man qualified, gulping). Click to next picture: His first night at the Hotel Excelsior, which they called the Hotel Exercise; across the street there were people sleeping at the State Hotel on tables outside; and what I find most astonishing about that is that he was astonished, because at that time there weren't so many people in his country who had to sleep that way; if I went to Pakistan now and saw them I probably wouldn't even notice.

On the Afghans:

> They have their faults, but so do we. Let us give them what we can.
> And let's accept whatever they can give us.

That's really what he wrote and thought; it seems so sweet to me now, like something that a child might have written. He had the feeling of being rich, his notebook and cassettes now filled weightlessly with information susceptible to understanding. He would comb it like a head of hair, having whipped out his long- and fine-toothed analyses. Now that the Soviets have left (whether or not they come back), it is funny to see how much of it has turned to ashes.

On the Pakistanis:

> **The same.**

It was an overcast day when the Young Man disembarked at Karachi Cantt. Everyone invited him to stay. He went instead to a youth hostel, drinking Sprite after Sprite until his Pakistani money was gone. Then he lay listening to the call to evening prayers.

. . . *"wie fromme viktorianische Kriegsgeschrei . . ."* said the *Süddeutscher Zeitung* as they flew out of German airspace, the Young Man rolling back home like the proverbial foul ball to the fallow field. — "Sorry about the turbulence," the captain said. — The Young Man didn't mind it. It kept him awake. But his eyes flicked down to his belly, where he felt the familiar cramps begin—was it that grape-leaf stuff from the Turkish caterer, or simple intestinal incredulity at preservatives, meat 'n' cheese? A glut of food for whatever reason on airplanes, and never enough to drink—half the volume in the glass is ice cubes, and after ten 7-Ups a day in Pakistan he needed it, oh how he needed it—even the air conditioning seemed fake, and his body could not stop preparing itself for the shock that must come when it ended, as when he stepped out of Levi's car, or the Habib Bank, or the American Center, into the reality of dear old p-p-Peshawar—and every time a hair moved on his head he raised his hand, expecting to dislodge a cloud of flies, for the moment too ill and exhausted to plan out the action-steps of his Help to the Afghans stage by stage;* closing his eyes, he did not see the narrow café in Peshawar with its counter topped with long-necked bottles of Mango Squash and rose-flavored syrup, the racks of Sprites and Fantas in the cooler with its magnificently transparent double doors (although it was not cool inside), where the customers sat, dark-mustached, with wide giving eyes, and someone always bought the Young Man a soda when he came in; and it took him years to think the thought: What if I had bought everybody there a soda?—since after all that's all I could have done for them—but he had selfishly hoarded in order to be selfless, as for instance in Afghanistan when the Mujahideen were sitting under a tree with him and they wanted to play an Indian rock-and-roll cassette on his tape player but he said no because he had to save the batteries for interviews; after all, interviewing them was the only way to begin helping them (to his credit, he did at least feel bad about it—he honestly was not stingy even though he acted that way; he was convinced of himself just as Pakistanis and Afghans were each convinced that the other was dirtier); and the plane descended toward this—ISLE, this— WHIMSY, this—POMP AND CIRCUMSTANCE where all topics are mediated through sports and weather and people read books like *All Quiet in the Garden* and (look at the lovely unveiled face of that girl across the aisle!) now here they all were in this—ENGLAND . . . He had lost thirty pounds. He had taken about twelve hundred slides, most of which were worthless. Soon he would be organizing his Afghan relief presentations, to which hardly anyone would come; he would scrupulously send his pure-got contributions to Pakistan, in doses so small that they ought to have been homeopathic, instead of simply useless. — Oh, he was determined to be of use, all right. Two years after his return, he began learning to shoot a gun . . .

---

* "Bill," wrote the General six months later, "get well soon. If the American Doctors can't take care of you—come back to Pakistan, we shall look after you. The weather is nice and chilly. Please accept Xmas and New Year's greetings from all of us. May the New Year bring happiness and prosperity. Are you still reading the holy Qur'ān?"

Why I failed: A letter from the General (1984)

MEMBER
SENATE OF PAKISTAN

My dear Bill,

Thanks for your nice letter. There is an old saying — Health is wealth. You ought to take good care of your health. Three things are needed for every Project:

    a. brain
    b. hands — Physical fitness to do things
    c. money.

You have the brain — but you are not physically fit and you have no money — hence forget about the AFGHANS — for the time being. My advice to you is to get down to serious profession — any of your own choice . . . . and take good care of your health . . . .

"ROOS" is at our doorstep . . . . We will keep her at a distance ourselves, if we live as Muslims . . . . . The other day a young Afghan orphan boy came to see me. He had a bullet injury in his head. A C.R.C.* doctor removed it but he has gone blind now . . . . . Surely they could arrange Eye transplant etc. . . . . . "T.B." is on the increase — sitting in America you can't appreciate the problems of the Refugees in Pakistan and the problems inside Afghanistan.

More in my next.

                    With best wishes,
                    Yours sincerely,

---

* Committee of the Red Cross.

THE END

14
POSTSCRIPT

A letter from the general (1987)

Bill – your First Book is a "hit" – now get down to serious business of writing. I read the book reviews at least ten times and side-lined/under-lined the remarks – try to eradicate your failings in printed ink.

Your book on Afghanistan must reflect the following:

a. Afghanistan – its importance to the Free World & USA, if any, prior to the Russian invasion.

b. Why Russia invaded Afghanistan. Has Russia achieved its aim?

c. How the Afghans kept the Russians – a superpower – at bay! with outmoded weapons.

d. Will the Russians quit Afghanistan – for good.

e. Spell out the Russian and the USA interest in clear terms, in this Region – before invasion, during invasion and after the Russian pull-out.

f. The role played by Pakistan – its physical and economical contribution – Afghanistan's impact on Pakistan's economy.

g. Has the Free World adequately compensated Pakistan and the victims of Russian aggression by air and blasts?

h. A friend in need is a friend indeed. Has Pakistan lived up to this role?

I ask the reader: What would your list of important issues be? Have I addressed them? How can *you* help?

The Soviet view (San Francisco, 1987)

Because I am a believer in the Fairness Doctrine, I decided to contact the consulate of the U.S.S.R. to obtain their opinion of this book. Here is what I wrote.

3065 Pacific Ave.
San Francisco, CA 94115
6 November 1987

Consulate General of the
  Soviet Union
279 Green Street
San Francisco, CA

Ladies and Gentlemen:

. . . Being somewhat of an empiricist, I place a high value on what I see and hear myself. It causes me some regret, therefore, to admit that when I was in Afghanistan I never spoke with Soviet or pro-Occupation personnel. This makes my book seriously flawed. I have, of course, read a few key documents which present the Soviet point of view: the 1980 interview with Brezhnev given shortly after Babrak Karmal took office, those two or three of Babrak's speeches which are available, some *Tass* statements, etc. But the fact remains that almost all of my sources have a very strong anti-Soviet bias.

For this reason, I would like to give you the opportunity to read and comment on the manuscript draft of my book (which is about 250 double-spaced pages). Any suggestions or corrections to errors of fact would be gratefully appreciated. I frankly believe that the Soviet presence in Afghanistan is wrong. I do my best to make my readers believe this, too. I challenge you to convince them otherwise. If you care to comment on the book, I will give you five or ten pages in it to do so. I will not edit or alter your remarks in any way without your permission. If you sincerely feel that the views of my book are in error, well, as Lenin said ("All Out For the Fight Against Denikin!"), "All our agitation and propaganda must serve to inform the people of the truth." If not, your silence will speak for itself . . .

Yours truly,

William T. Vollmann

Their silence spoke for itself.

APPENDIX

CHRONOLOGY

1734–1979

This is a story about how various big fishes gobbled up the little fishes and then turned their attention to a certain medium-sized fish . . .

1734 The Russians make conquests in Kazakhstan.

1747 Afghanistan is unified under Ahmad Shah in an absolute monarchy.

1765 The British take Calcutta.

1813 Persia signs the Treaty of Gulistan, yielding most of its territory in the Caucasus to Russia.

1828 Persia signs the Treaty of Turkmanchai, relinquishing the southern Caucasus to Russia.

1837 Lord Auckland, Governor-General of India, sends a Captain Burnes to Kabul "to work out the policy of opening the River Indus to commerce." Meanwhile, the Tsar sends a Captain Vitkievitch on the same errand.

1838 The British undertake the forcible restoration of Shah Shuja to the Afghan throne, a project which launches the First Afghan War (1838–42). Severe casualties are inflicted on both sides.

1839 The first Russian attempt to conquer Bokhara fails.

1842 The First Afghan War having proved to be a disaster, the British withdraw from Afghanistan, paying compensation and leaving hostages. Later they take their retribution, and a Colonel Sutherland writes, "It is a comfort to be able to look a native in the face again with confidence." Then they leave again.

1843 Sind falls to the British.

1844 Russia and Great Britain agree to act in the spirit of Count Nesselrode's memorandum, which recommends that the two powers preserve the internal peace of Persia by leaving Bokhara, Khiva and Samarkand as buffer states.

(1846 Kashmir falls to the British.

1849 The Punjab falls to the British.)

1853 The Crimean War ends this happy cooperation.

1855 The Afghans annex Kandahar, which, with Herat, has often changed hands between Afghanistan and Persia.

1856 The Persians seize Herat in retaliation, and announce that they will next occupy Kandahar and establish themselves on the borders of the Punjab, a British area. The British therefore join cause with the Afghans against the Persians and defeat them.

1859 The British occupy Baluchistan.

1863 The Afghans regain Herat.

1865 The Russians occupy Tashkent.

1867 The new province of Russian Turkestan is established.
   Bokhara falls to Russia.

1869 Referring to the Nesselrode memorandum, the Russian Prince Gort-chakoff suggests Afghanistan as the next buffer zone. The British put him off, saying that the frontiers are too ill defined.

1873 Khiva falls to Russia.
   Russia gives up Badakhshan and Wakhan to Afghanistan in exchange for British recognition of the new frontier. Afghanistan is now the only neutral area between the British and the Russians. Sher Ali, the Afghan monarch, asks Lord Northbrook for assurance of British assistance in the event of a Russian invasion of his country. The British refuse. Sher Ali decides that he must cultivate the Russians.

1875 The British become alarmed at the frequent correspondence between Russia and Afghanistan. They become more so when a Russian mission is established at Kabul.

1876 The British sign a treaty with the Khan of Kalat, allowing Empire troops to occupy Quetta. Meanwhile, the Russians make a similar arrangement in Kokand.

1878 Following rejection of their ultimatum demanding the establishment of a British Resident in Kabul, the British invade Afghanistan, precipitating the Second Afghan War (1878–81).

1879 The British retire the bulk of their army after obtaining acquiescence to the presence of a British Resident and the annexation of the Khyber Pass. They begin paying a subsidy to the Amir of Kabul. At the right moment, the Afghans attack the Residence and slaughter all the defenders. Fierce guerrilla-style clashes occur for the next two years, with the Afghans inflicting very respectable casualties. In the end a pro-British government is installed.

1881 The British evacuate Afghanistan.

1884 Baron de Staal, the Russian Ambassador in London, receives his instructions: Russia will maintain its "expansion in Central Asia, leading us to occupy to-day in Turkestan and the Turkestan steppes a military position strong enough to keep England in check by the threat of intervention in India."

At this opportune moment, the chieftains of Merv are persuaded to tender allegiance to the Russian Emperor.

1893 The Durand Line is drawn to delineate the border between Afghanistan and the North-West Frontier Province of British India. Peshawar and the Khyber Pass are included in the British dominions.

1896 Pamir falls to Russia.

1901 The British draw another line, and the North-West Frontier Province becomes a separate entity from the Punjab.

In Afghanistan, Habibullah succeeds to the throne.

1907 At the Anglo-Russian Convention, Russia agrees that Afghanistan is outside its sphere of influence, and Britain agrees not to occupy or annex the country.

1914 World War I breaks out. Afghanistan is neutral.

1917 The Great October Socialist Revolution takes place in Russia. The Bolsheviki abrogate the secret protocols of the Tsarist regime, and grant independence to previous rump states such as Bokhara. Later they change their minds and nibble them up again.

1919 Constitutional monarchy is adopted in Afghanistan. Amanullah Khan succeeds to the throne. At this point the issue of Afghan independence is as inflammatory as Pushtunistan will be after World War II. Declaring his country's complete autonomy from any foreign power, Amanullah strikes at British holdings along the frontier, precipitating the Third Afghan War. Allegations are made that the British use chemical warfare against the Afghans. After some inconclusively bloody events, the British recognize Afghanistan's independence, but not before the Russians do. This year Afghanistan receives its first Soviet subsidy.

1921 A Soviet-Afghan treaty is signed recognizing current frontiers. The Khanate of Bokhara falls to the Soviets. Throughout the decade, various revolts against Soviet power take place in Central Asia, but without success.

1926 The Soviets and the Afghans sign a Pact of Neutrality and Mutual Non-Aggression.

1928 Having taken a leaf from Peter the Great's book, Amanullah tours Europe and returns to abolish the veil, open coeducational schools, and begin construction of a new capitol. Religious leaders encourage revolt. Amanullah is deposed by Bacha Saqqao.

1929 One of Amanullah's generals, Muhammed Nadir Khan, comes out of exile to depose and execute Bacha Saqqao. He then takes the throne as Nadir Shah, and repeals Amanullah's reforms.

1931 "Soviet-Afghan economic relations unfailingly responded to the interests of Afghanistan. A new Soviet-Afghan treaty in 1931 on neutrality and mutual nonaggression helped strengthen Afghanistan's independence" (*Great Soviet Encyclopedia*, 3rd ed. [trans.], vol. II).

1933 Zaher Shah, last king of Afghanistan, succeeds to the throne upon the assassination of his father (8 November).

1934 The United States officially recognizes Afghanistan.

1935 The Germans, Japanese and Italians begin economic activities in Afghanistan. The Nazis explain that whereas Japanese are only "honorary Aryans," Afghans are true Aryans.

1936 The Soviets are refused permission to establish a trade mission in Afghanistan.

1939 World War II breaks out. Afghanistan is again neutral.

1940 The Soviet Union agrees in principle to Nazi Germany's suggested Four-Power Pact, in which "the Soviet Union declares that its territorial aspirations center south of the national territory of the U.S.S.R. in the direction of the Indian Ocean." Buhrhanuddin Rabbani, future leader of Jamiat-i-Islami, is born in Faizabad.

1941 Britain and Russia request that Afghanistan expel all nondiplomatic Axis personnel. Afghanistan responds by expelling *all* nondiplomatic personnel.

1942–43 The U.S. and Afghanistan exchange diplomatic missions.

1946 A year after the end of World War II, American firms begin operating in Afghanistan. Over the next few years, the U.S. and the U.S.S.R. both give the country development loans and aid.

1947 British India is partitioned into India and Pakistan. Hindu-Muslim hostility creates bad feeling between the two countries from the start. Resettlement of Indian Muslims in Pakistan and Pakistani Hindus in India is accompanied by mutual atrocities. The North-West Frontier Province is given the choice of belonging to India or to Pakistan. It selects the latter. But some Pathans say it should have been given the option of independence, since the tribal areas in the N.W.F.P. are not mere territories, but sovereign khanates.

In both Pakistan and Afghanistan there is growing agitation for a "Pushtunistan," or separate state for the Pathan tribes, who live in the border areas of both countries. Afghan Pathans call upon Pakistan to hold a plebiscite in the N.W.F.P.; Pakistan refuses. When Pakistan applies for membership in the United Nations, Afghanistan casts the sole dissenting vote by reason of the Pushtunistan issue.

1948 Pakistan and Afghanistan exchange ambassadors.

1949 In the course of quelling unrest in the tribal areas, Pakistan air-bombs the village of Moghulgai, 2,100 yards inside Afghanistan. Meanwhile, Afghan Afridi tribesmen meet inside Pakistan to found Pushtunistan. Riots ensue.

The "Liberal Parliament" is established in Afghanistan. Some freedom of the press is permitted. A student movement springs up.

1950 Pakistan stops petroleum traffic to Afghanistan for three months. Afghanistan and the Soviet Union sign a four-year barter agreement. The student movement becomes more aggressive, attacking Islam and the Royal Family.

1951 Pakistan's Prime Minister, Liaquat Ali Khan, is assassinated by an Afghan. In Afghanistan, the student union is dissolved.

1952 The Soviets establish a trade office in Kabul. They export enough grain and cement to allow the Afghans to lift rationing on these commodities. Due to continuing unrest, all non-government newspapers are closed. Mr. Hafizullah Amin, a man of considerable ambition, becomes Cultural Officer of the Embassy of the Royal Government of Afghanistan in Washington, D.C. "The future is hidden from us," says Wittgenstein. "But does the astronomer think like this when he calculates an eclipse of the sun?"*

1953 Muhammed Daoud, first cousin of Zaher Shah, becomes Prime Minister of Afghanistan. Daoud requests military aid from the United States and is refused.

1954 The U.S.S.R. loans Afghanistan $3.5 million. Pakistan signs a Mutual Security Agreement with the U.S.A. Daoud requests military aid from the United States and is refused.

---

* *Phil. Inv.*, IIxi, p. 223ʳ.

1955 A war almost breaks out over the Pushtunistan question. Pakistan closes the border for five months. Soviet Premier Bulganin says that his country supports Afghanistan's demands for a plebiscite. The peace-loving democratic peoples of the U.S.S.R. offer the Afghans arms to use against the Pakistanis, and award them a $100 million development loan. Daoud requests military aid from the United States and is refused. Amin joins the staff of U.S.A.I.D. in Kabul. The 1931 Soviet-Afghan Treaty of Neutrality and Non-Aggression is extended for another ten years.

1956 The Afghans make "major development agreements" with the Soviet Union. The United States funds a $15 million airport in Kandahar. Amir Sayyid 'Alim Khan, the last ruler of Bokhara, dies in exile. Afghanistan receives $25 million in military aid from the Soviet Union and East Bloc countries. Some of this money is used to construct airfields, which the Soviets will find very convenient in 1979. In reaction to Daoud, the Islamic Movement, the nucleus of the religious Mujahideen factions, is formed by professors in Kabul. Rabbani becomes a member.

1957 Women announcers begin working for Radio Afghanistan.

1959 During Independence Week celebration, the wives and daughters of the Royal Family and dignitaries appear unveiled. When the mullahs protest to Daoud, he has them thrown in jail.

1961 On 23 August, Pakistan and Afghanistan break diplomatic relations, and the Pakistan-Afghanistan border is closed. Various skirmishes occur in the N.W.F.P. over the Pushtunistan question.

1962 Amin becomes a translator for the U.S. Embassy in Kabul.

1963 Prime Minister Daoud resigns (9 March). He is succeeded by the commoner Dr. Muhammed Yousuf. The border with Pakistan is re-opened, and diplomatic relations re-established.

1964 A liberalized Islamic constitution is promulgated. Women are given equality under the law. Zaher Shah remains king, but the Royal Family is prohibited from entering politics. (This bars Daoud, for instance, from returning to power, because he is a member of the Royal Family.) The Doshi-Jabal Us-Seraj road is completed between Kabul and the Soviet border.

1965 The first national elections are held. (With what ironic sadness does one remember this now!) Political parties appear on the scene: conservatives, centrists, liberals and leftists. In July, the newspaper *Khalq* ("The Masses") first appears. Its publisher is a man named Nur Muhammad Taraki, about whom Louis Dupree remarks: "The novel as found in the West is rare in the Middle East and virtually unknown in Afghanistan. One well-known leftist journalist, Nur Muhammad Taraki, is considered to be a budding

Persian-language novelist, however."★ *Khalq* is the organ of the Democratic People's Party, formed by Taraki on 1 January. A more extremist wing of the D.P.P. publishes *Parcham* ("The Flag"), a magazine to which Mr. Babrak Karmal is a frequent contributor. Babrak calls for the formation of a "United Democratic Front" to achieve socialism by evolution from within the system. (Both wings, Parcham and Khalq, are politically right of a third group within the D.P.P. called Shu'la-yi-Jawed, "the Eternal Flame.") Babrak and a woman deputy of the D.P.P., Dr. Ananhita, are elected to Parliament. Babrak urges the students to come and demonstrate, which they do with such vigor that Parliament must be adjourned. On 25 October, government troops fire on student demonstrators, killing three. On 29 October, Mohammad Hashim Mawamdal succeeds Dr. Yousuf as Prime Minister.

The Soviet-Afghan Treaty of Neutrality and Non-Aggression of 1931 is renewed. Meanwhile, U.S. assistance to Afghanistan continues to average $22 million a year.

1966 *Khalq* is closed by the government.

1967 Prime Minister Mawamdal is replaced by Nur Ahmad Etemadi. A split occurs in the D.P.P. between the Khalq and the Parcham (which remains affiliated with the Shu'la-yi-Jawed).

1968 The share of socialist countries in the total foreign trade turnover of Afghanistan reaches 47%. Some conservative members of Parliament propose that Afghan women be prohibited from studying abroad. A demonstration of Afghan women students makes them change their minds. The Parcham and the Shu'la-yi-Jawed split apart.

1969 *Parcham* is closed by the government. In a melee in Parliament, Babrak is severely injured and sent to the hospital. His and Ananhita's terms expire.

1970 The magazine *Mujalla-i-Shariat* (*Shariat Journal*) appears, edited by Prof. Rabbani.

1971 Pakistan and India go to war. Pakistan loses. As a result, East Pakistan becomes the sovereign state of Bangladesh. In Afghanistan, Dr. Abdul Zahil becomes Prime Minister, and a student strike begins which lasts until 1972.

1972 Rabbani becomes head of the Jamiat-i-Islami.

1973 Supported by the Parcham and others, Daoud overthrows the monarchy while Zaher Shah is in Italy (17 July).† Daoud becomes both President and Prime Minister. He declares martial law. Over the next half-decade he strives to continue the policy of gracious nonalignment, but with increasingly less success. The Soviets improve the border routes of Afghanistan and strengthen the roads between major Afghan cities. Some Cassandras say that

---

★ Louis Dupree, *Afghanistan*, p. 92.
† Afghan calendar: 26th of Saratan, 1352.

the roads are being given a much greater weight capacity than the Afghans require. It is almost as if (ignoble thought!) the roads had been designed to accommodate Soviet tanks. Daoud meanwhile sends 1,600 Parcham cadres to the country to assist in modernization. This effort fails, and many of them leave their posts, convinced that a more radical approach is needed.

On 20 October, former Prime Minister Mawamdal, convicted of a plot against Daoud, "commits suicide" in prison.

1975 Dissatisfied with what they see as increasingly anti-Islamic tendencies of the government, Gulbuddin et al. begin to build up their own political organizations in the provinces and in Peshawar, where they are given support by Pakistan's Bhutto government in retaliation for Afghan-supported subversive activities in Pakistan. On the night of 21–22 July, religious leaders launch the "Panjsher Insurgency," which is not limited to Panjsher but includes Paktiya, Jalalabad and many other areas. Ninety-three people are brought to trial, and three executed. In September, a military plot against Daoud is uncovered.

1976 Daoud and Bhutto exchange visits.

1977 In February, a new constitution is passed, and the country officially becomes the Republic of Afghanistan. In July, the Parcham and the Shu'la-yi-Jawed reunite. General Zia seizes power in Pakistan and arrests Bhutto, who is imprisoned for two years. Zia visits Daoud for consultations in October. In December, another plan for a military coup against Daoud is discovered, and the perpetrators arrested.

1978 On 17 April, Daoud tells confidants that he will soon announce sweeping reforms. But ten days later he and his family are efficiently liquidated. Nur Muhammad Taraki accepts the call of the nation and becomes President and Prime Minister.* The Soviet Union expresses congratulations; the United States does not. Surviving members of the Royal Family are arrested and deprived of citizenship. The Democratic Republic of Afghanistan is now governed by a coalition of Khalq and Parcham members. Babrak Karmal becomes Deputy Prime Minister for a little while, and Hafizullah Amin, who had set the coup in motion through his party contacts in the army, becomes Deputy Prime Minister and Minister of Foreign Affairs. Taraki signs a treaty of friendship with the Soviet Union, kindly reaffirms the equality of women in a Decree Number Seven, and then gets to work. In July, when he feels secure, he reduces the Parcham leadership to ambassadors and packs them off —Babrak to Prague, Ananhita to Belgrade, etc. In August, the remaining Parcham members are arrested on charges of conspiring against the government. Babrak, Ananhita and the other ambassadors are stripped of their powers and recalled home, but they wisely go to Moscow instead.

---

* "After the bloody coup of 7th of Saur," says a Jamiat-i-Islami publication, " . . . our dear country was falling in the mouth of social Imperialism dragon. Inferior slaves and country-selling elements have changed this country into a horrible prison."

1979 *(January)* 12,000 Afghan troops are moved to Konar Province to fight 5,000 guerrillas.

(March) Radio Kabul claims that Iran has sent 4,000 troops in disguise across the border, along with 7,000 Afghan dissidents, in order to unseat Taraki. Iran denies this. The Afghan government also accuses Pakistan of harboring and supporting the Mujahideen (as of course it is doing). A new all-Khalq cabinet is announced. Amin becomes Prime Minister, and thereby takes on responsibility for pacifying the countryside. Nuristani rebels commence operations. In Herat, rebels kill Soviet technicians and their wives and children.

(April) Bhutto is hanged in Pakistan.

(July) Guerrilla activity is reported in all 28 provinces of Afghanistan. Amin asks Taraki to request increased Soviet military aid.

(August) 30 Soviets are killed by Afghans in Kandahar. It is fair to say that Amin's pacification of the countryside is not going swimmingly.

(September) Taraki meets with Brezhnev in Moscow. What they discuss is a secret. But shortly thereafter Taraki summons Amin to his office, and gunshots are heard.

(October) Taraki's death is officially announced on Radio Kabul. The Soviets are silent. Amin releases some political prisoners, appoints a constitutional convention (here I must laugh), and launches major offensives against the Mujahideen in Paktiya and Badakhshan.

Christmas Day, 1979 The Soviets airlift troops and tanks into Kabul. Amin is liquidated, together with his family. Succeeding him is Mr. Babrak Karmal, a man for whom the Soviets have the warmest feelings.

1980–1989

In these hideous years the Soviets followed a principle of counterinsurgency set forth by Brigadier Frank Kitson. Borrowing an analogy from Mao, Kitson describes the insurgents as a fish, and the population is the water in which the fish swims. "If a fish has got to be destroyed it can be attacked directly by rod or net, providing it is in the sort of position which gives these methods a chance of success. But if rod and net cannot succeed by themselves it may be necessary to do something to the water which will force the fish into a position where it can be caught. Conceivably it might be necessary to kill the fish by polluting the water, but this is unlikely to be a desirable course of action."★ *The chaos of the invasion years gave way to a system of liquidation based on the establishment of zones of terror, which continued until the Soviet pullout.*

★ Frank Kitson, *Low-Intensity Operations: Subversion, Insurgency, Peace-keeping*, p. 49.

Soviet deserters
describe atrocities
in Afghanistan

Mercury News Wire Service

LONDON — Two soldiers who deserted the Soviet army in Afghanistan
. . . spoke publicly for the first time of atrocities committed by the Soviet
army on unarmed civilians.

They said that entire villages of as many as 200 people were being massacred on the orders of senior Soviet commanders in regular sweeps of the
mountains in search of Afghan rebel forces. In one village, Bazartcha near
the town of Kandahar, where spent cartridges were found, all the men and
boys were shot where they stood. The women were then herded into a
house, into which the Soviet officer in charge, Lt. Vyacheslav Osdchi, threw
grenades.

. . . [Igor] Rykov, an armored personnel carrier driver of the 70th mo-
torized infantry brigade, described one incident in search of settlements
around Nangarkhar in which a senior official ordered a young private to
kill a 16-year-old Afghan boy with a knife.

Slaying

"Our lieutenant, 1st Lt. Anatoly Gevorkyan, ordered the members of
our platoon to bring out a young Afghan boy, about 16 years old. He then
ordered Pvt. Oleg Sotnik to kill him with a knife, saying: 'Now then,
Sotnik, here is the knife. Stick it into this young man. They tell me you
are afraid of blood. You must get used to killing in cold blood, like I do.' "

When the private's attempt was unsuccessful, the lieutenant cut the boy's
throat himself . . .

1988 In Pakistan, General Zia is killed in a mysterious plane crash.

1989 Soviet troops pull out of Afghanistan.
Benazir Bhutto comes to power in Pakistan.

SOURCES

ACKNOWLEDGMENTS

My thanks to various Pakistanis and Afghans whose names I promised not to mention. Information which in my opinion could conceivably be of any value to the Soviets or their successors has been omitted. Such deletions only involve dates, places, etc., and in no way bias the record.

The Afghanistan National Liberation Front took me into Afghanistan and out again, fed me, guarded my safety, and was patient with my limitations. To all my friends there, especially to Suleiman, and to "Poor Man," the leader I went in with, I wish to express my thanks. I cannot say how much I appreciate their kindness.

I owe even more, however, to General N. and his family—so much more that I cannot begin to write it all here. I hope that they will take this book as an earnest of an intention that I sought, however unsuccessfully, to fulfill.

Mr. Don Climent, Mr. Mark Ice, Dr. Levi Roque, Ms. Mary McMorrow and other International Rescue Committee (I.R.C.) personnel were extremely hospitable and helpful in arranging for me to visit their refugee camp operation near the border. I will always cherish my memories of Mary and Levi's friendship. Mr. Hassan Ghulam of the Austrian Relief Committee (A.R.C.) permitted me to visit his organization's camps near Mardan.

I thank all the people that I interviewed. Most of the transcripts have been considerably abbreviated in this book. Many crying necessities in 1982 are irrelevant now. Yet my purpose and theirs is not.

My thanks to the Ella Lyman Cabot Trust, which gave me $990 for use in distributing my fund-raising slide-tape presentation (which, like this book, was called "An Afghanistan Picture Show"), and to Aid For Afghan Refugees (A.F.A.R.), which provided $150 to duplicate the show. Mr. John Schaecher, then president of A.F.A.R., furthered my trip in many ways. I am very grateful to him. Mr. Seth Pilsk and Ms. Linda Ohde put in many hours with me preparing the slide show (and later a radio presentation). Both also gave generously of their resources for fund-raising. Mr. John Hotaki of Bennett Photo went beyond the call of duty in his help with photo reproduction for various fund-raising events.

Mr. S.P. translated the taped Pushtu interviews which I have transcribed here. I wish that I could thank him by name. Mr. Lindsey Grant gave me valuable advice on film and equipment accessories. I am very grateful to Mr. Robert Kvaal for his kind efforts to place the manuscript. The late James R. Withrow, Jr., provided encouragement and support. Professor Alan Paskow taught me my Wittgenstein. I would also like to thank Ms. Erica Bright, Professor Galya Diment, Mr. Paul Foster, Mr. John Glusman, Mr. Garth Pritchard, Ms. Catherine Reynolds, Dr. Janice K. Ryu, Mr. Scott Swanson and Mr. David Traub.

I apologize to anyone whose name I have forgotten. Eleven years is a long enough period of time for even the infallible Young Man to make mistakes.

CONSULATE GENERAL OF PAKISTAN
NEW YORK, U.S.A.

Visa No. 975182
Type of Visa Transit / Entry 1982
Date of Issue May 07, 1982
Date of expiry August 06, 1982
Provided the passport remains valid.

Number of entries permitted
multiple / single

Authorized duration of each stay
WILL BE DETERMINED AT THE PORT OF ARRIVAL
Purpose of Visit TOURIST

VICE CONSUL

Consulate General of Pakistan
New York

Dear William:

February 9, 1983

Thanks again for the look at this, and my apologies again for my slowness. As I told you over the phone, I especially like the "young man" sections of this. I only wish that I thought I could get someone to buy it. Do keep on, though, and don't hesitate to try me again. I'll try to be more prompt.

Hope your intestinal parasites are a thing of the past. I've had them once and that was more than enough.

Best,

Barney M. Karpfinger

PAN AM   LHK
                          PAN AM

GOVERNMENT OF PAKISTAN
DEPTT OF CIVIL AVIATION
No. 506919 7
AIRPORT EMBARKATION FEE
Rs. 100

IRC

39-C Sahibzada Abdul Qayum
University Town
(off Park Rd.)

MARK E. ICE
Administrative Coordinator
INTERNATIONAL RESCUE COMMITTEE, INC.

G P O 504
Peshawar
Pakistan

TEL: 4127

CARE.
660 FIRST AVENUE, NEW YORK, N.Y. 10016   (212) 686-3110
                                  CABLE PARCELUS N.Y.

THE WORLD'S MOST NEEDED GIFT

EDWIN J. WESLEY
CHAIRMAN

May 29, 1981

Mr. William T. Vollmann
217 West Avenue
Ithaca, NY 14850

Dear Mr. Vollmann:

You are not entirely crazy. It is possible, but perhaps remotely. Whether you can get any funding depends on what you want to do. The International Rescue Committee is very significantly involved in operating some 20 mobile medical units in Afghan refugee camps in Pakistan. Currently, CARE is much less involved. You might have a shot at the IRC operation if you have the capability of getting involved in a medical way.

Best regards. Good luck.

Very sincerely yours,

Ed Wesley

مسافرخانه
کراچی ائرپورٹ

رسید نمبر 17182

رقم سے Mr. William James Vollmann

Twenty Only

بصورت نقد/چیک نمبر A — S

بینک — نبام — موصوف — پلانگ نمبر

برائے مسافرخانہ — ماتوا وصول پائی.

خدائی بخش